Final Report of the Forty-fourth Antarctic Treaty Consultative Meeting

ANTARCTIC TREATY
CONSULTATIVE MEETING

Final Report
of the Forty-fourth
Antarctic Treaty
Consultative Meeting

Berlin, Germany
23 May - 2 June 2022

Volume I

Secretariat of the Antarctic Treaty
Buenos Aires
2022

Antarctic Treaty Consultative Meeting (44th : 2022 : Berlin)
    Final Report of the Forty-fourth Antarctic Treaty Consultative Meeting. Berlin,
    Germany, 23 May – 2 June 2022.
    Buenos Aires : Secretariat of the Antarctic Treaty, 2022.
    288 p.

    ISBN 978-987-8929-19-4

    1. International law – Environmental issues. 2. Antarctic Treaty system.
    3. Environmental law – Antarctica. 4. Environmental protection – Antarctica.

    DDC 341.762 5

Published by:

Secretariat of the Antarctic Treaty
Secrétariat du Traité sur l'Antarctique
Секретариат Договора об Антарктике
Secretaría del Tratado Antártico

Maipú 757, Piso 4
C1006ACI - Buenos Aires
Argentina
Tel: +54 11 3991 4250
ats@ats.aq

This book is available for free in digital format from www.ats.aq and in hard
copy from https://www.amazon.com/.

ISSN 2346-9897
ISBN 978-987-8929-19-4

Contents

VOLUME I

3. Resolutions   **245**

VOLUME II
(Available at www.ats.aq)

PART II. MEASURES, DECISIONS AND RESOLUTIONS (CONT.)

4. Management Plans

Antarctic Specially Managed Area No 7 (Southwest Anvers Island and Palmer
Basin): Revised Management Plan

Antarctic Specially Protected Area No 109 (Moe Island, South Orkney Islands):
Revised Management Plan

Antarctic Specially Protected Area No 110 (Lynch Island, South Orkney
Islands): Revised Management Plan

Antarctic Specially Protected Area No 111 (Southern Powell Island and
adjacent islands, South Orkney Islands): Revised Management Plan

Antarctic Specially Protected Area No 113 (Litchfield Island, Arthur Harbor,
Anvers Island, Palmer Archipelago): Revised Management Plan

Antarctic Specially Protected Area No 115 (Lagotellerie Island, Marguerite Bay,
Graham Land): Revised Management Plan

Antarctic Specially Protected Area No 119 (Davis Valley and Forlidas Pond,
Dufek Massif, Pensacola Mountains): Revised Management Plan

Antarctic Specially Protected Area No 122 (Arrival Heights, Hut Point Peninsula, Ross Island): Revised Management Plan

Antarctic Specially Protected Area No 124 (Cape Crozier, Ross Island): Revised Management Plan

Antarctic Specially Protected Area No 126 (Byers Peninsula, Livingston Island, South Shetland Islands): Revised Management Plan

Antarctic Specially Protected Area No 127 (Haswell Island): Revised Management Plan

Antarctic Specially Protected Area No 129 (Rothera Point, Adelaide Island): Revised Management Plan

Antarctic Specially Protected Area No 133 (Harmony Point, Nelson Island, South Shetland Islands): Revised Management Plan

Antarctic Specially Protected Area No 139 (Biscoe Point, Anvers Island, Palmer Archipelago): Revised Management Plan

Antarctic Specially Protected Area No 140 (Parts of Deception Island, South Shetland Islands): Revised Management Plan

Antarctic Specially Protected Area No 149 (Cape Shirreff and San Telmo Island, Livingston Island, South Shetland Islands): Revised Management Plan

Antarctic Specially Protected Area No 164 (Scullin and Murray Monoliths, Mac.Robertson Land): Revised Management Plan

PART III. OPENING AND CLOSING ADDRESSES AND REPORTS

1. Opening and Closing Addresses

2. Reports by Depositaries and Observers

Report of the USA as Depositary Government of the Antarctic Treaty and its Protocol

Report of Australia as Depositary Government of CCAMLR

Report of Australia as Depositary Government of ACAP

Report of the UK as Depositary Government of CCAS

Report by the CCAMLR Observer

Report of SCAR

Report of COMNAP

3. Reports by Experts

Report by ASOC

Report by IAATO

Report by WMO

PART IV. ADDITIONAL DOCUMENTS FROM ATCM XLIV

1. List of Documents

2. List of Participants

Acronyms and abbreviations

ACAP	Agreement on the Conservation of Albatrosses and Petrels
ACBR	Antarctic Conservation Biogeographic Region
ASMA	Antarctic Specially Managed Area
ASOC	Antarctic and Southern Ocean Coalition
ASPA	Antarctic Specially Protected Area
ATS	Antarctic Treaty System or Antarctic Treaty Secretariat
ATCM	Antarctic Treaty Consultative Meeting
ATCP	Antarctic Treaty Consultative Party
ATME	Antarctic Treaty Meeting of Experts
BP	Background Paper
CCAMLR	Convention on the Conservation of Antarctic Marine Living Resources and/or Commission for the Conservation of Antarctic Marine Living Resources
CCAS	Convention for the Conservation of Antarctic Seals
CCRWP	Climate Change Response Work Programme
CEE	Comprehensive Environmental Evaluation
CEP	Committee for Environmental Protection
COMNAP	Council of Managers of National Antarctic Programs
EIA	Environmental Impact Assessment
EIES	Electronic Information Exchange System
HCA	Hydrographic Committee on Antarctica
HSM	Historic Site or Monument
IAATO	International Association of Antarctica Tour Operators
IBA	Important Bird Area
ICAO	International Civil Aviation Organization
ICG	Intersessional Contact Group
IEE	Initial Environmental Evaluation
IGP&I Clubs	International Group of Protection and Indemnity Clubs
IHO	International Hydrographic Organization
IMO	International Maritime Organization
IOC	Intergovernmental Oceanographic Commission
IOPC Funds	International Oil Pollution Compensation Funds
IP	Information Paper
IPCC	Intergovernmental Panel on Climate Change
IUCN	International Union for Conservation of Nature
MPA	Marine Protected Area
NCA	National Competent Authority
RCC	Rescue Coordination Centre
SAR	Search and Rescue
SCAR	Scientific Committee on Antarctic Research
SC-CAMLR	Scientific Committee of CCAMLR
SGCCR	Subsidiary Group on Climate Change Response
SGMP	Subsidiary Group on Management Plans
SOLAS	International Convention for the Safety of Life at Sea
SOOS	Southern Ocean Observi ng System
SP	Secretariat Paper
ToR	Term of Reference
UAV/RPAS	Unmanned Aerial Vehicle / Remotely Piloted Aircraft System
UNEP	United Nations Environment Programme
UNFCCC	United Nations Framework Convention on Climate Change
VSSOS	Vessel-Supported Short Overnight Stay
WMO	World Meteorological Organization
WP	Working Paper
WTO	World Tourism Organization

PART I

Final Report

1. ATCM XLIV Final Report

Final Report of the Forty-fourth Antarctic Treaty Consultative Meeting

Berlin, Germany, 24 May – 2 June 2022

(1) Pursuant to Article IX of the Antarctic Treaty, Representatives of the Consultative Parties (Argentina, Australia, Belgium, Brazil, Bulgaria, Chile, China, Czech Republic, Ecuador, Finland, France, Germany, India, Italy, Japan, the Republic of Korea, the Netherlands, New Zealand, Norway, Peru, Poland, the Russian Federation, South Africa, Spain, Sweden, Ukraine, the United Kingdom of Great Britain and Northern Ireland, the United States of America, and Uruguay) met from 24 May to 2 June 2022, for the purpose of exchanging information, holding consultations, and formulating, considering, and recommending to their Governments, measures in furtherance of the principles and objectives of the Treaty. The Meeting was held in a hybrid format, with participants meeting either in person in Berlin, or virtually.

(2) The Meeting was also attended by delegations from the following Contracting Parties to the Antarctic Treaty which are not Consultative Parties: Belarus, Canada, Colombia, Malaysia, Monaco, Portugal, Romania, Switzerland, Türkiye, and Venezuela.

(3) In accordance with Rules 2 and 31 of the ATCM Rules of Procedure, Observers from: the Commission for the Conservation of Antarctic Marine Living Resources (CCAMLR), the Scientific Committee on Antarctic Research (SCAR), and the Council of Managers of National Antarctic Programs (COMNAP) attended the meeting.

(4) In accordance with Rule 39 and Rule 42 of the Rules of Procedure, Experts from the following international organisations and non-governmental organisations attended the Meeting: the International Hydrographic Organization (IHO), the International Union for Conservation of Nature (IUCN), the World Meteorological Organization (WMO), the Antarctic and Southern Ocean Coalition (ASOC), and the International Association of Antarctica Tour Operators (IAATO).

(5) Germany, as Host Country of ATCM XLIV, fulfilled its information requirements towards the Contracting Parties, Observers and Experts through the Secretariat Notes, letters and a dedicated website.

Item 1: Opening of the Meeting

(6) The Meeting was officially opened on 24 May 2022. On behalf of the Host Government, in accordance with Rules 5 and 6 of the Rules of Procedure, the Head of the Host Government Secretariat, Dr Manfred Reinke, called the Meeting to order and proposed the candidacy of Mrs Tania von Uslar-Gleichen as Chair of ATCM XLIV. The proposal was accepted and Mrs von Uslar-Gleichen was elected as Chair of ATCM XLIV in accordance with Rule 6.

(7) The Chair warmly welcomed all Parties, Observers and Experts to Berlin and thanked them for their confidence in appointing her as Chair of the Meeting. The Chair expressed her hope that Parties would interact productively and act towards the good of Antarctica and the Treaty.

(8) The Chair also noted that ATCM XLIV would be carried out in a hybrid format, in accordance with the Rules of Procedure and the *Ad-Hoc Guidelines for ATCM XLIV – CEP XXIV Hybrid Meeting*, which had been agreed to and adopted for ATCM XLIV by all Consultative Parties, and which complemented, but were not intended to replace or have precedence over, the Rules of Procedure (see Appendix 1).

(9) Delegates observed a minute of silence in honour of friends, colleagues and service members who were active in the Antarctic community and passed away in the previous year. The Chair mentioned especially the passing of Dr Yves Frenot, former director of the French Polar Institute and former Chair of the CEP (2010-14).

(10) Ms Jennifer Lee Morgan, State Secretary and Special Envoy for International Climate Action at the Federal Foreign Office, welcomed delegates to Berlin, noting that this was the first physical ATCM after two years of pandemic. She noted that it was Antarctica and its vital role in humankind's efforts to live in balance with the earth and its protected status under the Environmental Protocol that drew Parties together, and highlighted the celebration of the 30th anniversary of the Environmental Protocol last year in Madrid. She thanked the scientists who had worked together over the decades to protect Antarctica, and reminded Parties of their important tasks to discuss and decide measures on the management and protection of Antarctica. She underlined that shifts in the Antarctic climate would have consequences for the climate around the world, noting that the mass loss of Antarctic ice sheet was projected to contribute substantially to global sea level rise. While encouraging Parties to move forward with their important work, Ms Lee Morgan recognised that it was not an easy decision to come together in Berlin while one Consultative Party was waging war on another Consultative Party. She stated that the Russian Federation was waging an unjustifiable, unprovoked and illegal war against Ukraine, violating the United Nations Charter and other fundamental principles of international law. She called on the Russian Federation to put an end to the war it had started and stop its military aggression, noting that this breach of international law was contrary to the spirit of the Antarctic Treaty, which was widely seen as a prominent example of well-functioning multilateralism. She also called on Parties to take responsibility for the protection of the unique and vulnerable ecosystem of the Antarctic and to not block important decisions for reasons not related to Antarctic interests. Ms Lee Morgan stressed that there was a strong urgency to care for the white continent, noting that Antarctica had recently sent out some worrisome signals to us. She highlighted the importance of understanding and monitoring the Antarctic climate for the survival of humankind. Based on scientific results, the right decisions for protection could be taken. She noted that the establishment of a network of protected areas was key to protecting and maintaining biodiversity in Antarctica as well as to counteract the effects of climate change. She noted that Parties would discuss proposals in this regard and also mentioned that, although in a different context, the work on new marine protected areas had to be continued as well. Noting the likely expansion of Antarctic tourism following the pandemic, she also encouraged Parties to be prudent and adopt a strategic approach on how to sustainably manage tourism in Antarctica, and to ensure that tourism activities met the strict requirements of environmental protection. Finally, Ms Lee Morgan stated that it was essential to maintain the integrity of the Antarctic Treaty System, in order to keep Antarctica a demilitarised continent, where peaceful and international cooperation prevailed. She affirmed that Germany was ready to accept this responsibility both by hosting this ATCM even in these difficult times, and by its commitment to strive, with all Parties, to ensure Antarctica would remain a beautiful, essential place.

(11) Dr Bettina Hoffmann, Parliamentary State Secretary at the Federal Ministry for the Environment, Nature Conservation, Nuclear Safety and Consumer Protection, welcomed Parties and noted the hybrid nature of the Meeting, which allowed virtual participants to contribute across multiple time zones. She recalled that Antarctica had always been a continent that embodied the idea of peaceful use, even at times when nations were at great odds. During the Cold War, the Antarctic Treaty had served as a platform for different sides to meet and work together towards a common goal. Dr Hoffmann stated that the Treaty faced new political challenges and condemned in the strongest possible terms the Russian Federation's war of aggression against Ukraine, which was a violation of international law. She added that the ATCM's work for peace, research and

environmental protection should not be compromised because of the aggression of one Party against another. The global crises of climate change, biodiversity loss and pollution would not wait for the war to end. Dr Hoffmann recalled the 30th anniversary of the Environmental Protocol and underlined the need to protect and preserve what Parties have been working towards over the past 30 years. She noted that the Treaty principles, among them the precautionary principle, should continue to guide Parties. In this regard, she highlighted three priority issues requiring action from the ATCM. First, she highlighted the impact of the global climate crisis on Antarctica and, in particular, on the emperor penguin, and encouraged Parties to take immediate actions towards a stronger conservation status for it. Second, she emphasised the important role of area protection in preventing biodiversity loss, and encouraged Parties to further develop management plans to protect Antarctica's unique flora and fauna. She also referred to ongoing work under the German G7 Presidency on marine protected areas. Third, Dr Hoffmann emphasised that the global pollution crisis was also affecting Antarctica and noted that micro plastics posed a serious threat. She recalled the United Nations Environment Assembly, which mandated negotiations aimed to complete a draft legally binding agreement on plastics by the end of 2024. She also called on Parties to work towards the reduction of noise levels in Antarctic waters, noting it was particularly important to whales and other Antarctic wildlife. Finally, she highlighted the importance of working together collaboratively to further strengthen the preventative protection and preservation of Antarctica while setting an example for peaceful coexistence and multilateralism.

(12) The Russian Federation asserted its right to reply and they made a full statement on their position, which is recorded at paragraph 38.

Item 2: Election of Officers and Creation of Working Groups

(13) Ms Jenny Haukka, Head of Delegation of Finland, Host Country of ATCM XLV, was elected Vice-Chair. In accordance with Rule 7 of the Rules of Procedure, Mr Albert Lluberas Bonaba, Executive Secretary of the Antarctic Treaty Secretariat, acted as Secretary to the Meeting. Dr Manfred Reinke, head of the Host Country Secretariat, acted as Deputy Secretary.

(14) The Meeting noted that the meeting of the Committee for Environmental Protection was led by its chair Ms Birgit Njåstad of Norway.

(15) Two Working Groups were established:

- Working Group 1: Policy, Legal and Institutional Issues;
- Working Group 2: Operations, Science and Tourism; and

(16) The following Chairs of the Working Groups were elected:

- Working Group 1: Mr Theodore Kill from the United States;
- Working Group 2: Ms Sonia Ramos García from Spain and Dr Phillip Tracey from Australia.

Item 3: Adoption of the Agenda and Allocation of Items to Working Groups

(17) The following Agenda was adopted:

1. Opening of the Meeting
2. Election of Officers and Creation of Working Groups
3. Adoption of the Agenda and Allocation of Items to Working Groups and Consideration of the Multi-year Strategic Work Plan

4. Operation of the Antarctic Treaty System: Reports by Parties, Observers and Experts

5. Report of the Committee for Environmental Protection

6. Operation of the Antarctic Treaty System

    a. Request from Canada to become a Consultative Party

    b. General matters

7. Operation of the Antarctic Treaty System: Matters related to the Secretariat

8. Liability

9. Biological Prospecting in Antarctica

10. Exchange of Information

11. Education Issues

12. Multi-year Strategic Work Plan

13. Safety and Operations in Antarctica

14. Inspections under the Antarctic Treaty and the Environment Protocol

15. Science issues, future science challenges, scientific cooperation and facilitation

16. Implications of Climate Change for Management of the Antarctic Treaty Area

17. Tourism and Non-Governmental Activities in the Antarctic Treaty Area, including Competent Authorities Issues

18. Preparation of ATCM XLV

19. Any Other Business

20. Adoption of the Final Report

21. Close of the Meeting

(18)   The Meeting adopted the following allocation of agenda items:

- Plenary: Items 1, 2, 3, 4, 5, 6a, 18, 19, 20, 21.
- Working Group 1: Items 6b, 7, 8, 9, 10, 11, 12.
- Working Group 2: 13, 14, 15, 16, 17.

(19)   The Meeting also decided to allocate draft instruments arising out of the work of the Committee for Environmental Protection and the Working Groups to a legal drafting group for consideration of their legal and institutional aspects.

Item 4: Operation of the Antarctic Treaty System:
Reports by Parties, Observers and Experts

(20)   Pursuant to Recommendation XIII-2, the Meeting received reports from depositary governments and secretariats.

(21)   The United States, in its capacity as Depositary Government of the Antarctic Treaty and its Environmental Protocol, reported on the status of the Antarctic Treaty and the Protocol on Environmental Protection to the Antarctic Treaty (IP 52). Since the last report, there had been no accessions to the Treaty and one approval of the Protocol. Austria had deposited an instrument of approval of the Protocol on 27 July 2021, and the Protocol had entered into force for Austria on 26 August 2021. The United States noted that there were currently 54 Parties to the Treaty and 42 Parties to the Protocol. It further noted that, in respect to Measure 1 (2005) recommending that Annex VI on Liability Arising from Environmental Emergencies form part of the Environmental Protocol, Chile and France approved Measure 1 (2005), respectively, on 15 June 2021 and 18 November 2021. It also reported that Canada deposited instruments of acceptance of Annex V and the Amendment of Annex II to the Environmental Protocol on 23 February 2022.

(22)   Australia, in its capacity as Depositary for the Convention on the Conservation of Antarctic Marine Living Resources (CCAMLR), reported that there had been no new accessions to the Convention since ATCM XLIII. It noted that there were currently 36 Parties to the Convention (IP 46).

(23)   The United Kingdom, in its capacity as Depositary of the Convention for the Conservation of Antarctic Seals (CCAS), reported that it had not received any requests to accede to the Convention, or any instruments of accession, since ATCM XLIII (IP 18 rev. 2). The United Kingdom encouraged all Contracting Parties to CCAS to submit their returns on time.

(24)   Australia, in its capacity as Depositary for the Agreement on the Conservation of Albatrosses and Petrels (ACAP), reported that there had been no new accessions to the Agreement since ATCM XLIII, and that there were 13 Parties to the Agreement (IP 45). Australia encouraged Parties to join ACAP.

(25)   CCAMLR presented IP 14 *Report by the CCAMLR Observer to the Forty Fourth Antarctic Treaty Consultative Meeting*, which reported on the 40th annual CCAMLR Meeting, held online from 18 to 29 October 2021 and chaired by Dr Jakob Granit (Sweden). CCAMLR reported that SC-CAMLR and its working groups undertook significant work in 2021 on developing a revised krill management strategy. CCAMLR also reported that the Commission had added one vessel to the Non-Contracting Party IUU list and one vessel to the Contracting Party IUU list. It further noted that most compliance rates in the CCAMLR Summary Compliance Report were greater than 92%. CCAMLR noted the issue of seabird strikes on warps and net monitoring cables in the krill fishery as well as seal and humpback whale by-catch events. It reported that the Commission approved the reconvening of the Working Group on Incidental Mortality Associated with Fishing (WG-IMAF) to address this issue. CCAMLR also noted the establishment of two MPAs in South Orkney and the Ross Sea, as well as three additional proposals for MPAs, including an East Antarctica MPA, Weddell Sea MPA and an Antarctic Peninsula Region MPA. The Commission considered but could not reach agreement on a revised resolution on climate change, and agreed to reconsider the proposed revision of the resolution at CCAMLR 41. CCAMLR informed the Meeting that the Pine Island Glacier area had reduced by 22% since 2017, thus meeting the criteria for designation of a Special Area for Scientific Study. It was designated as Stage 1, pursuant to Conservation Measure 24-04, on 12 June 2021. CCAMLR concluded by reporting that the 41st Meeting of the Commission would be held in Hobart, Australia, from 24 October to 4 November 2022.

(26)   The Meeting thanked CCAMLR for its report, noting the significance of the 40th Meeting of the Commission and the common areas of work: climate change, non-native species, species protection, marine spatial management, and monitoring. The Meeting highlighted that the Declaration on the occasion of CCAMLR's 40th anniversary was attached to CCAMLR's report, and emphasised its relevance to the ATCM including, for example, the determination to further address the effects and impacts of climate change and the reaffirmation of the Commission's commitment to developing a representative network of marine protected areas.

(27)   SCAR presented IP 16 *The Scientific Committee on Antarctic Research Annual Report 2022 to the XLIV Antarctic Treaty Consultative Meeting*, which summarised its recent work to promote scientific knowledge, understanding and education on Antarctica. SCAR highlighted the work of its three scientific research programmes: the Integrated Science to Inform Antarctic and Southern Ocean Conservation (Ant-ICON); INStabilities and Thresholds in ANTarctica (INSTANT) and Near-term Variability and Prediction of the Antarctic Climate System (AntClimnow). SCAR reported that, as part of the United Nations Decade of Ocean Science for Sustainable Development (2021-

2030), it had coordinated the Southern Ocean Task Force which was established to develop the Southern Ocean Action Plan launched in April 2022. SCAR had also organised two events at the 26th United Nations Climate Change Conference of the Parties (COP26) in Glasgow in 2021: an official side event titled "Antarctic and Overshoot Scenarios: Risk of Irreversible Sea-Level Rise" and, as part of Polar Oceans Day at the Cryosphere Pavilion, an event titled "Antarctic Marine Ecosystems Under Pressure: Protection Needs Action Locally and Globally". SCAR also referred to IP 5, noting that its Fellowship Programme aimed to encourage the active involvement of early career researchers in Antarctic scientific research and build new connections and further strengthen international capacity and cooperation in Antarctic research. SCAR highlighted its film, "Peace and Science" and encouraged Parties to access the film via the SCAR website. SCAR further reported on its work with intergovernmental fora, numerous capacity building and outreach initiatives as well as collaborative projects undertaken with IAATO for the development of a systematic conservation plan for the Antarctic Peninsula, which aimed to facilitate the concurrent management of biodiversity, science and tourism. Finally, SCAR reported that the 10th SCAR Open Science Conference would be a virtual event, hosted by India from 1-10 August 2022, with the theme "Antarctica in a Changing World".

(28) COMNAP presented IP 19 *Annual Report 2021/22 Council of Managers of National Antarctic Programs*, which summarised its activities during the previous year. Despite continued challenges presented by the COVID-19 pandemic, COMNAP had remained committed to its work facilitating the cooperation of national Antarctic programmes that supported approximately 500 scientific projects in Antarctica, and coordinating the maintenance and security of critical Antarctic infrastructures. During its 33rd Annual General Meeting, held in July 2021, COMNAP welcomed the TÜBITAK Marmara Research Center, Polar Research Institute of Turkey among its membership, making it COMNAP's 31st member. COMNAP reported that it also renewed its *COVID-19 Outbreak Prevention and Management Guidelines for the 2021/22 Antarctic Season* to assist national Antarctic programmes in the preparation of their own protocols. Other highlights of the year included the widespread participation of the Antarctic community in the COMNAP aviation workshop and improvements in COMNAP air operations products such as the Antarctic Flight Information Manual and the COMNAP RPAS Operator's Handbook. COMNAP also remarked that it was looking forward to further active participation and cooperation among its membership in the upcoming Search and Rescue workshop in 2023.

(29) The Meeting thanked COMNAP for its report and, in particular, for its competent and steadfast work in coordinating the international response of Antarctic stations, researchers and personnel to the ongoing COVID-19 pandemic. The Parties noted the overall effectiveness of the sanitary measures taken by national Antarctic programmes under COMNAP guidance and leadership, and expressed particular gratitude to Executive Secretary, Michelle Rogan-Finnemore, for her efforts during the season.

(30) In relation to Article III-2 of the Antarctic Treaty, the Meeting received reports from other international organisations.

(31) WMO presented IP 21 rev.1 *WMO Annual Report*, which reported on a range of WMO activities of relevance to the Antarctic Treaty System. This included activities of the World Climate Research Programme, World Weather Research Programme, the Global Cryosphere Watch and the Antarctic Regional Climate Centre network. WMO highlighted its ongoing work in coordinating research and modelling activities on ice sheet mass balance and sea level, ice shelves and alpine glaciers, sea ice, and permafrost, often in collaboration with SCAR. Several modelling activities were also of relevance to the ATCM, contributing science and climate scenarios used in the global assessment reports of the IPCC. The report also highlighted the ongoing Year of Polar Prediction,

the final summit of which was to take place in August 2022, as well as WMO's research opportunities for early career researchers. WMO referred Parties to IP 71 and IP 74 for further information. WMO thanked all the Parties for their cooperation and support, and restated its continued commitment to further scientific and meteorological research, publications and other long-term collaboration with the ATCM.

(32) The Meeting thanked WMO for its paper and took note of the broad and diverse engagement of its membership in vital research on climate change, weather prediction and cryosphere research.

(33) ASOC presented IP 88 *ASOC report to the ATCM* and reported on its activities to promote Antarctic conservation over the past year. ASOC reported that it, and its members, had participated in CCAMLR meetings, meetings of the IMO, and the United Nations Conference of the Parties, where ASOC member WWF hosted an event on blue carbon and Antarctic krill. ASOC also noted its support for policy-relevant scientific research, including funding biodiversity indicators research for the Southern Ocean. In addition, ASOC member Greenpeace undertook an expedition to the Weddell Sea that included a number of scientific submarine dives. ASOC member, the Pew Charitable Trusts, organised a climate workshop that brought together international experts to discuss the global impact of changes to the Southern Ocean, and the policy responses needed to address these climate risks. ASOC highlighted the need to embark on a new era of Antarctic preservation and conservation, including designating new protected areas, assigning emperor penguins the status of Specially Protected Species (SPS), and taking action on climate change. ASOC therefore urged Parties, along with all Antarctic bodies and actors, to engage in international discussions to increase the conservation outcomes of the Antarctic Treaty System.

(34) IAATO introduced IP 41 *Annual Report of the International Association of Antarctica Tour Operators*. In its report IAATO noted that its membership currently comprises 106 Operators and Associates, representing businesses based in 21 different Antarctic Treaty Party countries and that IAATO Operators annually carried nationals from nearly all Treaty Parties in addition to nationals from a further 44 non-Treaty Party countries. IAATO stated that the 2021-22 Antarctic season ran smoothly with no incidents to report. The 2020-21 and 2021-22 seasons saw reduced operations due to the challenges of the global pandemic. However, IAATO anticipated that the 2022-23 season would see the growth observed in prior years to continue. IAATO had invested in various tools during its history to manage the challenges that may occur during growth. During the annual meeting additional measures were agreed upon to enhance IAATO's response, such as extending the requirement for IAATO's online assessment to captains and certain officers. IAATO reported the tools and measures that it had implemented would further evolve with the continued growth.

(35) Ukraine presented IP 85 rev.1 *Implementation of the National Antarctic Program of Ukraine in the Conditions of Hybrid Warfare and Open Military Aggression of the Russian Federation: Challenges and Lessons Learned*. The paper outlined the main challenges faced by Ukraine's national Antarctic programme in the context of a hybrid war and military intervention by the Russian Federation. Ukraine informed the Meeting that the Russian Federation's unfriendly actions had had a significant negative impact on the work and progress of its Antarctic programme. It reported that the *Noosfera* had set out on its first Antarctic voyage under the flag of Ukraine from the port of Odessa on 28 January 2022, and that, since February, Odessa has been under continuous missile and artillery fire, blocking the return to Ukraine of the vessel and all Ukrainian researchers in Antarctica. Ukraine also reported that, after the collapse of the Soviet Union in 1991, the Russian Federation left all Soviet Antarctic stations under its jurisdiction, despite the fact that 16.37% of the assets of the Soviet Union should have been moved to Ukraine. It further noted that Russia's military actions had led to budget cuts in all areas of the

economy, including the budget of Ukraine's national Antarctic programme. Ukraine expressed gratitude to those Parties whose governments and Antarctic programmes had offered their assistance. Ukraine called on Parties to initiate discussions over the proper response of the Antarctic community to the unfriendly actions of one Consultative Party towards another. It also urged the Meeting to deprive the Russian Federation of its right to vote in future ATCMs, to reject any initiatives made by the Russian Federation, to terminate ongoing joint projects with the Russian Federation, and to refuse to purchase services from, or supply services to, the Russian Federation or other actors directly or indirectly affiliated with the Russian Federation.

(36) Most Parties expressed their solidarity with Ukraine and the Ukrainian people, and condemned the Russian Federation's unjustified, unprovoked and illegal war of aggression against Ukraine, noting that it violated international law and the United Nations Charter, and undermined international security and stability. Many Parties also condemned Belarus' involvement in this unlawful use of force against Ukraine. Most Parties thanked Ukraine for its time and effort in presenting its paper, noting that it raised international awareness of the plight of Ukrainian scientists working in Antarctica. Recalling previous collaboration with Ukraine, most Parties offered support to Ukraine's national Antarctic programme, and its efforts to make a full contribution to the Antarctic Treaty System. Most Parties noted the wider negative impacts of the Russian Federation's invasion of Ukraine on world and energy security, and multilateral cooperation in general. These Parties called for an immediate end to all hostilities against Ukraine, and urged the Russian Federation to withdraw its troops from Ukraine and to respect Ukraine's territorial integrity.

(37) Several Parties reported that they had condemned the Russian Federation for the invasion of Ukrainian territory, and urged that the illegitimate use of force cease, in the relevant international fora. These Parties acknowledged the challenges facing the Ukrainian national Antarctic programme and some offered them help with regards to logistics in Antarctica. These Parties stressed that the Antarctic Treaty had overcome difficult political challenges throughout its 60-year history resorting to its basic principles, like peace and international cooperation, and that the Meeting should strive to advance pressing issues that fall within the mandate of the Antarctic Treaty System.

(38) The Russian Federation condemned IP 85 rev. 1, stating that many of the statements in the paper were false. It noted that the paper, as well as comments made by many Parties posed a threat to the tradition of international cooperation that underpinned the Antarctic Treaty System. The Russian Federation expressed its outrage at the characterisation of its activities in Ukraine as unprovoked and unjustified, also referring to parts of the opening addresses during the official opening ceremony of ATCM XLIV. It stated that its military operation in the Donetsk and Luhansk regions of Ukraine was necessary to protect Russians from Ukrainian aggression, and was being carried out in accordance with Article 51 of the United Nations Charter. The Russian Federation called on Parties to ignore the paper, refrain from any accusatory rhetoric, and remain within the bounds of the ATCM's mandate.

(39) The Chair noted that a substantial number of Parties stood and walked out of the meeting room for the duration of the intervention of the Russian Federation.

(40) While acknowledging the challenges facing the Ukrainian national Antarctic programme, China suggested that the ATCM was not an appropriate venue to discuss geopolitical issues. China cautioned that the ATCM should focus on its work and not go beyond its mandate, and reminded the Meeting that multilateral mechanisms like ATCM should not be politicised. China called for the peaceful settlement of the crisis in Ukraine.

Item 5: Report of the Committee for Environmental Protection

(41) Ms Birgit Njåstad, Chair of the Committee for Environmental Protection, introduced the report of CEP XXIV. The CEP had considered 44 Working Papers and 63 Information Papers. In addition, 4 Secretariat Papers and 4 Background Papers had been submitted under CEP agenda items.

(42) Reflecting on the outcomes and achievements of CEP XXIV, the Meeting expressed its appreciation for the excellent leadership demonstrated by the CEP Chair and Vice-Chairs and the extensive amount of work the Committee had completed during its full work programme. In doing so, Parties stressed the importance of the Committee's responsibilities and roles: in the comprehensive protection of the Antarctic environment under the Environmental Protocol; in advising the ATCM using the best scientific advice available; and in the broader Antarctic Treaty System. Parties emphasised that the role of the CEP was growing increasingly urgent as Antarctica faced the impacts of climate change, non-native species introductions, and other pressures clearly articulated in reports such as those presented by SCAR, and where the effectiveness and timeliness of measures taken pursuant to the Protocol was critical.

(43) Recalling the actions taken by one Member at CEP XXIII to undermine consensus, most Parties expressed frustration that similar actions had been taken again at CEP XXIV. Some Parties raised concerns that this Member had proposed parallel, or counter-proposals, rather than engaging constructively in related intersessional work that was open to all Members and had been developed over many years by many Members as part of agreed priority work or as part of the work of CEP Subsidiary Bodies. This placed obstacles in the way of agreed priority work, and led to a lack of agreement on otherwise critical outcomes.

(44) Most Parties called on the Member to uphold the spirit of consensus and to move forward together, working constructively to maintain a regular flow of high-quality advice to the ATCM, prevent any departure from science and technical discussion and ensure outcomes that benefited the Antarctic environment in accordance with Article 12 of the Protocol. Some Parties also recalled the Paris Declaration adopted at ATCM XLIII, in which all Parties reaffirmed their strong and unwavering commitment to the objectives of the Antarctic Treaty, its Environmental Protocol and other instruments of the Antarctic Treaty System, and also reaffirmed the commitment of drawing upon the best available scientific and technical advice.

(45) China stated its continued commitment to the comprehensive protection of the Antarctic ecosystem and supported the decision-making system already established under the Antarctic Treaty System. In response to comments made by most Parties, China reiterated its willingness to work towards consensus in accordance with the Antarctic Treaty and Environmental Protocol on the basis of sound science, and emphasised that Parties needed to abide by those rules that had been agreed to, including those contained in the CEP and ATCM Rules and Procedures.

Opening of the Meeting (CEP Agenda Item 1)

(46) The Chair of the CEP advised that the CEP had welcomed Austria as a new Member, following its accession to the Environmental Protocol on 26 August 2021, and had noted that the CEP now comprised 42 members.

(47) The Meeting welcomed Austria as a new Member of the Committee and congratulated it for its accession to the Environmental Protocol.

(48)   The Committee had expressed sincere condolences for the passing of Dr Yves Frenot, who had served as CEP Chair from 2010 to 2014, and had acknowledged Dr Frenot's immense contributions to the Committee.

(49)   The Meeting also extended its sincere condolences for the passing of Dr Frenot and acknowledged his invaluable contributions to the Committee.

Strategic Discussions on the Future Work of the CEP (CEP Agenda Item 3)

(50)   The Chair of the CEP advised that the Committee had discussed a proposal to revisit the CEP's strategic priorities and Five-year Work Plan. While emphasising that the CEP had been functioning well within the current Work Plan, and that it had been successfully delivering on its mandate as outlined in Article 12 of the Environmental Protocol, the Committee had recognised the timeliness of reviewing strategic priorities in light of changing circumstances and emerging issues.

(51)   The CEP had therefore agreed to advise the ATCM that it would revisit its priorities, the functioning of the Committee, and its Five-year Work Plan at CEP XXV. The Committee had noted that, during these considerations of CEP strategic priorities, efforts would be made to identify existing and new challenges. The CEP had agreed that this would take the form of a workshop hosted in collaboration with Finland prior to CEP XXV, and that Members and Observers would be encouraged to, where appropriate, facilitate broad participation in intersessional discussions to ensure diversity and inclusivity in the workshop. The Committee had further noted that participants would be guided by the principles of the Environmental Protocol, drawing on the best available science.

(52)   The Chair of CEP noted that the Committee had updated its Five-year Work Plan to incorporate actions arising from CEP XXIV.

(53)   The Meeting commended and appreciated the process initiated by the CEP to revisit its strategic priorities and Five-year Work Plan, in particular in light of changing pressures, the urgent action required to attend to the implications of climate change, and attending to the ATCM's requests for advice. The Meeting welcomed the workshop to be held in Helsinki, and looked forward to the outcomes which would also be relevant to the work of the ATCM.

Operation of the CEP (CEP Agenda Item 4)

(54)   The Chair of the CEP advised that the Committee had discussed the utility of providing information on its two subsidiary groups, the Subsidiary Group on Management Plans (SGMP) and the Subsidiary Group on Climate Change Response (SGCCR), on the Secretariat's website. The CEP had agreed that webpages would be useful tools for disseminating information to existing and new Members. The Committee had supported the development of individual dedicated Secretariat webpages for the two Subsidiary Groups, approved initial content for these webpages to be posted, and noted that any future updates would need to be approved by consensus by the Committee.

Cooperation with other Organisations (CEP Agenda Item 5)

(55)   The Chair of the CEP reported that the Committee had received annual reports from SC-CAMLR, COMNAP, IAATO, SCAR and WMO and had nominated CEP representatives to attend the meetings of other organisations. The Committee had noted the importance of the Observers to the work of the CEP.

Climate Change Implications for the Environment: Strategic approach (CEP Agenda Item 7)

Strategic Approach

(56) The Chair of the CEP noted that the Committee had considered the decadal update of the Antarctic Climate Change and the Environment report (ACCE) and discussed policy and research recommendations put forth by SCAR on the basis of this. The Committee had congratulated SCAR on its milestone decadal update. The Committee had noted that the update underscored the urgency to conduct further research to fill science gaps and to implement response actions. It had noted the important value of the ACCE report, which had drawn on the best available science, to support the Committee's deliberations on management responses to climate change in Antarctica and the relevance of the findings for the work of the SGCCR and for the CCRWP. Finally, the Committee had highlighted the importance of communicating and disseminating the findings of this report to the wider global community.

(57) The Meeting thanked the CEP for its work and welcomed its advice. Parties also welcomed the ongoing work by SCAR to inform the CEP and ATCM on climate change in Antarctica using the best available science, noting that climate change had become one of the largest threats to Antarctica. Noting the outcomes of the ACCE Report, Parties highlighted the necessity of timely action on climate change.

(58) SCAR reiterated its encouragement for strong action related to climate change, and its appreciation that Parties had acknowledged the need for urgency in this regard.

Implementation and Review of the Climate Change Response Work Programme

(59) The Chair of the CEP noted that under this agenda item the Committee had considered a report relating to the communication, implementation and review of the Climate Change Response Work Programme (CCRWP) from the Subsidiary Group on Climate Change Response (SGCCR), as well as other papers relevant to this issue. The Committee had expressed support for the work undertaken by members of the SGCCR during the 2021-22 intersessional period and had asserted the need to continue to implement the CCRWP on the basis of knowledge of climate change and the challenges it presented. The Committee also had agreed to inform the ATCM on the progress in implementing CCRWP actions.

(60) The Chair of the CEP reported that the Committee had not reached consensus on updates to the CCRWP proposed by the SGCCR, and that the SGCCR therefore would continue working in the coming intersessional period to implement the existing CCRWP (2016) in accordance with its current Terms of Reference.

(61) The Meeting thanked the CEP and emphasised the importance of understanding the implications of climate change in Antarctica and the necessity of acting on the basis of the best available science. The Meeting welcomed the CEP's strategic approach and its focus on implementing the CCRWP. It also underscored the value of the CEP's annual progress reports to the ATCM.

(62) The Meeting called on Parties to support the continuation of this work as a priority and encouraged all Parties to actively engage in the work of the SGCCR. Parties highlighted that intersessional exchanges should be pragmatic and promote understanding among participants, particularly when different views existed, in order to facilitate Members reaching consensus.

(63)   Most Parties expressed disappointment that consensus on an updated version of the CCRWP had not been reached. These Parties voiced their frustration that one Member had individually submitted a paper with different views than those of the SGCCR, rather than engaging constructively in the work of the SGCCR, and had not sought to build agreements on its proposals blocking the process of reaching consensus on this matter. Most Parties supported keeping the CCRWP up-to-date, and emphasised that the CCRWP did not establish legally binding requirements. These Parties called for all CEP Members to engage in intersessional discussions and work towards consensus, as all Parties were obliged to do in accordance with the Antarctic Treaty.

(64)   In response to these comments, China stated that it had engaged constructively in intersessional discussions, where it had suggested that the CEP should focus on the implementation of the existing CCRWP rather than on its update. China stated that the Committee should focus on research and monitoring to narrow the knowledge gaps of the CCRWP. Given that almost all the gaps/needs and actions/tasks remained to be done under the current version of the CCRWP, China saw no need to update it at that stage. China emphasised the importance of recognising different opinions among CEP Members, and noted there was a need to improve the way to effectively and efficiently update the CCRWP.

(65)   The Chair of the CEP noted that the Committee had also agreed to advise the ATCM that it was moving to a phase more focused on CCRWP implementation, and had delivered or initiated work on almost all of the 34 Actions identified within the CCRWP, providing examples to this effect.

(66)   The Chair of the CEP further advised that the Committee had also agreed to report to the ATCM that much remained to be done to fully implement all the CCRWP Actions. The Committee had noted priority actions where effort may usefully be focused.

(67)   The Chair of the CEP reported that the Committee had noted that, for some of these priority actions, work had been underway or planned for the 2022-23 intersessional period.

(68)   The Meeting commended the CEP for having delivered or initiated work on almost all the 34 Actions identified within the CCRWP. In particular, it acknowledged the work undertaken by Dr Kevin Hughes (United Kingdom) in convening and leading the work of the SGCCR. Parties noted that during the intersessional period great progress had been made to update the CCRWP, with many CEP Members engaging constructively in discussions.

(69)   The Chair of the CEP advised that under this agenda item the Committee had also considered a review of progress in the implementation of the recommendations identified at the Joint CEP/SC-CAMLR Workshop on Climate Change and Monitoring (2016). Emphasising the importance of collaboration and communication between the CEP and SC-CAMLR, the Committee had agreed to, during the next intersessional period, initiate a process to develop a next joint CEP/SC-CAMLR workshop to take place at the latest in 2024.

(70)   The Meeting welcomed the plans for a further Joint CEP/SC-CAMLR Workshop and emphasised the importance of the collaboration between the CEP and SC-CAMLR to address the challenges of climate change in the Antarctic region.

(71)   The Chair of the CEP noted that under this agenda item the Committee had also initiated discussions on the risk of climate change impacts on Antarctic heritage values and a proposed two-year work plan to progress the development of a climate change risk assessment tool for Antarctic heritage. The Committee had expressed full support for the proposed work.

(72) The Meeting conveyed to the CEP Chair its decision to hold a joint session with the CEP, and also SCAR and COMNAP in the following year to consider the implementation of the recommendations of SCAR's Antarctic climate change and the environment (ACCE) report, and requested the CEP to provide input to the session on recommendations that fall within its functions. The CEP Chair indicated the CEP's willingness and eagerness to engage.

Draft Comprehensive Environmental Evaluations

(73) The Chair of the CEP reported that no Draft Comprehensive Environmental Evaluations had been submitted to the Committee for consideration at this Meeting.

Other EIA Matters

(74) The Chair of the CEP reported that under this agenda item the Committee had considered a paper relating to the effectiveness of EIA in Antarctica, summarising the findings of an independent assessment on this matter. The Committee had underlined the importance of the EIA process for the protection of the Antarctic environment, and had engaged in a broad discussion on the topics highlighted in the full report. The Committee advised the ATCM that it had agreed to progress on this issue through informal discussion during the intersessional period and had agreed to a work plan to that effect, but that it also had agreed that opportunities for improving the Antarctic EIA system needed to be handled carefully so as not to cause additional challenges.

(75) The Meeting thanked the United Kingdom for leading work on opportunities to improve EIA in Antarctica, including to modernise the EIA process taking into account current best practices. It encouraged all Parties to implement domestic legislation on EIA requirements for Antarctica. The Meeting agreed that the EIA process was a cornerstone of the Environmental Protocol. Some Parties also highlighted the value of keeping the Annexes up to date as a broader principle. The Meeting furthermore thanked CEP for its advice and looked forward to hearing the results from the further intersessional discussions to take place.

(76) The Chair of the CEP noted that under this agenda item the Committee also had considered the preliminary results of a project aimed at mapping coastline sensitivity and to develop an oil spill sensitivity map for the coastline of the Antarctic Peninsula region. The Committee had agreed on the usefulness of the preliminary sensitivity map for assisting with oil spill contingency planning and response, and had encouraged Members and Observers to provide suggestions for improving the map's accuracy and utility to enhance the management of potential oil spills in the Antarctic Peninsula region. The CEP Chair also noted that the Committee had considered the preliminary sensitivity map a useful tool for the EIA processes.

Area Protection and Management Plans (CEP Agenda Item 9)

Management Plans

(77) The CEP Chair reported that the Committee had considered papers that presented seventeen revised Antarctic Specially Protected Area (ASPA) management plans and one revised Antarctic Specially Managed Area (ASMA) management plan.

(78) Accepting the CEP's advice, the Meeting adopted the following Measures on Protected Areas:

- Measure 1 (2022) *Antarctic Specially Managed Area No 7 (Southwest Anvers Island and Palmer Basin): Revised Management Plan.*

- Measure 2 (2022) *Antarctic Specially Protected Area 109 (Moe Island, South Orkney Islands): Revised Management Plan.*

- Measure 3 (2022) *Antarctic Specially Protected Area No 110 (Lynch Island, South Orkney Islands): Revised Management Plan.*

- Measure 4 (2022) *Antarctic Specially Protected Area No 111 (Southern Powell Island and adjacent islands, South Orkney Islands): Revised Management Plan.*

- Measure 5 (2022) *Antarctic Specially Protected Area No 113 (Litchfield Island, Arthur Harbor, Anvers Island, Palmer Archipelago): Revised Management Plan.*

- Measure 6 (2022) *Antarctic Specially Protected Area No 115 (Lagotellerie Island, Marguerite Bay, Graham Land): Revised Management Plan.*

- Measure 7 (2022) *Antarctic Specially Protected Area No 119 (Davis Valley and Forlidas Pond, Dufek Massif, Pensacola Mountains): Revised Management Plan.*

- Measure 8 (2022) *Antarctic Specially Protected Area No 122 (Arrival Heights, Hut Point Peninsula, Ross Island): Revised Management Plan.*

- Measure 9 (2022) *Antarctic Specially Protected Area No 124 (Cape Crozier, Ross Island): Revised Management Plan.*

- Measure 10 (2022) *Antarctic Specially Protected Area No 126 (Byers Peninsula, Livingston Island, South Shetland Islands): Revised Management Plan.*

- Measure 11 (2022) *Antarctic Specially Protected Area No 127 (Haswell Island): Revised Management Plan.*

- Measure 12 (2022) *Antarctic Specially Protected Area No 129 (Rothera Point, Adelaide Island): Revised Management Plan.*

- Measure 13 (2022) *Antarctic Specially Protected Area No 133 (Harmony Point, Nelson Island, South Shetland Islands): Revised Management Plan.*

- Measure 14 (2022) *Antarctic Specially Protected Area No 139 (Biscoe Point, Anvers Island, Palmer Archipelago): Revised Management Plan.*

- Measure 15 (2022) *Antarctic Specially Protected Area No 140 (Parts of Deception Island, South Shetland Islands): Revised Management Plan.*

- Measure 16 (2022) *Antarctic Specially Protected Area No 149 (Cape Shirreff and San Telmo Island, Livingston Island, South Shetland Islands): Revised Management Plan.*

- Measure 17 (2022) *Antarctic Specially Protected Area No 164 Scullin and Murray Monoliths, Mac.Robertson Land: Revised Management Plan.*

(79) The Committee had agreed to forward the draft revised management plan for the suggested merger between ASPA 152 and ASPA 153 to the SGMP for review.

(80) The Committee had not been able to endorse the revised management plans for ASPA 145, due to differing understandings of the requirements of Decision 9 (2005). The Committee had invited the CEP Observer to SC-CAMLR to draw SC-CAMLR's attention to the issue discussed with respect to the trigger criteria in Decision 9 (2005).

(81) The Committee had also considered a draft management plan for a new protected area in Western Sør Rondane Mountains, Dronning Maud Land, East Antarctica and had reaffirmed that it had recognised that the outstanding values of the site warranted protection and had forwarded the draft management plan for the area to the SGMP for review.

(82) Under this agenda item the Committee had also considered the prior assessment of three proposed new protected areas, in accordance with the *Guidelines: A prior assessment*

process for the designation of ASPAs and ASMAs: i) Otto-von-Gruber-Gebirge (Dronning Maud Land, East Antarctica); ii) Danger Islands Archipelago (North-eastern Antarctic Peninsula); and iii) Farrier Col, Horseshoe Island, Marguerite Bay. The Committee had agreed that the values of the three proposed ASPAs merited special protection and had endorsed the development of management plans for these areas. The Committee had further highlighted the usefulness of the prior assessment procedure, which had offered the opportunity to consider proposed new areas before the majority of work toward designation had been implemented.

(83) Germany thanked the CEP for considering the prior assessments for the proposed ASPAs in Otto-von-Gruber-Gebirge (Dronning Maud Land, East Antarctica and the Danger Islands Archipelago (North-eastern Antarctic Peninsula). Referring to the results of the joint SCAR-CEP workshop held prior to CEP XXII (CEP XXII-WP 70), Germany expressed its willingness to further contribute to the systematic development of the Antarctic protected areas management system.

Historic Sites and Monuments

(84) The CEP Chair noted that the Committee had agreed to forward proposals for modifications to sites 26, 29, 36, 38, 39, 40, 41, 42, 43 and 93 of the List of Historic Sites and Monuments to the ATCM for adoption by the way of a Measure, utilising the mechanisms of Decision 1 (2021) for the first time. The Committee furthermore advised that it had made additional updates in fields that do not require adoption through a Measure to the listing for HSM 93. The CEP Chair also highlighted the finding of the wreck of the *Endurance* (HSM 93).

(85) Australia remarked that it was highly fitting to update the HSM details for the wreck of the *Endurance*, and congratulated the team of researchers on their work to locate it. The Meeting adopted Measure 18 (2022) *Revised List of Antarctic Historic Sites and Monuments: Updating information for Historic Sites and Monuments No 26, 29, 36, 38, 39, 40, 41, 42, 43 and 93.*

(86) The Committee had also considered guidance to support Parties in developing conservation management plans as tools to protect Antarctic heritage. The Committee had highlighted that, although they were not required for all HSMs, conservation management plans were a useful tool for protecting HSMs. The Committee had agreed to update the *Guidelines for the assessment and management of Heritage in Antarctica*. The Committee had encouraged Members to continue to share their conservation management plans and expertise with each other so as to raise the standard of heritage stewardship and to consider how this could be facilitated.

(87) The Meeting adopted Resolution 1 (2022) *Revised Guidelines for the assessment and management of Heritage in Antarctica*.

Site Guidelines

(88) Regarding the Committee's work on Site Guidelines, the CEP Chair reported that it had revised the site guidelines for Wordie House, Winter Island, and that it had agreed to request Torgersen Island, Arthur Harbour be removed from the list of Site Guidelines maintained by the Secretariat, as it was no longer relevant due to the closing of the Visitor's zone in ASMA 7.

(89) Accepting the CEP's advice, the Meeting considered and approved the revised Site Guidelines for Wordie House, Winter Island, agreed to remove Torgersen Island, Arthur Harbour from the list of Site Guidelines, and adopted Resolution 2 (2022) *Site Guidelines for Visitors*.

Marine Spatial Protection and Management

(90) The CEP Chair reported that no papers had been submitted under this item and made a note of the Committee's pending obligation to respond to the request from the ATCM in Resolution 5 (2017).

Other Annex V Matters

(91) The CEP Chair reported that the Committee had, recalling the positive experience the Committee had had with pre-meeting reviews on revised draft management plans prior to the virtual CEP XXIII meeting, considered and agreed to procedures for the efficient pre-meeting review of revised management plans submitted to the CEP within the remit of the SGMP. The Committee had agreed to revise the SGMP's Terms of Reference to reflect this regular task of pre-meeting review of management plans. The Committee had also adopted the SGMP work plan for 2022/23.

(92) The CEP had also considered a report on recent research to develop an inventory of type localities for terrestrial and freshwater species on the Antarctic continent and offshore islands within the Antarctic Treaty area. The Committee had recognised the value of this work in enhancing the systematic protection of Antarctica and had encouraged Members to draw on this research, as well as other relevant tools, when reviewing management plans for existing ASPAs. The Committee had also encouraged Members to continue to support efforts to improve Antarctic biodiversity knowledge, including research to determine the distribution, as well as status and trends, of species with type localities in the Antarctic Treaty area.

Conservation of Antarctic Flora and Fauna (CEP Agenda Item 10)

Quarantine and Non-native Species

(93) The CEP Chair reported that no Working Papers had been submitted under this agenda item. However, the Committee had been informed about ongoing work related to non-native species relevant to this priority item on the CEP Five-year Work Plan, and had been encouraged to see a great deal of commitment and engagement on the issue.

Specially Protected Species

(94) The Chair of the CEP reported that under this agenda item the Committee had considered the report from the CEP Intersessional Contact Group established to develop a Specially Protected Species Action Plan for the emperor penguin to support this species' designation as a Specially Protected Species and other related papers. The Committee had emphasised the importance of drawing on best available science to support CEP management decisions such as listing Specially Protected Species, and had recalled SCAR's advice on the need for the conservation of the emperor penguin. With one exception, Members voiced strong support for the recommendations that the emperor penguin should be designated a SPS under Annex II of the Protocol, and that the Action Plan should be implemented. The Committee did not, however, reach consensus on this matter despite receiving full support from all but one Member. With one exception, Members had also agreed that the current legal framework on SPS presented no impediments to advancing efforts to designate emperor penguins as SPS and that, although there was room to revisit some aspects of its guidance, the framework had not required further immediate consideration.

(95) The Meeting commended the Committee and, in particular, the SGCCR convenor, Dr Kevin Hughes (United Kingdom), for its work on this issue. Most Parties also expressed regret that an agreement could not be reached on designation of the emperor penguin as an Antarctic SPS.

(96) Most Parties expressed full support to the recommendations put forward to designate the emperor penguin as a Specially Protected Species. These Parties noted this to be a reasonable recommendation, consistent with the provision of Annex II and the relevant guidelines, and based on best available science as comprehensively synthesised by SCAR. Most Parties highlighted the high quality of SCAR's analysis based on peer-reviewed science as well as its impartial, multilateral approach to scientific research and collaboration, and that SCAR contributed its expertise and experience as an Observer to the ATCM in a manner consistent with the ATCM Rules of Procedure. Most Parties further emphasised that there was no legal or practical impediment to designating the emperor penguin as an SPS.

(97) Most Parties noted with regret that, despite the extensive work of the ICG to seek common ground, and the compelling advice of SCAR, one CEP Member had submitted a parallel Working Paper with the goal of countering the ICG's recommendations, rather than engaging constructively in the ICG. Most Parties emphasised concerns about the unwillingness of that Party to engage in consensus-building and hoped that its submission of parallel papers did not establish precedent.

(98) Several Parties commented that the information presented by this Member did not reflect the best available science, and further cautioned that, if the ATCM did not act on SCAR's clear advice to protect the emperor penguin, it might fail to meet its responsibilities under the Environmental Protocol. Most Parties indicated that they would take action to implement the advice of the ICG based on best available science and the precautionary approach, even if one Member continued to obstruct coordinated action to protect the species.

(99) China thanked the convenor of the SGCCR for his work during the intersessional period, and expressed its willingness to join any consensus in accordance with ATCM and CEP Rules and Procedure, and on the basis of best available science. China noted that it worked with other CEP members and contributed a lot of data and information on emperor penguins to the draft Action Plan, which built on ATCM XLIII-WP 37 submitted by SCAR and thus constituted the real best available science on this matter. It also noted that according to the assessment process charter in the CEP Antarctic SPS Guidelines endorsed by the ATCM in 2005, the CEP should give further assessment to potential future threats to a species, which was listed on the IUCN Red List but at a lower extinction risk level than "Vulnerable". The draft Action Plan submitted by the ICG drew on the best available science both from the CEP members and SCAR, and clearly provided the following conclusion: the emperor penguins were currently listed as Near Threatened in the IUCN Red List; the observed population of the species had been increasing in the regional (Antarctic) scale; the known and emerging terrestrial and marine threats affecting emperor penguin were considered relatively small if not negligible; the threat assessment of climate change and sea ice reduction on the species was considerably uncertain; and the threat was predicted to take place only until after 2050. Following the scientific advice from SCAR in the paper ATCM XXVIII/CEP VIII-WP 34 and ATCM XXIX/CEP IX-WP 38, China reiterated its position that the emperor penguin was not currently eligible for such a designation, and recommended the ATCM develop a targeted research and management plan for the emperor penguins as a Near - Threatened species to provide early-warning.

(100) ASOC expressed its regret that the Meeting could not agree to designate the emperor penguin as a Specially Protected Species. It commented that this would have been a precautionary, science-based, and concrete action that the ATCM could have taken to respond to the threat of climate change and to protect an important species. It highlighted that this action would be in full alignment with the Antarctic Treaty and Environmental Protocol. ASOC found it baffling that the ATCM could not agree to take this step.

(101) SCAR reiterated its appreciation to the CEP for considering and supporting its scientific advice on the conservation status of the emperor penguin. SCAR thanked the Committee for its strong motivation to take action based on its advice. It reiterated that SCAR's experts had undertaken a scientifically robust assessment concluding that designation of the emperor penguin as an SPS was warranted, based on the best available, peer-reviewed science and detailed consideration of the most up-to-date IUCN criteria and processes. SCAR further highlighted its understanding that there was no legal or practical impediment to designating the emperor penguin as an SPS. It noted that it would continue to advise the ATCM as further scientific information became available but cautioned that waiting for additional evidence before acting could mean missing the window of opportunity to protect the emperor penguin. SCAR further noted that such a designation would have been a powerful signal from Parties on their level of concern about the impacts of climate change and the need to reduce greenhouse gas emissions.

(102) Most Parties called for movement toward consensus on the issues outlined under this item and encouraged Parties to retain the conservation status of the emperor penguin as a priority for consideration at ATCM XLV - CEP XXV.

Other Annex II Matters

(103) The CEP Chair reported that the Committee had considered a paper on Important Marine Mammals Areas (IMMAs), which had suggested that IMMAs could be a useful tool to assist Parties when planning and conducting a range of Antarctic activities. The CEP Chair reported that the Committee had encouraged Members to consider this matter further and revisit discussions on IMMAs in a future meeting, and that Members had expressed their interest in doing so.

(104) The CEP Chair also reported that the Committee had considered a proposal suggesting that the *Environmental Guidelines for operation of Remotely Piloted Aircraft Systems in Antarctica*, adopted in Resolution 4 (2018), should be revised. The Committee had noted that the use of Remotely Piloted Aircraft Systems (RPAS) in Antarctica had been an increasingly frequent activity and that it required special attention, but the Committee had noted that there was no clear agreement on the immediate need to revise the RPAS guidelines. The Committee had encouraged further intersessional discussion between interested Members and a report from such discussions at a future CEP meeting.

Environmental Monitoring and Reporting (CEP Agenda Item 11)

(105) The CEP Chair reported that the Committee had discussed and had considered recommendations on the Antarctic Environments Portal. The Committee had thanked SCAR for its work and had reiterated its continued support for the Portal, noting once more its value as a source of high-quality scientific information on subjects of relevance for the work of the Committee.

(106) Recognising the value of the Portal also to the ATCM and the relevant information that SCAR provided to the Portal, New Zealand encouraged all Parties to make use of it.

(107) The CEP Chair also reported that the Committee had considered a paper drawing Members' attention to the need for a more structured system of sampling and data collection for chemical contamination in the Antarctic. The Committee had acknowledged the value of enhancing collective efforts towards the development of a structured sample data base of environmental contamination in Antarctica. The Committee had expressed broad support for the recommendations in the paper, had requested SCAR to submit recommendations to CEP XXV on how a more systematic sampling and data collection of chemical contamination in the Antarctic could be delivered, and also had encouraged Members to intensify cooperation between all stakeholders, to initiate a more structured sample and data collection of environmental contamination in Antarctica.

(108) Noting the CEP's growing emphasis on pollution in Antarctica, Germany expressed its broad support for systematic sampling and data collection in Antarctica, called for more collaboration on this issue and thanked SCAR for its willingness to submit scientific advice on the matter to a future ATCM.

(109) In addition, the CEP Chair noted that the Committee had considered a paper regarding monitoring as a key tool for decision-making for an adaptive and sustainable management of Antarctic tourism. Following broad discussions, the Committee had highlighted the importance of developing programmes to assess impacts arising from tourism activities, had expressed its support for the recommendations in the paper, and had encouraged Members and Observers to work together to progress this work.

General Matters (CEP Agenda Item 13)

(110) The Chair of the CEP advised that the Committee had considered a paper aiming to strengthen the communication of CEP science needs to researchers and national science funding agencies. The Committee had noted that the issues highlighted in the paper were relevant to all Members, especially those Members whose funding agencies and national Antarctic programmes were not closely linked. The Committee had agreed to: i) initiate a process to consider how the list of CEP science needs for Antarctic management, in the CEP Five-year Work Plan, could be further developed to clarify research needs in a way that could be more easily understood and actioned by researchers and funding agencies; and ii) advise the ATCM that Parties should ensure that CEP science needs were regularly communicated to national science funding agencies with the aim of supporting timely delivery of science to inform CEP advice to the ATCM.

(111) Several Parties noted that good science required adequate funding and requested Parties communicate CEP needs to national science funding agencies. Parties also noted that the CEP's scientific priorities should be reported with clarity to appropriate funding agencies.

(112) The CEP Chair also reported that the Committee had considered a paper from the Secretariat on an analysis of information in the EIES on Waste Management Plans and Contingency Plans. The Committee had highlighted the importance of having easily accessible information on waste management plans and contingency plans, and recalled that Article 9 (3) of Annex III to the Environmental Protocol clearly outlined Members' responsibilities to circulate and review waste management plans. The Committee had encouraged Members to share relevant information through the EIES tool.

Election of Officers (CEP Agenda Item 14)

(113) The Chair of the CEP noted that the Committee had elected Dr Heike Herata (Germany) to serve a first two-year term as the Vice-Chair. The Committee had thanked Dr Kevin Hughes for his effective, friendly and systematic approach to the work he had completed during his four-year term of service.

(114) The Meeting warmly thanked Dr Hughes for his excellent work and contributions as CEP Vice-Chair and SGCCR convenor. The Meeting also congratulated Dr Herata on her election as Vice-Chair.

Preparation for Next Meeting (CEP Agenda Item 15)

(115) The Chair of the CEP noted that the Committee had adopted the Preliminary Agenda for CEP XXV, reflecting the agenda for CEP XXIV.

(116) The Meeting expressed its appreciation to the CEP, noting the significance of the Committee's advice and recommendations to the ATCM with respect to the implementation of the Environmental Protocol.

(117) The Meeting warmly thanked Ms Birgit Njåstad for her excellent leadership of the Committee, which allowed for a productive CEP meeting. It also thanked her for her preparatory work and for facilitating the high quality of discussions despite the hybrid nature and difficult circumstances of the meeting.

Item 6a: Operation of the Antarctic Treaty System: Request from Canada to become a Consultative Party

(118) Canada informed the Meeting that it had formally submitted a request for Consultative Party status to the Depositary Government on 21 October 2021. Canada had been a non-Consultative Party since 1988, and became a full Member to the Environmental Protocol in 2003. It had implemented all Annexes that were currently in force and was on a path to approve Annex VI, with which it was already in compliance.

(119) The United States, in its capacity as Depositary Government of the Antarctic Treaty and the Environmental Protocol, confirmed that Canada had complied with the guidelines set out in Decision 2 (2017).

(120) The Consultative Parties thanked Canada for its presentation. All but two Consultative Parties agreed that Canada's application met the requirements of the guidelines set out in Decision 2 (2017), including the requirement for substantial scientific research activity in accordance with paragraph 2 of Article IX to the Antarctic Treaty.

(121) Two Consultative Parties raised concerns regarding Canada's request. Both China and the Russian Federation stated procedural as well as substantive grounds for not taking a decision at this ATCM.

(122) Following discussions and consultations, the Consultative Parties did not take a position on Canada's request for Consultative Party status. They agreed that Canada's application would be placed on the agenda for further consideration and decision at ATCM XLV in Helsinki.

Item 6b: Operation of the Antarctic Treaty System: General Matters

(123) The Executive Secretary presented SP 3 rev. 1 *List of measures with status "not yet effective"*, and reported that, according to the Antarctic Treaty database, several Measures were not yet effective. These included Measures adopted at ATCM XXVII (Cape Town, 2004), ATCM XXVIII (Stockholm, 2005) and ATCM XXXII (Baltimore, 2009).

(124) The Russian Federation introduced WP 50 *Continuing Discussion on Relevant Issues, Trends and Challenges to the Antarctic Treaty System*. It recalled that ATCM XLII had added a new priority issue (number 16) to the Multi-year Strategic Work Plan to encourage Parties to proactively identify and address current and future trends related to the Antarctic Treaty System. This had been followed by two rounds of informal intersessional discussion in which many Parties had participated. Expressing the view that conditions allowed for the launch of a new, more practically focused, stage of work on the topic, the Russian Federation proposed that the first issue to be considered under this framework would be the challenge of climate change. The Russian Federation suggested that further deliberations on the issue focus both on the impacts of climate change on the Antarctic as well as on activities within the Antarctic Treaty area that affected global climate change. Referencing earlier climate change related work within the Antarctic Treaty System, the Russian Federation emphasised that relevant decisions

of all Antarctic Treaty System bodies be taken into account in further deliberations. It stressed the need for the ATCM to decide on how to implement legal instruments of certain relevance that were outside the Antarctic Treaty System such as the Paris Climate Agreement and the Intergovernmental Panel on Climate Change. The Russian Federation recommended that the Meeting: discuss further steps for considering relevant issues, trends and challenges to the Antarctic Treaty System; consider identification of climate change as a priority issue without prejudice to the scope of the topic as reflected in the Multi-year Strategic Work Plan of 2019 and of 2021; consider prolonging informal discussions at the ATCM Forum; and update the Multi-year Strategic Work Plan as appropriate.

(125) Some Parties thanked the Russian Federation for its work during the intersessional period and underscored the importance of working together in a cooperative manner to address emerging issues and challenges to the Antarctic Treaty System. Parties also reiterated the need to address climate change in the Antarctic.

(126) Some Parties expressed support for the proposed recommendations. Noting that climate change was already being addressed under other relevant ATCM and CEP agenda items, the Meeting agreed not to continue informal discussions on relevant issues, trends and challenges to the Antarctic Treaty System on the ATCM Forum.

(127) While welcoming further efforts to address climate change, WMO highlighted that climate change was not only a natural phenomenon as had been noted in WP 50. WMO pointed out that even though natural variation was an important source of the changing climate, human influence was dominant, as confirmed by the IPCC Sixth Assessment Report.

(128) The Republic of Korea presented IP 11 *The Act on the Promotion of Polar Activities of the Republic of Korea*, which described the Act on the Promotion of Polar Activities that the government of the Republic of Korea had enacted in April 2021. It indicated that its purpose was to promote and provide the institutional foundation for the activities of the Republic of Korea in the Arctic and Antarctic, and to enhance its contribution towards addressing the global challenges faced by humanity, such as climate change. The Republic of Korea expressed its interest in developing effective arrangements that could coordinate similar assets and resources utilised in dissimilar tasks, and learning from other Parties' experiences.

(129) Argentina presented IP 34 *Commemoration of the 62nd Anniversary of the signing of the Antarctic Treaty by the APAL countries*, prepared jointly with Brazil, Chile, Ecuador, Peru, Uruguay, Colombia and Venezuela. The paper described the commemoration of the 62nd anniversary of the signing of the Antarctic Treaty in the Administrators of Latin American Antarctic Programs (APAL) countries. The commemorations had focused on public outreach activities and events, including the participation of the Secretariat, SCAR, COMNAP and other organisations.

(130) The Meeting thanked the co-authors for their paper, and some Parties joined Argentina in emphasising the importance of public outreach and communication such as this and other similar events.

(131) Ecuador presented IP 124 *Organización en Ecuador de la XXXIII Reunión de Administradores de Programas Antárticos Latinoamericanos - RAPAL 2022*. It reported that the 33rd meeting of the RAPAL countries would be held from 23 to 26 August 2022 in Quito.

(132) China introduced WP 24 *An Overview on the Legal Framework on Antarctic Specially Protected Species and Its Application*, and referred to IP 44 *An Overview on the Legal Framework on Antarctic Specially Protected Species and Its Application*. China reported that it had reviewed the legal framework on Antarctic Specially Protected Species (SPS)

and its application within the ATCM and the CEP, along with scientific advice from SCAR, with a view to providing useful guidance on future designation of Antarctic SPS. It highlighted several observations of relevance to the legal framework on Antarctic SPS with examples from past ATCM processes. These observations included: that the designation of an SPS would normally be a temporary measure; that some protection of the species was already afforded by the Environmental Protocol and other treaties; and that the Antarctic SPS category should be applied for the whole of a species' Antarctic population. China further highlighted its views, both that the IUCN red list category "Vulnerable" or higher was the threshold for considering potential designation of Antarctic SPS, and that the ATCM decision-making and consultation processes were ultimately independent from the IUCN and other bodies. China recommended that the ATCM align the future designation of SPS with its view of previous ATCM and CEP practices; encourage SCAR to assess the risk of extinction of species, using the most up-to-date IUCN criteria; and review and harmonise the inconsistency between the Guidelines and Annex II to the Protocol.

(133) Most Parties indicated that the current legal framework on SPS presented no impediments to advancing efforts to designate emperor penguins as SPS. Responding to the concerns expressed in the paper, most Parties noted that they did not consider there were material inconsistencies between Annex II and the Guidelines, and that the legal framework did not require further immediate consideration. Most Parties further emphasised that, according to the Guidelines, an IUCN listing as "Vulnerable" was not a prerequisite for designation of an SPS. All Parties affirmed that the ATCM was an independent decision-making body that was not bound by IUCN's categorisation of a species, and affirmed the importance of designating Antarctic SPS consistent with Annex II and the Guidelines.

(134) Highlighting that the information provided by SCAR indicated a need for urgent action, most Parties cautioned that further delay in designating the emperor penguin as an SPS would undermine the precautionary approach to decision making as a fundamental part of the Protocol and the work of the CEP. Most Parties emphasised the value of SCAR's expert advice as representative of best available science. Most Parties expressed specific concern that China's assertion that the emperor penguin was not currently threatened ignored projections of poor prospects for the species by the end of the century.

(135) SCAR reiterated that its experts had assessed the risk to the emperor penguin based on the most up-to-date criteria and information, and determined its conservation status to be vulnerable. SCAR noted that it had accordingly advised the CEP that it should consider the designation of the emperor penguin as an SPS. It thanked many Parties for reaffirming that SCAR was the primary source of scientific information related to SPS designation. SCAR affirmed that it would continue to provide further scientific advice as it became available, consistent with Annex II and the current Guidelines.

(136) China thanked Parties and SCAR for the comments and questions provided in respect of WP 24. China noted its conclusion that the emperor penguin was not threatened was drawn from the draft action plan provided to the CEP by the intersessional contact group considering this issue. China also clarified that SCAR was an important, but not the only, source of information for the decision-making process of the ATCM. Although China considered that there were minor inconsistencies between the Guidelines and Annex II, it reiterated its support of designating Antarctic SPS consistent with Annex II and the Guidelines.

(137) The Meeting thanked China for its paper and the accompanying IP. There was no consensus around the recommendations put forward in WP 24.

(138) The United Kingdom introduced WP 33 *Report on Effectiveness of Environmental Impact Assessment in Antarctica*, prepared jointly with the Netherlands. It reported on

the results of an independent assessment commissioned by the United Kingdom on the effectiveness of EIA in Antarctica. The United Kingdom noted that the assessment report had found that the Antarctic EIA system remained a meaningful tool in helping to protect the Antarctic environment, but that the effectiveness of the system could be improved in response to increasing pressures on the Antarctic environment. The proponents had asked the CEP for its views on taking forward any of the improvement opportunities they had identified, and the Committee had advised that it agreed to review and progress work to improve the effectiveness of the EIA system through informal intersessional discussions. The United Kingdom and the Netherlands invited the ATCM to continue encouraging all Parties to the Environmental Protocol who had yet to do so, to develop and bring into force domestic implementing legislation, particularly in respect of the EIA requirements of Annex I. They also invited the ATCM, on reviewing the advice of the CEP, to consider any further actions which could improve the effectiveness of the Antarctic EIA system, and discuss whether any work should commence on preparing for a review of Annex I of the Environmental Protocol.

(139) The Meeting thanked the United Kingdom and the Netherlands for their valuable work to review the effectiveness of the Antarctic EIA system. It confirmed that the Antarctic EIA system was an important tool to protect the Antarctic environment while agreeing that improvements could be made. Many Parties suggested that the EIA experiences gained by Parties as well as developments in national and international EIA and cumulative impact assessment processes could be considered as resources. Noting that the proponents had recommended that Parties who had not yet done so develop and bring into force domestic implementing legislation, several Parties offered to share their experience in this regard. Some Parties requested access to the document through which the conclusions, which were included in the Working Paper, had been reached. Some Parties also cautioned that further improvements to the EIA system should avoid imposing unnecessary burdens. The United Kingdom confirmed that it was ready to circulate the document to all interested Parties.

(140) The Meeting expressed support for the course of action charted by the CEP on this topic and for the actions relevant to the ATCM. The Meeting agreed that it should proceed first with improvements that could be realised under the existing legal framework, and indicated that any suggestion of revising Annex I should proceed with caution. The Meeting noted improvements requiring revisions to the text of Annex I could be discussed at a later time. The Meeting looked forward to updates from the Committee after the intersessional period, and many Parties expressed their willingness to participate in future discussions and contribute to this ongoing work.

(141) Spain noted that the current process for drafting CEP and ATCM papers could be simplified for the benefit of all Parties, especially new Parties that were not accustomed to submitting meeting documents. Spain also highlighted the high volumes of papers submitted, and the large amount of time and effort required by meeting chairs to consider and classify them for discussion. Spain proposed that the Secretariat prepare a dossier or guideline with relevant information to assist Parties in the submission of papers to the ATCM and CEP.

(142) The Meeting thanked Spain and expressed support for its proposal. It agreed to request the Secretariat to develop a guide for the presentation of papers to the CEP and ATCM, to be presented for consideration at CEP XXV and ATCM XLV.

(143) The following paper was also submitted under this agenda item and taken as presented:

- IP 51 *Communicating the Antarctic Treaty System to the United Nations* (Argentina, Australia, Chile, France, New Zealand, Norway, the United Kingdom, the United States).

(144) The following papers were also submitted under this agenda item:

- BP 8 *South Africa's Antarctic Treaties Regulations* (South Africa).
- BP 12 *Establishment of the Advisory Committee on the National Polar Policy* (Poland).
- BP 27 *Postergación de la XXVI Expedición Antártica Ecuatoriana* (Ecuador).

Item 7: Operation of the Antarctic Treaty System: Matters related to the Secretariat

(145) The Executive Secretary introduced SP 4 *Secretariat Report 2021/2022*, which provided details on the Secretariat's activities in the Financial Year 2021/22 (1 April 2021 to 31 March 2022) including addressing challenges in preparation for the virtual ATCM XLIII and CEP XXIII meetings in France, and preparation for the hybrid ATCM XLIV and CEP XXIV in Berlin. The Executive Secretary drew the Meeting's attention to the redesign of the EIES, and other improvements on its website, including a new platform for submitting meeting documents. With regard to financial matters, the Executive Secretary provided an overview of contributions it had received and presented its externally audited financial report for the financial year 2020/21. He also presented the provisional Financial Report 2021/22, remarking that the appropriation lines, which had already been adjusted for the virtual format of ATCM XLIII, were further reduced given that many of its travel plans were cancelled due to the pandemic, and that the Secretariat ended with a provisional surplus for this period of USD 253 302. The Executive Secretary reported that there had been no changes to personnel and that progress had been made on updating its human resources policy. The Executive Secretary also mentioned that the organisational review process announced at previous meetings had been resumed in this period and several recommended actions had been applied.

(146) The Executive Secretary introduced SP 5 *Secretariat Programme 2022/2023*, which outlined the activities proposed for the Secretariat in the Financial Year 2022/23 (1 April 2022 to 31 March 2023). He outlined the Secretariat's regular activities such as the preparation of ATCM XLV, the publication of reports, and other tasks assigned to the Secretariat under Measure 1 (2003). The Executive Secretary did not foresee any personnel changes in the upcoming period. In accordance with Staff Regulation 6.3 (e), the Executive Secretary reported that he intended to renew the Assistant Executive Secretary's contract for an additional four years. With regard to financial matters, the Executive Secretary drew the Meeting's attention to the rising cost of living in Argentina, which was only minimally compensated by the US Dollar's rise against the Argentine Peso. The Executive Secretary reported that despite the impact of local and global inflation, a balanced budget was attained and that the contributions for the financial year 2023/24 would not rise. In terms of intersessional activities, he announced several website and information systems developments, such as the redesign of the Contacts Database, which would include improvements to delegates' registration to the meeting. The Secretariat also extended the offer for EIES virtual training and discussion sessions, which had been implemented following a request from several Parties at ATCM XLIII.

(147) The Executive Secretary introduced SP 6 *Five Year Forward Budget Profile 2023/2024 – 2027/28*, which provided the Secretariat's budget profile for the period 2023-28. He noted that, despite local and global inflation, the accumulated surplus in the General Fund allowed for a zero-nominal increase in contributions until 2027/28.

(148) The Meeting expressed its gratitude to the Secretariat for the support it had provided and continued to provide during a challenging time. It also commended the Executive Secretary for his calm leadership.

(149) Reflecting on their positive experience with the EIES virtual training, a number of Parties encouraged Parties to utilise this opportunity. The Meeting also requested that the Secretariat prepare a paper for ATCM XLV on the utilisation of the EIES by Parties, in order to encourage transparency, which the Secretariat agreed to do.

(150) Following further discussion the Meeting adopted Decision 1 (2022) *Secretariat Report, Programme and Budget.*

Item 8: Liability

(151) The Executive Secretary introduced SP 9 *Limits of liability and environmental remediation,* which constituted a response to a request from ATCM XLII (ATCM XLII Final Report para. 174). The paper included two Annexes: a summary of all relevant Measures and Resolutions and previous advice from the CEP relating to environmental remediation and liability matters (Annex 1); and a report on the limits of liability in relevant international instruments (Annex 2), for the potential future amendment of the limits in Article 9(2) of Annex VI to the Protocol on Environmental Protection to the Antarctic Treaty.

(152) The Meeting thanked the Secretariat for preparing the paper, noting that it contained valuable information for future discussions concerning the improvement of the Antarctic liability regime.

(153) Consultative Parties provided updated information on the status of their approval of Annex VI of the Environmental Protocol, and implementation of Annex VI in domestic legislation. Chile and France informed the Meeting that they had approved Annex VI during the previous year. Several Parties congratulated Chile and France on the grounds of their approval and noted the positive progress made towards the entry into force of Annex VI. Nineteen Consultative Parties had approved Annex VI (Australia, Chile, Ecuador, Finland, France, Germany, Italy, the Netherlands, New Zealand, Norway, Peru, Poland, the Russian Federation, South Africa, Spain, Sweden, Ukraine, the United Kingdom and Uruguay). Five Consultative Parties reported that they were applying domestic legislation implementing Annex VI pending the entry into force of Annex VI (Belgium, Finland, Norway, South Africa and Sweden). Several Parties reported that they were in the process of implementing Annex VI in domestic legislation. Some Parties indicated they might complete implementation within their current legislative period.

(154) Some Parties expressed their wish to obtain further information and advice from Parties that had already completed the adoption of Annex VI. Several Parties that had already approved Annex VI to the Protocol noted that they stood ready to share their experiences, as did those in the process of implementing Annex VI into their domestic legislation. Some of these Parties offered to share their experiences and were encouraged to do so via the EIES.

(155) Several Parties noted that they considered the entry into force of Annex VI to be the current priority with respect to liability questions. Some Parties, citing possible difficulties in securing sufficient support from domestic legislatures, encouraged all Parties to continue a broader exchange on the subject while the adoption of the Annex was still ongoing.

(156) The Meeting agreed to continue to evaluate the progress made by Consultative Parties to ratify and adopt Annex VI on Liability Arising from Environmental Emergencies and bring the Annex into effect in accordance with Article IX of the Antarctic Treaty. Parties that had not yet approved Annex VI were encouraged to do so as a matter of priority. The Meeting commended the efforts of Parties working towards implementation and welcomed further reports on progress at ATCM XLV.

(157) The Meeting noted that, under Decision 5 (2015), the ATCM was to take a decision in 2020 on the establishment of a timeframe for the resumption of negotiations on liability, and that discussions on this matter had been on hold for two years. It also noted the progress that was being made towards the entry into force of Annex VI, and that many Parties considered this to be the current priority with respect to liability. The Meeting agreed to return to the matter of establishing a timeframe for the resumption of negotiations on liability in 2025 and to update the Multi-year Strategic Work Plan accordingly.

(158) Following further discussion, the Meeting adopted Decision 2 (2022) *Liability arising from environmental emergencies.*

Item 9: Biological Prospecting in Antarctica

(159) The Meeting noted that biological prospecting in Antarctica remained an item on the Multi-year Strategic Work Plan, and recommended that the agenda item should remain a priority in future meetings. The Meeting also noted the recommendations that SCAR had provided in its Survey of Member Countries regarding the collection of biological samples (ATCM XLIII-IP 12). Most Parties supported retaining the item on the Multi-year Strategic Work Plan and retaining the ATCM Forum on bioprospecting to continue intersessional discussions.

(160) One Party noted the absence of papers submitted to ATCM XLIV, and the low effectiveness of the ATCM Forum, and proposed closing the ATCM Forum on biological prospecting. Some Parties were not in favour of retaining the item in the Multi-year Strategic Work Plan in 2023. These Parties expressed readiness to consider re-inclusion of the issue on the Multi-year Strategic Work Plan in future meetings.

(161) The Meeting reaffirmed that the Antarctic Treaty System was the appropriate framework for managing the collection of biological material in the Antarctic Treaty area and for considering its use. The Meeting agreed to retain the item on the agenda, but did not reach consensus on continuing the ATCM forum on biological prospecting or retaining this item on the Multi-year Strategic Work Plan. It was stated that Parties do not need a forum to continue exchanging views on this subject during the intersessional period. Some Parties expressed an interest in continuing discussions on the collection of biological material during informal intersessional consultations. Several Parties also stated that they were working on papers related to biological prospecting in Antarctica, which they planned to submit to a future ATCM.

Item 10: Exchange of Information

(162) Spain introduced WP 9 *Review of the scientific information contained in the EIES.* It reminded the Meeting that information exchange was a commitment undertaken by the Parties under Article III (1) (a) and Article VII (5) of the Antarctic Treaty, as well as under Article 17 of the Environmental Protocol and its annexes. Spain recalled that ATCM XLIII-SP 10 had identified a gradual decrease in scientific information exchanged between Parties, and suggested that a review be conducted on the scientific information sent to the EIES. Spain proposed that the Meeting establish an ICG to initiate the review as well as to discuss and exchange ideas that would enable and encourage the development of useful tools for Parties. Spain encouraged Observers and Experts to contribute to this work to ensure the interoperability of data across different relevant databases.

(163) The Meeting thanked Spain for its paper and underscored that the exchange of information was a cornerstone of the Antarctic Treaty System. The Meeting also noted recent improvements made by the Secretariat to the EIES and thanked the Secretariat for

this work. The Meeting highlighted that scientific data and information was already shared through a number of other national and international repositories such as the Antarctic Metadata Directory (AMD) managed by SCAR. The Meeting agreed that future work should aim to simplify information sharing and ensure interoperability between different systems.

(164) SCAR thanked Spain for its paper and emphasised its long-standing interest in scientific information exchange and data management. SCAR reminded the Meeting of its Standing Committee on Antarctic Data Management (SCADM), which facilitated co-operation between scientists and Parties with regard to scientific data. SCAR further highlighted the principle of FAIR data, noting that data was only useful if it was Findable, Accessible, Interoperable, and Reusable. It stated that achieving data interoperability was particularly challenging. SCAR also welcomed Spain's invitation to participate in a potential ICG.

(165) The Meeting requested the Secretariat to commission information from all Parties on how evidence of non-compliance with the Treaty or Protocol in Antarctica should be recorded and presented to their competent authorities. The Secretariat agreed to issue such a commission during the intersessional period and welcomed the offer of the United Kingdom to assist with drafting. The Secretariat noted it would collate responses and present a paper to ATCM XLV.

(166) Welcoming the proposal in WP 9, IAATO noted its prior work with competent authorities to simplify data input in EIES and expressed its interest in participating in an ICG. Additionally, IAATO acknowledged the difficulties for national competent authorities to penalise unauthorised vessels, noting that it appeared some of these unauthorised vessels were becoming bolder in their activities, which continued to undermine the Antarctic Treaty System. IAATO offered its support in collecting appropriate information and requested additional guidance on what was needed.

(167) The Executive Secretary noted that, in an effort to avoid redundancy and duplication with other existing efforts, the Secretariat would collaborate with SCAR, and provide updates of the information presented in SP 7 and ATCM XLIII-SP 10. On the matter of non-authorised activities, the Secretariat recalled that a specific forum had been created on the Secretariat website to allow communication among national competent authorities, as well as to make information on the denial of authorisations available as one of the Summarised Reports of the EIES.

(168) The Meeting agreed to establish an ICG on Scientific Information in EIES with the aim of:

- Discussing the advisability of reporting on the existence of international scientific cooperation among the Parties;

- Examining the fields contained in item 2.1.2. (Science Activities in Previous Year) of the Annex to Decision 7 (2021) to determine whether it was necessary to include other customisable fields that would allow to generate summarised reports and thematic maps;

- Analysing the advisability of including a section in item 1 (Pre-season Information) of said Annex on science projects foreseen to be developed in the following year's campaign;

- Avoiding duplicating information already submitted to prevent overload in fulfilling the exchange requirements;

- Reporting on the results and proposals of the ICG at the ATCM XLV in order to update Decision 7 (2021); and

- Identifying any specific trends in EIES reporting by Parties with the view of increasing utilisation of the EIES.

(169) It was further agreed that:

- Observers and Experts participating in the ATCM would be invited to provide input;

- The Executive Secretary would open the ATCM forum for the ICG and provide assistance to the ICG; and

- Spain would act as convener and report to the next ATCM on the progress made in the ICG.

(170) Ecuador presented IP 116 *Propuesta ecuatoriana de catálogo de objetos geográficos antárticos*. It highlighted the value of geo-object catalogues for defining geographic data by optimising the information production processes, increasing its consistency and logic, and harmonising information structuring. Ecuador highlighted examples in which spatial information on Antarctic geo-objects was being expanded by SCAR and Australia. Ecuador intended to present a catalogue and accompanying proposal on how to move this work forward to the 33rd Meeting of the Administrators of Latin American Antarctic Programmes (RAPAL).

(171) The Executive Secretary noted that the spatial information it made available on the Secretariat website was standardised according to international norms.

Item 11: Education Issues

(172) Bulgaria introduced WP 23 *Fifth report of the Intersessional Contact Group on Education and Outreach*, prepared jointly with Belgium, Brazil, Chile, Portugal, Spain and the United Kingdom. Bulgaria recalled that ATCM XLIII had supported the continuation of the ICG on Education and Outreach and reported on the ICG's work over the past year, which it had conducted via the online ATCM Discussion Forum. This forum included seven posts from four Parties focusing on national and international education and outreach activities. Highlights of the activities included celebrations surrounding the 30th anniversary of the signing of the Environmental Protocol, and "Polar Week" celebrations, which involved almost 3000 students. The ICG recommended that the ATCM: recognise the usefulness of the Forum on Education and Outreach and support the work of the ICG during one more intersessional period; advise Parties to keep promoting the use of the Forum and provide information on their activities related to education and outreach; and advise Parties to continue to promote, not only Antarctica and Antarctic research, but also the Antarctic Treaty and Environmental Protocol, through their education and outreach activities.

(173) The Meeting thanked the proponents for WP 23 and congratulated the ICG on its work through the intersessional period. Parties emphasised the essential role of education and outreach in increasing our understanding of Antarctica, particularly in the context of climate change impacts. Parties highlighted the importance of promoting inclusivity and diversity in Antarctic programmes and activities, and noted some of the initiatives already underway. Some Parties and Observers also highlighted the educational opportunities available through SCAR, COMNAP and IAATO, including various fellowship programs for early career researchers. One Party also noted its view that education and outreach efforts should follow the ATCM Rules of Procedure.

(174) The Meeting agreed to continue the ICG on Education and Outreach for another intersessional period with the aim of:

- Fostering collaboration at both the national and international level, on Education and Outreach;

- Identifying key international activities/events related to education and outreach for possible engagement by the Antarctic Treaty Parties;

- Sharing results of education and outreach initiatives that demonstrate the work of Antarctic Treaty Parties in managing the Antarctic Treaty area;

- Emphasising ongoing environmental protection initiatives that had been informed by scientific observations and results, in order to reinforce the importance of the Antarctic Treaty and its Protocol on Environmental Protection;

- Promoting related education and outreach activities by Experts and Observers, and encouraging cooperation with these groups;

- Sharing best practices and encouraging, enhancing and promoting diversity and inclusion across the global Antarctic community, including among scientists, logisticians, policy-makers and all others engaged in Antarctic matters, in order to lower any barrier to the engagement of all the talents needed to tackle the challenges of the future of Antarctica;

- Encouraging Parties to provide the Secretariat with link(s) to their web page(s) with educational and outreach resources (the Secretariat will include these links in its "Educational Resources" section of the Secretariat webpage); and

- Inviting Parties, Observers and Experts to review, during the intersessional period at the ATCM Education and Outreach Forum, the work carried out by the ICG and discuss its future development.

(175) It was further agreed that:

- Observers and Experts participating in the ATCM would be invited to provide input;

- The Executive Secretary would open the ATCM forum for the ICG and provide assistance to the ICG; and

- Bulgaria would act as convener and report to the next ATCM on the progress made in the ICG.

(176) WMO presented IP 74 *Education and Outreach Activities of the World Climate Research Programme*, which discussed the education and outreach activities of WMO's co-sponsored World Climate Research Programme (WCRP). WMO highlighted two new WCRP initiatives: the WCRP Climate Science Academy and the Climate and Cryosphere (CliC) Fellowships and Grants. These two initiatives aimed to ensure that the next generation of climate science leaders would be ready to take on important roles in guiding the climate research agenda and would equip scientists to engage with the public in the context of climate change.

(177) The following papers were also submitted and taken as presented under this agenda item:

- IP 17 *Celebración del 30° Aniversario del Protocolo al Tratado Antártico sobre Protección del Medio Ambiente entre Chile y España* (Chile, Spain).

- IP 105 *Education & Outreach Activities of Turkey in 2021-2022* (Türkiye).

- IP 126 *Actividades en Educación y Comunicación Antártica* (Chile).

(178) The following papers were also submitted under this agenda item:

- BP 24 *Ventana de Tiempo: primera película colombiana filmada en la Antártica* (Colombia).

- BP 28 *Antarctic education and outreach activities along 2021* (Uruguay).

- BP 32 *Romanian Education and Outreach Activities in 2020-2022 Pandemic* (Romania).

Item 12: Multi-year Strategic Work Plan

(179) The Meeting considered the Multi-year Strategic Work Plan adopted at ATCM XLIII (SP 11). It considered how to take each priority item forward in the coming years, and whether to delete current priorities and add new priorities.

(180) After discussion, the Meeting adopted Decision 3 (2022) *Multi-year Strategic Work Plan for the Antarctic Treaty Consultative Meeting.*

(181) The Meeting reaffirmed that the Multi-year Strategic Work Plan was a useful tool to support its work. Noting that it had been ten years since the Work Plan had been first adopted at ATCM XXXV, the Meeting considered it timely to dedicate attention to the Work Plan by engaging the Secretariat to assist the Meeting in making the Work Plan more effective and efficient. It was also suggested that Parties consider bringing forward papers to ATCM XLV on how the Meeting could use, maintain and optimise the Work Plan.

(182) The Meeting requested that the Secretariat review the ATCM's use of the Multi-year Strategic Work Plan and report its findings back to ATCM XLV.

Item 13: Safety and Operations in Antarctica

Safety and Operations: Aviation

(183) COMNAP introduced WP 17 *Additional COMNAP advice in regards to ATCM review of Resolution on Air Safety in Antarctica*, referred to IP 6 *Antarctic Aviation Workshop 2022 Report*, and thanked all experts who contributed to the Workshop. The paper provided additional advice in regards to Resolution 6 (2021) *Air Safety in Antarctica.* COMNAP suggested updates based on the outcomes of the Antarctic Aviation project and Workshop 2022. Key recommendations included: the removal of the words "hard copy"; consider the addition of a new operative sub-paragraph in regards to requiring transponders be turned on in all aircraft operating in the Antarctic Treaty area and in regards to strongly recommending ADS-B In technology on all aircraft operating in the area; to add the words "and other operators" to paragraph 8; and to add a new operative paragraph to refer to minimum recommended survival equipment on-board aircraft.

(184) IAATO stated that it strongly supported COMNAP's work on air safety, and noted that IAATO air operators had been pleased to contribute to the workshop and intersessional discussions. IAATO supported the proposal that all operators, both non-governmental and governmental, should install technologies to support safe air operations.

(185) Many Parties congratulated COMNAP on the air safety work and for convening the Antarctic Aviation Workshop 2022. The Meeting welcomed this additional advice from COMNAP in support of the ATCM review of Air Safety in Antarctica Resolution. After discussion, and consultation, the Meeting broadly agreed to the recommendations as presented by COMNAP in WP 17

(186) The Meeting adopted Resolution 3 (2022) *Air Safety in Antarctica.*

(187) Colombia presented IP 110 *Identificación de peligros de la operación aérea en la Antártida para gestionar la seguridad operacional de la Fuerza Aérea Colombiana - Fase II.* It reported on an ongoing study by the Colombian Air Force aimed at identifying potential risks involved in aerial operations on the Antarctic Peninsula. The objective of the study was to effectively design procedures to improve the safety of aerial activities in the area. Colombia noted that the study had paid particular attention to the improvement and maintenance of runways, and the use of aerial photography and drones to acquire more detailed knowledge about flight conditions on the Antarctic Peninsula.

Operations: Maritime

(188) Brazil presented IP 64 *Hydrographic and Cartographic Activities of Brazil in the Antarctic Region carried out during the last two campaigns of the Brazilian Antarctic Program (OPERANTAR XXXIX e XL)*. It reported on the recent work of the Directorate of Hydrography and Navigation (DHN), the agency representing Brazil in the IHO. It also presented an overview of bathymetric and hydrographic surveys undertaken and the nautical publications and charts that the Brazilian Antarctic programme updated during the last two seasons.

(189) Argentina presented IP 87 *Report on the 24th edition of the Joint Antarctic Naval Patrol between Argentina and Chile – 2021/2022*, prepared jointly with Chile. Argentina noted that its joint Antarctic naval patrols with Chile had been ongoing since 1998. The patrols included search and rescue activities, salvaging operations, pollution monitoring, and remediation actions to safeguard navigation and the environment.

(190) Bulgaria informed the Meeting that it would be sending a Bulgarian vessel to the Bulgarian St. Kliment Ohridski station in the upcoming Antarctic season.

(191) Referring to IP 92, the United Kingdom noted that its researchers had observed large volumes of plastic pollution deriving from fishing vessels in the Southern Ocean. The United Kingdom encouraged ASOC to continue reporting on this issue.

(192) Regarding the papers presented on maritime matters, the Meeting reflected on the importance of strengthening the exchange of points of view on national experiences of hydrographic surveys, as well as on the implementation of the Polar Code in Antarctica. The Meeting therefore invited Parties to share papers on these matters at the next ATCM. Following a proposal from Finland, the Meeting supported the organisation of a topical session to the agenda of the ATCM XLV to enhance and support harmonised implementation of the IMO Polar Code in waters around both poles.

(193) The following paper was submitted and taken as presented under this agenda item:

- IP 92 *Developments to enhance the safety of pleasure yachts and fishing boats operating in the Antarctic Treaty area* (ASOC).

Safety and Operations: Stations

(194) COMNAP introduced WP 18 *Report on emergency plans and implementation of natural disaster risk assessment at Antarctic stations*. It recalled that Resolution 7 (2021) invited COMNAP to present a report to assess the general situation of emergency plans at Antarctic bases and its support operations, and the degree of implementation of natural disaster risk assessment programmes. COMNAP reported that it undertook a survey to assess the general situation of emergency and evacuation plans, procedures and the availability of shelters or evacuation locations in case of a natural disaster affecting Antarctic stations and their support operations. All Member programmes with stations responded to the survey. Survey results indicated that 20 of the 29 COMNAP Member national Antarctic programmes with one or more stations in the Antarctic Treaty area had emergency plans in the event of a natural disaster. They also indicated that 23 of these national Antarctic programmes had shelters in case of a natural disaster. COMNAP invited the Parties to consider these results during any review of their emergency management plans and future work within the ATCM on this topic. COMNAP also stressed that this survey was a first step to a larger project on these issues.

(195) The Meeting thanked COMNAP for its comprehensive paper on emergency plans and natural disaster risk assessment at Antarctic stations. Many Parties emphasised the

importance of this work and stated that they would consider these results in developing future emergency plans. Many Parties and IAATO also expressed a willingness to continue working with COMNAP on this issue.

(196) The United Kingdom and Argentina noted that, when further assessing the situation of emergency and evacuation plans, procedures and the availability of shelters or evacuation locations in Antarctic stations, the risk of occurrence of natural disasters at such stations should be taken into account, so as to concentrate efforts on the stations that need it most. It was suggested that this work could be expanded to other natural disasters.

(197) Finally, the Meeting stressed the importance of promoting wide participation in the Technical Collaboration Group that COMNAP would organize to identify knowledge gaps and be prepared to respond to the risks associated with seismic activity. COMNAP agreed to bring further information on this work to a future ATCM.

(198) Germany presented IP 59 *Report on Refurbishment and Modernization of the German Antarctic Receiving Station GARS O'Higgins* It highlighted the need for the modernisation of GARS O'Higgins Station to reduce the human footprint, and noted that the station had been in operation for more than 30 years. Germany noted that crane access had only been allowed to the east of the station, where the Chilean site was located, to protect the breeding Gentoo Penguin colonies in immediate vicinity of the station buildings. Efforts to protect the Gentoo Penguin also included a penguin protection fence. Germany thanked in particular Chile and also Brazil for their logistic support.

(199) Germany presented IP 70 *Energetic modernisation of the German Neumayer-Station III*, which investigated the possibilities of modernising the energy infrastructure, enhancing renewable energy technologies, and reducing operational costs. Although Neumayer-Station III was considerably larger than Neumayer-Station II, it consumed 50 per cent less fuel due to energy optimisation. It also informed the Meeting that as the start of the upgrade a new wind turbine planned with a nominal power of 50 kW will be installed in January 2023 and tested for at least one year.

(200) The Meeting thanked Germany for its papers, and highlighted its interest in cooperating and learning from Germany regarding future modernisation plans in order to collectively reduce the human footprint in Antarctica.

(201) Several Parties mentioned that, in addition to modernisation, joining stations or sharing logistics in the future could also be a way forward in combatting climate change. Noting the increased amount of construction work in Antarctica, the Meeting suggested that Parties should continue sharing information and experiences on the environmental, safety and cultural aspects of their construction work for the benefit of all Parties.

(202) COMNAP referred the Meeting to its ATCM XLII-IP 47 and to the COMNAP Symposium Proceedings on Station Modernization. COMNAP also noted its willingness to continue to provide practical and technical advice to assist the ATCM in its decision-making on the modernisation topic.

(203) Ecuador presented IP 115 *Análisis de riesgos de desastres naturales en la zona de influencia de la Estación Científica "Pedro Vicente Maldonado"* which proposed an analysis of climatic, environmental, and anthropic aspects to reduce the risk of possible natural disasters at its scientific station. Ecuador highlighted COMNAP's initiative on the evaluation of the status of emergency plans in Antarctic bases and their implementation of disaster risk programmes, as set out in Resolution 7 (2021). Ecuador reported that it planned to cooperate with Chile to establish joint emergency procedures as both Parties had experience regarding tsunami alerts.

(204) Uruguay presented IP 33 *Proyecto Cambio de matriz energética Base Científica Antártica Artigas. Instalación de Generador Eólico* which reported on the installation of a portable

wind turbine at the General Artigas Station. Uruguay stated that it was currently undertaking a trial period to be assessed in the 2022/23 season, and that it intended to eventually construct a wind park in order to minimise its greenhouse gas emissions and eliminate the use of fossil fuels in Antarctica.

(205) The Secretariat presented SP 7 *Waste Management Plans and Contingency Plans: Analysis of the information provided by the Parties in the EIES*. This paper analysed the status and evolution of the data that corresponded to the information exchange requirements for waste management plans and contingency plans contained in the annual report and permanent information that Parties submitted to the EIES during the period 2012-2021. This study revealed that, regarding the provisions of Annex III and Annex IV to the Protocol, the data submitted on waste management and contingency plans appeared to be incomplete and was not consistent among the Parties. The Secretariat noted that the general lack of accessible and updated waste management plans and contingency plans on the EIES did not necessarily preclude the existence of such plans. The Secretariat mentioned that it stood ready to assist Parties in the utilisation of the EIES.

(206) IAATO welcomed the exchange of information on waste management and contingency plans. It noted that Annex III and IV also applied to non-governmental operators, and IAATO operators were keen to have their contingency plans and, where relevant, waste management plans accessible through the EIES.

(207) The Meeting thanked the Secretariat for its analysis and encouraged it to keep presenting these kinds of reports. It observed that waste management was an essential aspect of the Environmental Protocol and required continuous improvement. Further, the Meeting reaffirmed the importance of information exchange in complying with transparency requirements of the Antarctic Treaty System and the need to continue working on its enhancement. The Meeting also encouraged Parties to make use of the Secretariat's offer of virtual training sessions in using the EIES.

(208) The following papers were also submitted under this agenda item:

- BP 1 *Indoor Farming Facility at the Antarctic King Sejong Station* (Republic of Korea).

- BP 4 *Resumen sobre la Campaña Antártica de Verano 2021-2022* (Uruguay).

- BP 5 *Update of the Information on the Progress of the Renovation of the Henryk Arctowski Polish Antarctic Station on King George Island, South Shetland Islands.* (Poland).

- BP 6 *40th Brazilian Antarctic Operation (OPERANTAR XL) – 2021/2022* (Brazil).

- BP 7 *Celebrating the 40 years of the Brazilian Antarctic Program (PROANTAR)* (Brazil).

- BP 16 *Monitoring of hazardous objects on the glacier in the Larsemann Hills region (East Antarctica)* (Russian Federation).

- BP 20 *Installation of the VHF Repeater Module on Horseshoe Island* (Türkiye).

- BP 22 *On the Progress of Work on the Assembly of a New Wintering Complex at Vostok Station in the 2021/2022 Season* (Russian Federation).

- BP 27 *Postergación de la XXVI Expedición Antártica Ecuatoriana* (Ecuador).

Issues relating to the management of the COVID-19 pandemic

(209) COMNAP presented IP 94 *National Antarctic Programs' operations as the global pandemic continued*. COMNAP stated that national Antarctic programmes working together to respond to the COVID-19 challenge might have been the greatest example of

international collaboration in relation to Antarctic activities that it had witnessed in recent times. The paper reported on the 2021/22 season, the COMNAP COVID-19 guidance, and the implementation of that guidance by national Antarctic programmes in order to facilitate Antarctic science. It commended all national Antarctic programmes for their commitment to the implementation of the protocols.

(210) The Meeting thanked COMNAP for the update and highlighted the extraordinarily challenging circumstances for research in Antarctica during 2021/22 season. The Meeting commended COMNAP for its leadership in facilitating exchange of experiences and in establishing recommendations that had helped Parties to facilitate world-leading science through the pandemic. Particular reference was made to the SCAR-COMNAP Joint Expert Group on Human Biology & Medicine and the COMNAP COVID-19 *ad hoc* Subcommittee for its excellent and tireless work during the pandemic.

(211) The Meeting extended a special thanks to all scientists and personnel of national Antarctic programmes who had worked collaboratively to save lives and to ensure that science could continue regardless of the pandemic. It acknowledged the work of the national Antarctic programmes in the gateways of Argentina, Australia, Chile, New Zealand and South Africa in facilitating and liaising for the safe passage of other programmes through their airports and ports while also managing their own complex programmes. The Meeting also recognised the valuable work of the Joint Expert Group on Human Biology & Medicine, with leadership from the British Antarctic Survey Medical Unit, and the COMNAP COVID-19 *ad hoc* Subcommittee, with leadership from the Alfred Wegener Institute, Helmholtz Centre for Polar and Marine Research.

(212) IAATO thanked COMNAP for its close collaboration and communication during the pandemic. While IAATO operators did not conduct tourist visits to research stations during the 2020-21 season, five IAATO operators had provided logistical assistance to national Antarctic programmes. IAATO noted that these operators followed COMNAP and national Antarctic programme protocols and would continue to do so in the future. IAATO also noted the collaborative work and communication with Parties with Gateway cities to Antarctica.

(213) SCAR noted that long-term research was essential for understanding the current and future conditions of Antarctic and Southern Ocean environments, the dynamics of our solar system, and the fundamentals of how the universe worked. On behalf of the scientific community, SCAR thanked COMNAP and the national Antarctic programmes for enabling such long-term science to continue under the challenging circumstances of the pandemic, and for keeping the scientific community safe during an extraordinary time.

(214) COMNAP thanked the Parties for their overwhelming support and noted that responding to pandemic challenges was only possible to achieve because of the engagement of national Antarctic programmes and with open communication with the IAATO Secretariat. COMNAP confirmed that it was already working on updated guidance for the 2022/23 season.

(215) The following papers were also submitted and taken as presented under this agenda item:

- IP 57 *DROMLAN's efforts to prevent the spread of SARS-CoV-2 virus within the Dronning Maud Land, Antarctica* (Germany, India).

- IP 58 rev.1 *Efficiently and Safely Conducting Expeditions in the Arctic and Antarctic During the SARS-CoV-2 Pandemic* (Germany).

(216) The following paper was also submitted under this agenda item:

- BP 29 *Outcome of the application of the Sanitary Protocol for Uruguay's Antarctic activities during 2021-2022, and its update* (Uruguay).

Item 14: Inspections under the Antarctic Treaty and the Environment Protocol

(217) Chile presented IP 29 *Seminario sobre inspecciones Antárticas*. The paper highlighted inspections as a key mechanism of the Antarctic Treaty System and introduced the concept of a seminar to allow Parties that had carried out Antarctic inspections to share their learning and create opportunities to cooperate. Chile informed the Meeting that, together with Argentina, it would organize an Antarctic Inspection Seminar in November 2022, and would circulate its terms of reference to other Parties in due course.

(218) The Meeting recalled that, during ATCM XLII, it had agreed to informally discuss items linked to inspections. The Meeting thanked Chile and Argentina for organising the seminar in response to that request. Many Parties noted they would be willing to attend the seminar.

Item 15: Science issues, future science challenges, scientific cooperation and facilitation

Scientific cooperation and facilitation

(219) Türkiye presented IP 99 *Czechia-Turkey Scientific and Logistic Collaboration in Antarctica*, prepared jointly with the Czech Republic, which presented information on the collaboration between the Czech Republic and Türkiye during the 6th Turkish Antarctic Expedition (TAE-VI). Türkiye also presented IP 102 *Bulgaria-Turkey Scientific and Logistic Collaboration in Antarctica*, prepared jointly with Bulgaria, which presented information on the collaboration between the 30th Bulgarian Antarctic Expedition and TAE-VI. Türkiye reported that all Parties to these collaborations had fulfilled their commitments well and carried out their joint operations in a spirit of solidarity and mutual support. Türkiye noted that international scientific collaboration enhanced not only the interests of individual research projects but also helped reduce carbon footprints in Antarctica.

(220) Türkiye presented IP 103 *A Memorandum of Understanding between the Ministry of Science and Innovation of the Kingdom of Spain and the Scientific and Technological Research Council of Turkey*, prepared jointly with Spain, which reported on the signing of a memorandum of understanding between Spain and Türkiye regarding cooperation in polar sciences and logistics. Türkiye also presented IP 104 *A Memorandum of Understanding between the Scientific and Technological Research Council of Turkey, Marmara Research Center, Polar Research Institute and the National Institute of Polar Research, the Research Organization of Information and Systems*, prepared jointly with Japan, which reported on the signing of a memorandum of understanding between the national competent institutions of Türkiye and Japan dealing with polar research. Türkiye informed the Meeting that it looked forward to cooperative polar research, joint coordination of intellectual activities, improved utilisation of resources, cooperation in polar logistics, and enhanced exchange of scientific information and research materials.

(221) The Meeting thanked Türkiye and noted the usefulness of keeping the ATCM informed about the formal agreements they conclude in matters of Antarctic or polar scientific cooperation.

(222) WMO presented IP 106 *WMO Unified Data Policy and the Global Basic Observing Network (GBON)*, which reported on the adoption of a reviewed and updated data policy and information sharing network following the 2021 Extraordinary Session of the World Meteorological Congress. WMO reported that the Unified Data Policy established the general purposes, scope, and intent of data exchange between all WMO members, while the GBON was expected to significantly strengthen the global availability of observational data. The Policy sought to expand WMO information exchange practices to cover all relevant WMO earth data, going beyond weather, climate and water data to include domains such as atmospheric composition, oceanography, the cryosphere, and space

weather. WMO reported that the new instruments aimed to facilitate free and open exchange of data and measurements between various meteorological organisations, enhance numerical prediction models, and help meteorological institutions worldwide access critically-needed observations.

(223) The Meeting thanked WMO for its presentation and noted the potential of the newly implemented policy and network to benefit vital research and meteorological institutions worldwide.

(224) COMNAP presented IP 5 *Early Career Opportunities: Antarctic Fellowships & Scholarships*, prepared jointly with CCAMLR, SCAR and IAATO. The paper identified the joint work of the four proponents to support early career persons in their Antarctic research and engineering projects. COMNAP emphasised the importance of early career opportunities, both for aspiring scientists and engineers, as well as for the general wellbeing of Antarctic research. COMNAP encouraged all Parties to bring these opportunities to the attention of their early career persons.

(225) The Meeting thanked the co-authors for IP 5 and noted the great value of the past twenty years of collaboration in supporting early career persons in Antarctic research, science and engineering.

(226) Uruguay presented IP 28 *Uruguay, país anfitrión de la XXXII Reunión de Administradores de Programas Antárticos Latinoamericanos*, which reported on the latest RAPAL meeting in September 2021. Uruguay introduced RAPAL's key functions as a forum facilitating discussions and exchanges about Antarctic scientific, logistic and research matters between the Latin American countries and other invited parties. It noted that the collaboration had been carried out for over two decades in a spirit of solidarity that warmly complemented the spirit of cooperation within the Antarctic Treaty system.

(227) The Meeting thanked Uruguay for its paper. Argentina thanked Uruguay for hosting the event and highlighted the role of RAPAL among all Latin American national Antarctic programmes.

(228) The Meeting thanked Parties for their papers and reiterated its support for all further international collaboration in scientific cooperation and facilitation in Antarctica.

(229) The following papers were also submitted and taken as presented under this agenda item:

- IP 12 *Scientific and Science-related Cooperation with the Antarctic Community and Responses to COVID-19* (Republic of Korea).

- IP 13 *Korea-Chile Collaboration in Antarctic Research* (Republic of Korea, Chile).

(230) The following papers were submitted under this agenda item:

- BP 2 *Icebreaking polar class research vessels: New Antarctic fleet capabilities* (COMNAP).

- BP 17 *Colombia avanza en los propósitos de su Programa Antártico con la construcción de un buque de investigación científico-marina Ice Class 1C* (Colombia).

- BP 31 *Antarctic research skills acquired under cooperation between Romania and Republic of Korea 2015-2020* (Romania).

Science issues and future science challenges

(231) The United States presented IP 26 *International Thwaites Glacier Collaboration: The Future of Thwaites Glacier and its Contribution to Sea-Level Rise,* prepared jointly with the United Kingdom. The paper provided an update on a joint research programme of the US National Science Foundation (NSF) and the UK Natural Environment Research

Council (NERC), which sought to obtain reliable longer-term projections of ice loss and sea-level rise originating from Thwaites Glacier. It stressed the important role of Thwaites Glacier as an area of interest in the ongoing process of climate change. Current estimates suggested that the melting of the glacier alone had contributed up to four millimetres in global sea-level rise, of the total three metres of global sea-level rise that could result from a general loss of the West Antarctic ice sheet. The results of the project had been published through various channels and were made widely available to the global scientific community. In conclusion, the United States highlighted the importance of international cooperation in sustaining long-term research projects and reiterated its full commitment to advancing the scientific understanding of marine ice sheets and the climate conditions in the Thwaites Glacier area.

(232) The United Kingdom stressed the importance of international collaboration in carrying out research projects of this magnitude and noted that, in order to address crucial and complex questions related to global climate change, it was essential to engage in thorough collaboration with respect to science, logistics and information exchange.

(233) Norway presented IP 73 *Troll Observing Network (TONe) – A new research infrastructure supporting Earth System science with data from Dronning Maud Land,* which described a new research infrastructure project funded by the Norwegian Research Council. Norway highlighted that the Troll Observing Network (TONe) was a response to Resolution 8 (2021), which had called for Parties to support efforts to undertake research about Antarctic climate change and its impacts. It noted that TONe had benefited from a number of Norwegian and international stakeholders, and that data collected by TONe observatories would be openly available to the entire scientific community in line with Article III of the Antarctic Treaty.

(234) Switzerland presented IP 119 *Switzerland's contribution to snow research in Antarctica 2011-2021,* which summarised the past decade of research activities conducted by Swiss scientists concerning snow and firn in Antarctica at different host stations. Reviewing the various scientific contributions and achievements, Switzerland extended its thanks to all its international collaborators and, in particular, the Parties whose stations had hosted Swiss expeditions and researchers.

(235) WMO presented IP 71 *Winter Targeted Observing Periods and Further Plans of the Year of Polar Prediction in the Southern Hemisphere (YOPP-SH).* The paper provided an update on the activities undertaken in the Antarctic as part of the WMO's Polar Prediction Project since ATCM XLII. The paper described how the Year of Polar Prediction (YOPP), a hallmark activity of the PPP, had galvanised extra observation and modelling efforts in both the Arctic and Antarctic. WMO reported that the ongoing activities under YOPP included a second Antarctic Special Observing Period whose goal was to improve forecast capabilities during the non-summer months. The work and analysis of the results would continue until the season 2023-24. WMO noted that the upcoming YOPP Final Summit was scheduled to be held in Montreal in August 2022. In conclusion, WMO requested all Parties to share information about the YOPP data portal with their meteorological actors and networks in order to help create a comprehensive meteorological database for mutual benefit.

(236) The Meeting thanked WMO for its valuable contribution and highlighted the importance of the Year of Polar Prediction for the entire Antarctic community. It also congratulated WMO for its public outreach work and for its broad sharing of polar weather data.

(237) Ecuador presented IP 113 *Avances del proyecto de generación de un robot submarino para su uso en la Antártida,* which provided an overview of the development of a submarine robot suitable for Antarctic deep-sea research. Developed by a dedicated researcher in cooperation with universities in Ecuador, New Zealand and Australia, the device could be used to reach depths of up to 8000 metres with remote guidance

combining submarine robotics and artificial intelligence. Ecuador invited other Parties to consider assisting Ecuador to transport the submarine to Antarctic waters and to assist in facilitating its testing in Antarctic conditions.

(238) China presented IP 122 *Group-size effect on vigilance and flight initiation distances of Adélie penguins in south-eastern Antarctica*, which described the findings of the 36th Chinese National Antarctic Research Expedition in regards to the vigilance initiation distances and flight initiation distances of Adélie penguins to potential disturbances from human activities. Reporting its results that could help improve navigation practices and environmental protection in the Antarctic, China remained determined to continue to support this research. It concluded by inviting other Parties with similar interests to join it in further collaboration.

(239) Germany presented IP 60 *Information about the German concept paper "Polar Regions in Transition"*. The paper summarised the findings and recommendations of a detailed polar research concept paper composed by a new, dedicated advisory board commissioned by the German Federal Ministry of Education and Research. Germany directed the attention of other Parties to the structure of the concept paper, which sought to approach Antarctic research by presenting a number of guiding questions and providing concrete recommendations for further research agendas. It noted that the document had been made publicly available online in English for all interested Parties.

(240) The United States presented IP 27 *The Value of Long-term Ecological Datasets to Evaluate Ecosystem Response to Environmental Change along the Antarctic Peninsula*. The report highlighted the need to carry out research on the complex climatic feedbacks between the atmosphere, ice and oceans controlling the Antarctic ecosystem dynamics and evolution. It emphasised the value of long-term research programmes seeking to anticipate how global change might evolve over the coming decades and to build a scientific foundation for guiding future action plans towards enhancing the sustainability of ecosystems. The United States noted that its Long-Term Ecological Research (LTER) programme had been developed since the 1980s, with five polar sites of which two were in Antarctica. It was, therefore, able to provide unique information regarding regional environmental changes over three decades. Among the notable long-term results, in addition to data about the direct loss of ice sheets, were observations of critical impacts of the loss of sea ice leading to changes in habitats favouring some species and endangering others. The results had been published widely, and the United States welcomed all interested Parties to contact the US Antarctic Research Data Centre for further information.

(241) SCAR presented IP 107 rev. 1 *The Southern Ocean contribution to the United Nations Decade of Ocean Science for Sustainable Development*, prepared jointly with Belgium, the Netherlands, IAATO, WMO, and more generally, the Southern Ocean Task Force. It reported that the Task Force included organisations from across the scientific research community, industry sectors, and national and international management bodies. SCAR reported that the UN Decade of Ocean Science aimed to gather ocean stakeholders worldwide behind a common framework for research to support a sustainable future for the world's oceans. The Southern Ocean community had engaged in stakeholder-oriented processes to develop a Southern Ocean Action Plan, published in April 2022. SCAR noted that the Decade of Ocean Science was a unique opportunity to mobilise stakeholders together to focus on the research needs of the Southern Ocean. It further noted that the Action Plan aimed to identify research challenges, to strengthen the links between science, industry and policy, and to encourage internationally collaborative activities to address gaps in knowledge and data coverage. The Southern Ocean Action Plan was now freely available to download as indicated in the Information Paper.

(242) Colombia presented IP 109 *II Congreso Internacional "Colombia y su proyección en la Antártica"*, which introduced an annual international congress held in Colombia on the

protection of Antarctica as a space of academic research and scientific collaboration. In 2021, the congress had taken place in hybrid format and had aimed to promote discussions and awareness about Antarctic matters, as well as to help in formulating national Antarctic policy. Noting the participation of international partners from Brazil, Chile, Ecuador and elsewhere, Colombia expressed its gratitude to all national and international Antarctic institutes for their active cooperation.

(243) Türkiye presented IP 101 *Turkish Polar Science Workshops*, which reported on the annual National Polar Science Workshops held in Türkiye since 2017. Türkiye observed that the 5th National Polar Science Workshop had hosted over 500 participants, that over 100 abstracts had been submitted, and that over 80 institutions had been involved in the proceedings, with lectures by internationally noted speakers receiving considerable attention online.

(244) The Meeting thanked all the Parties and SCAR for their presentations on science issues and noted the many achievements and advancements which had been discussed.

(245) The following papers were submitted and taken as presented under this agenda item:

- IP 95 *Progress of glaciological research activities at the Dome Fuji station and its vicinity* (Japan).

- IP 108 *The Ice Memory Programme* (France, Italy).

(246) The following papers were also submitted under this item:

- BP 15 *Russian glaciological investigations at Vostok station during the 67th Russian Antarctic Expedition (January 2022)* (Russian Federation).

- BP 18 *Seeds for Future - Global Wild Plant Seed Vault* (Italy).

National Programmes' main scientific activities and results

(247) As a preliminary comment, the Chair suggested to Parties that, pursuant to the provisions of the ATCM Rules of Procedure (particularly Rules 50 and 51), the documents that provide information on the activities and results of their national Antarctic programmes should be presented to the Meeting in the form of Background Papers. She also noted that, for those papers that present scientific priorities in the medium and long term, and given the implications that they may have for identifying opportunities for cooperation, it would be appropriate to present these as Information Papers.

(248) Australia presented IP 50 *Australian Antarctic Science Program 2021-22*, which reported on highlights from its 2021/22 science programme. These included the arrival of Australia's new icebreaker RSV *Nuyina* and the testing and commissioning of the vessel's science systems; fieldwork to support projects on climate processes and change, and Southern Ocean ecosystems and environment protection and management; and the publication of a number of significant papers. Australia reported that it had begun developing a decadal plan for Antarctic science that would set out priority science questions and research priorities. Australia emphasised that the Australian Antarctic Science Program continued to benefit from national and international research and operational collaborations.

(249) Malaysia presented IP 63 *Malaysia's activities and achievements in Antarctic research and diplomacy*, which presented an update on its research activities and diplomatic efforts in the 2021/22 season. Malaysia thanked Chile, the Republic of Korea, and the United Kingdom for their continued support of its activities in Antarctica.

(250) Malaysia presented IP 69 *Report from Asian Forum of Polar Sciences to the ATCM XLIV*, which reported on the activities of the Asian Forum for Polar Sciences (AFoPS) to advance cooperation among Asian polar science institutions. Highlighting Malaysia's

chairmanship of AFoPS from 2021-22, it informed the Meeting that its recent work included: a webinar on capacity building; the 2021 AFoPS annual general meeting, held online 28 – 29 October 2021, where an MoU was signed between SCAR, the International Arctic Scientific Committee (IASC) and AFoPS; and a special meeting held online on 28 March 2022 in conjunction with the Arctic Science Summit Week (ASSW). Malaysia thanked AFoPS' members for their work.

(251) Japan presented IP 96 *Japan's Antarctic Research Highlights 2021- 22.* It outlined the research highlights of the 2021-22 season including high-resolution observations of the Antarctic atmosphere with the Program of the Antarctic Syowa Mesosphere, Stratosphere, and Troposphere/Incoherent Scatter (PANSY) radar and complementary instruments, and advanced balloon-borne observations of the Antarctic upper troposphere and lower stratosphere and hot water drilling at Laghovde Glacier. Japan noted that its scientific activities had returned to pre-pandemic levels.

(252) The Secretariat reminded Parties that, in response to a request made at the ATCM XLII (ATCM XLII Final Report, para 311) it had created a section on its website to highlight the key science priorities of national Antarctic programmes so as to make these easily accessible to all Parties. The Meeting encouraged Parties that had not yet done so, to provide information to the Secretariat to display on the website.

(253) The following papers were submitted and taken as presented:

- IP 78 *Update on the Australian Antarctic Strategy and 20 Year Action Plan and major initiatives* (Australia).

- IP 125 *Actividad de Chile en Glaciar Unión* (Chile).

(254) The following papers were submitted under this agenda item:

- BP 3 *Aotearoa New Zealand Antarctic Research Directions and Priorities 2021 - 2030* (New Zealand).

- BP 9 *Expedición Científica del Perú a la Antártida* (Peru).

- BP 10 *Actividades del Programa Nacional Antártico de Perú Período 2021 – 2022* (Peru).

- BP 19 *Antarctic Publications by Turkish Scientists (2021/2022 Update)* (Türkiye).

- BP 21 *The Sixth Turkish Antarctic Expedition (TAE-VI)* (Türkiye).

- BP 23 *Report on the scientific activity of the Argentine Antarctic Institute – 2021* (Argentina).

- BP 25 *VIII Expedición Científica de Colombia a la Antártica, verano austral 2020-2021* (Colombia).

- BP 30 *Indian Antarctic Scientific Activities During 2021-22* (India).

Diversity issues in Antarctic science

(255) Australia presented IP 55 *Diversity and inclusion in the Australian Antarctic program*, which described a range of activities aimed at increasing diversity across all aspects of the Australian Antarctic Program (AAP) over recent years. It welcomed the discussion on equality, diversity and inclusion at the Meeting. Australia noted that the AAP's diversity and inclusion activities aimed to ensure that all employees and expeditioners felt safe, welcome and respected as well as free from any discrimination. Australia highlighted that the Australian Antarctic Division was committed to increasing diversity across all aspects of the AAP.

(256) Argentina presented IP 114 rev.1 *Gender approach in the National Antarctic Program of Argentina*, which reported on the activities of Argentina's Antarctic Program with

regard to gender equality. It reported that women working within the National Directorate of the Antarctic and the Argentine Antarctic Institute held leadership positions as directors and managers. As for scientific personnel, Argentina noted that there had been gender parity among the personnel who carried out tasks in different Argentine Antarctic stations for several years. Regarding logistical support staff, it noted that women were being commissioned as motorists and drivers, and that parity had been achieved at the Carlini Station.

(257) SCAR welcomed the papers by Australia and Argentina and referred to its own efforts to further equality, diversity and inclusion through the establishment of its Equality, Diversity, and Inclusion (EDI) Action Group in January 2022.

(258) COMNAP thanked the Meeting for acknowledging its efforts on improving gender equality, inclusivity, and in developing recommendations that allowed for the safe reporting and communication of harassment, unwanted advances and inappropriate behaviour in Antarctica. It referred to its Preventing Harassment in Antarctica Safety Expert Group workshop held in 2018, and noted that it worked together with SCAR, IAATO and CCAMLR to ensure that its early-career opportunities also promoted equality, diversity and inclusion.

(259) The Meeting thanked Australia and Argentina for their papers, and recognised the increasing international interest in factors related to intersectionality and diversity. The Meeting also expressed its desire to ensure that everyone working on Antarctic matters was safe, welcomed, respected and free from discrimination. The Meeting expressed a firm commitment to this issue and welcomed further sharing of information on activities as well as best practices by Parties, Observers and Experts. The Meeting also commended SCAR and COMNAP for their extensive work on these matters.

Item 16: Implications of Climate Change for Management of the Antarctic Treaty Area

(260) The United Kingdom introduced WP 29 *Antarctica in a Changing Climate – Implementing ATCM Resolution 8 (2021)*, prepared jointly with Australia, Belgium, Finland, France, Germany, the Netherlands, Norway, Sweden, the United States, SCAR and ASOC. The paper provided an update on the implementation of Resolution 8 (2021), which was adopted at ATCM XLIII in response to the IPCC Special Report on the Ocean and Cryosphere in a Changing Climate (SROCC). It highlighted the many briefings and events undertaken since ATCM XLIII to share current science and to inform decision-makers about the implications of climate change in Antarctica. The United Kingdom thanked SCAR, the International Cryosphere Climate Initiative (ICCI), the Association of Polar Early Career Scientists (APECS), the UK Arctic and Antarctic Partnership (UKAAP) and ASOC member, World Wide Fund for Nature (WWF), for their support. The proponents highlighted the need for urgent action to mitigate climate change by focusing on two broad themes: the contribution of Antarctic ice sheets to irreversible global sea level rise with implications for coastal communities; and Southern Ocean ecosystems (including krill) under pressure from acidification and freshening and their role in helping to maintain a stable climate. The proponents also recommended that the ATCM: support research on the actual and potential implications of climate change; continue to support SCAR in the communication of the latest research and information on climate change and its impacts through its regular and valued updates to the ATCM; and support the work of the CEP to consider the environmental implications of climate change through the CCRWP. The United Kingdom also highlighted its IP 23 *Antarctic Blue Carbon*.

(261) ASOC thanked the proponents, expressed its support for the recommendations and its interest in contributing to the implementation of a Resolution. In support, ASOC also presented a short film titled "Krill: Superheroes of the Southern Ocean", produced by WWF.

(262) The Meeting thanked ASOC for its film presentation and, reflecting on the innovative nature of the film, emphasised the need for modern communication methods when interacting with the broader public on issues of climate change.

(263) Expressing its support for the recommendations outlined in the paper, WMO stated that it would continue working with Parties and SCAR as well as prepare papers relating to the issue of climate change. It also drew the Meeting's attention to the Intergovernmental Panel on Climate Change (IPCC)-WMO Pavilion at the 2021 United Nations Climate Change Conference (COP26) in Glasgow, and noted that it was planning similar events for the 2022 United Nations Climate Change Conference (COP27) in Egypt.

(264) SCAR thanked the Meeting for its support and highlighted its participation in many events at COP26.

(265) The Meeting thanked the proponents and expressed support for their recommendations. It further encouraged all Parties to communicate the urgency of taking actions to address climate change to governments, the economic sector, and civil society. Several Parties informed the Meeting of additional activities they were undertaking as part of implementing Resolution 8 (2021).

(266) The Meeting endorsed the recommendations in WP 29, and agreed to continue working to implement Resolution 8 (2021). With respect to the second recommendation in WP 29, which called on the ATCM to continue to support SCAR in the communication of the latest research and information on climate change and its impacts, the Meeting agreed to also support national Antarctic programmes in this endeavour.

(267) SCAR introduced WP 30 rev. 1 *Antarctic Climate Change and the Environment: A Decadal Synopsis. Findings and Policy Recommendations* and referred to IP 72 *Antarctic Climate Change and the Environment: A Decadal Synopsis and Recommendations for Action.* SCAR also introduced WP 31 rev. 1 *Antarctic Climate Change and the Environment: A Decadal Synopsis. Research Imperatives.* SCAR reported on the significant update to the ACCE Report, stating that the synopsis was based mainly on the findings of the IPCC's Sixth Assessment Report and drew on reports of the Intergovernmental Science-Policy Platform on Biodiversity and Ecosystem Services (IPBES). The ACCE Report included additional environmental research findings and outcomes of research prioritisation, undertaken by SCAR through its Antarctic and Southern Ocean Horizon Scan and through priorities identified by the SCAR Scientific Research Programs and other activities. SCAR emphasised that the report provided a global consensus, agreed by thousands of scientists, on the current physical and living environmental situation in the Antarctic, especially with respect to ice sheets, projections for the future, and implications, both globally, such as for sea level rise, and regionally, such as for Antarctic and Southern Ocean biodiversity. SCAR also presented a series of policy recommendations for Parties to consider based on the evidence presented in the synopsis.

(268) SCAR drew the Meeting's attention to several key messages that derived from its recommendations including: the urgency for action, both regional and global, for mitigating projected impacts of climate change; that the requirement for urgent action was not constrained by the need to reduce the uncertainty associated with future projections; the need to develop, with due urgency, large-scale integrated research approaches across national Antarctic programmes to reduce uncertainties in key areas, including improving projections of Antarctic cryosphere change, especially in a global

mean sea-level rise context, improving understanding of, and projections for, Antarctic biodiversity change, especially systems and species that were likely to be most vulnerable, and furthering the understanding of tropical-high latitude climate teleconnections and climate models, especially the Southern Annular Mode. The fourth and final key message was the requirement to develop clear, timely and regular communication about environmental changes in the Antarctic, and their implications for both Antarctic environments and the earth system, to governments, parties to related international agreements, the economic sector and to civil society. Finally, SCAR stressed that the report was based on an extraordinary body of internationally collaborative research, much of which had been supported by national Antarctic programmes, and the large majority of which had been drawn together through the voluntary work of researchers from most of the world's nations.

(269) The Meeting thanked SCAR for its significant update to the ACCE Report, and commended the scientists that had contributed to this considerable joint body of work. The Meeting also emphasised the value of receiving high-quality science syntheses. Many Parties highlighted the usefulness of the infographic attached to the papers and noted the teleconnections between Antarctica and the rest of the world, as well as the challenges the associated changed weather patterns posed for the stability of research infrastructure in Antarctica. Many Parties commended the ATCM XLIV Host Country for appropriately choosing "From Science via Policy to Protection" as the theme of the Meeting. Parties highlighted the value of the report for the CCRWP and agreed on the urgent need to take action to limit global warming to 1.5°C above pre-industrial levels.

(270) China, while generally supportive of the recommendations put forward in the papers, noted the scientific uncertainties in the rate of sea level rise trends, biodiversity and climate models SCAR had raised in its report, as well as the achievability of the proposed management goal to preserve the Southern Ocean environment in a state close to that known in the past 200 years. Recognising the crucial role of SCAR in providing independent and objective scientific advice to support and inform the work of the ATCM and CEP, as expressed in Resolution 7 (2019), China expressed concerns on whether SCAR was the appropriate body to provide policy recommendations.

(271) In response to China, many Parties recalled SCAR's important and long-standing role in providing for over sixty years sound advice and best available science to the Antarctic Treaty System, as reflected in Article 10 (2) of the Protocol.

(272) WMO thanked SCAR for the papers and informed the Meeting of its role in climate related research, including within the World Climate Research Programme (WCRP).

(273) ASOC thanked SCAR for its paper and stressed that Antarctica was of vital importance in combatting climate change, and that the need for curtailing emissions was present and urgent.

(274) COMNAP remarked that it would be sharing the SCAR report with its Science Facilitation Expert Group. It noted that maintaining sufficient government funding of national Antarctic programmes was imperative in order to meet science priorities.

(275) SCAR thanked Parties for their comments and their positive response the paper and the Decadal Synopsis. SCAR appreciated Parties' recognition of the urgency of these matters, including the research requirements and the need to meet Nationally Determined Contributions in keeping the world to 1.5 degrees of warming. In responding to the questions about preserving a state known for the past 200 years, SCAR made clear that system dynamics were included in such a state. In responding to the questions raised about whether it was an appropriate body to provide policy recommendations, SCAR noted that these were evidence-based recommendations and that it would be irresponsible not to put these recommendations forward.

(276) The Meeting welcomed SCAR's report and adopted Resolution 4 (2022) *Antarctic Climate Change and the Environment: A Decadal Synopsis and Recommendations for Action report*, recommending the dissemination of the report to departments and agencies charged with climate change negotiations, to Antarctic science and research bodies and funding agencies, and to the general public and media. The Meeting also continued to welcome updates from SCAR on climate change and its implications.

(277) The Meeting also adopted Decision 4 (2022*) Letters on Antarctic Climate Change and the Environment: A Decadal Synopsis and Recommendations for Action report* to send letters to the UNFCCC, IPCC, WMO, IPBES and IMO forwarding SCAR's Decadal Synopsis.

(278) The Meeting agreed to hold a full-day joint session of the CEP and the ATCM, with SCAR and COMNAP, to consider the implementation of the ACCE recommendations at ATCM XLV. The Meeting encouraged Parties, Observers and Experts to submit papers on the topic to ATCM XLV, and to bring experts to the meeting to support this work.

(279) China introduced WP 48 *The Implementation of the Climate Change Response Working Programme*. China recalled that Resolution 4 (2015) encouraged the CEP to begin to implement the CCRWP as a matter of priority. China noted that the CEP had established the SGCCR to facilitate the efficient and timely implementation of the CCRWP. On the basis of its initial review of the work of ATCM and the CEP in the past years, China recommended that the CEP focus its efforts on the implementation of the CCRWP and: adopt the reformatted CCRWP using the new format agreed in 2019; emphasise the important role of scientific research and monitoring as a centre piece of the implementation of CCRWP; re-confirm that the SGCCR should draft annual progress reports on the implementation of the CCRWP to the CEP, including the extent to which the related monitoring, research or management gaps/needs were fulfilled; and ask the SGCCR to update the CCRWP in accordance with the decisions of the ATCM or CEP, and report back the following year to further discuss the implementation of the CEP's CCRWP and the role of the SGCCR.

(280) The Meeting thanked China for its paper. While Parties agreed with the crucial role of scientific research and monitoring in reacting to climate change, they did not support the specific recommendations proposed by China in WP 48. Parties recalled the extensive discussions of WP 48 during the CEP meeting and expressed widespread support for the work of the SGCCR and its recommendations for revising the CCRWP as laid out in WP 37 *Report of the CEP Subsidiary Group on Climate Change Response (SGCCR) 2021- 2022* (United Kingdom). Reiterating the urgency of responding decisively to climate change, the Parties stressed the importance of moving forward in a productive manner towards further action.

(281) ASOC presented IP 90 *Ice Sheet Instability, Long-term Sea-level Rise, and Southern Ocean Acidification: Time for Coordinated Action by Antarctic Treaty Parties*, which advocated that the clear communication of the rapidly evolving findings of Antarctic science should comprise a matter of the highest concern to the Antarctic Treaty System. In particular, ASOC recommended that all participants should increasingly focus not only on the impacts of climate change on Antarctica but on the impact of these changes on the entire planet. To change the course of actions, ASOC proposed: that Parties should bring the findings of Antarctic science to strong global attention at the UNFCCC; that SCAR should do its utmost to voice the findings of Antarctic science at the upcoming COP27 and 2023 United Nations Climate Change Conference (COP28) meetings; and that the ATCM should regularly revise and communicate its priorities relating to the irreversible effects of climate change.

(282) The Meeting thanked ASOC for its paper. Many Parties expressed support for ASOC's efforts to enhance the communication of Antarctic research and policy priorities, as well as advancing global awareness about the role of the Antarctic in the global impacts of climate change. The Meeting commended ASOC on the examples of public communication and outreach it presented at ATCM XLIV, and noted ASOC's strong position as a facilitator for the public communication of Antarctic priorities, actions and findings.

(283) SCAR welcomed ASOC's paper and commended ASOC for its ongoing work in science and policy communication. It also thanked ASOC for its recommendations and agreed to continue to represent Antarctic science in the COP meetings in cooperation with other accompanying experts and participants such as the WMO.

(284) The following paper was submitted under this agenda item:

  • IP 89 *Banning Hydrocarbon Extraction in Antarctica Now: Reducing the Risks and Impacts of Global Climate Change* (ASOC).

Item 17: Tourism and Non-governmental Activities in the Antarctic Treaty Area, including Competent Authorities Issues

Policy and Management

(285) Spain introduced WP 22 *Towards adaptive and sustainable management of Antarctic tourism: Monitoring as a key tool for decision-making*, prepared jointly with Ecuador and the United States. It noted that tourism and non-governmental activities in the Antarctic had grown steadily since the 1960s, and recalled ATCM Recommendations IV-27 and VI-7, which recognised that tourism activities could jeopardise the conduct of scientific research, hinder the conservation of flora and fauna, and do lasting damage to the Antarctic environment. Noting the paucity of data on tourism impacts, the proponents proposed that: Parties promote the establishment of monitoring programmes to assess the actual impacts arising from tourism activities; the CEP promote the development of these monitoring programmes and continue with its work to understand the cumulative impacts of tourism on the environment; the monitoring programmes involve multiple stakeholders, including bodies such as SCAR, COMNAP and IAATO, which could contribute to the development and implementation of the programmes; and the monitoring programmes consider the needs identified in this document.

(286) The Meeting thanked the proponents and expressed support for the recommendations in WP 22.

(287) The Meeting emphasised the importance of data collection that contributed to the understanding and management of tourism and non-governmental activities and their cumulative impacts, particularly in the context of renewed growth of tourism activity. The Meeting emphasised the importance of monitoring programmes to assess the actual impacts arising from tourism activities, assessing the effectiveness of management measures, supporting the requirement to assess and verify impacts, and to understand the sensitivity of sites. The Meeting underscored the desirability of concrete action on the monitoring of tourism impacts to ensure the sustainability of tourism while protecting the Antarctic environment, and welcomed the attention of the CEP, and of SCAR, to monitoring issues. Several Parties highlighted national initiatives and projects that had collected data on tourism and carried out systematic monitoring over many decades and could serve as a basis of coordinated long-term monitoring programmes. The Meeting noted the challenges associated with establishing strategic long-term monitoring, including design of monitoring schemes, questions of spatial and temporal scale, funding, access to monitoring locations, and coordination across Parties and projects. Several Parties reflected on the importance of local scale monitoring efforts, in addition

to coordinated large-scale monitoring schemes.

(288) IAATO welcomed the recommendation to engage with a wide range of stakeholders, and noted the support provided by IAATO members for existing long-term monitoring programmes. It observed that it was not always easy to differentiate between the impacts arising from tourism, other activities, and climate change in Antarctica. IAATO noted the importance of a collaborative approach to help address practical and logistical challenges and offered its support in the development of a long-term monitoring programme.

(289) ASOC supported the initiatives proposed in WP 22 and noted that it was important for Parties to develop dedicated programmes for monitoring tourism impacts. ASOC emphasised that monitoring was important for collecting the scientific information needed to inform tourism management and policy development and to understand how tourism contributes to cumulative impacts. ASOC also noted its appreciation for data provided by IAATO and by Parties which complements other kinds of monitoring data.

(290) SCAR welcomed the recommendations and highlighted its long-standing history of undertaking science that sought to distinguish natural variability from anthropogenic forcing. It also noted many other international programmes undertaking focused work to develop effective monitoring that was financially and logistically efficient.

(291) The Netherlands introduced WP 36 *Report of the Intersessional Contact Group on Permanent Facilities for Tourism and other Non-Governmental Activities in Antarctica.* reporting on work in an ICG established at ATCM XLIII and convened by the Netherlands. The Netherlands noted the broad participation in the intersessional discussions and that they had covered a wide range of topics including: information on previous proposals to establish permanent tourism facilities in Antarctica; the definition of "permanent facilities"; and concerns related to the potential establishment of permanent facilities raised at previous meetings. The Netherlands indicated that even though interest in the development of these types of facilities remained limited, Parties had encountered some inquiries, and that there was a clear urgency to act. The ICG report recommended that the Meeting adopt a Resolution on permanent facilities for tourism and other non-governmental activities in Antarctica, and further proposed that the ICG continue, with the intention of conducting an inventory of existing facilities supporting tourism and other non-governmental activities, and discussing further regulation, including a possible Measure on this topic.

(292) The Meeting thanked the Netherlands for leading the intersessional discussions and expressed general support for the recommendations of WP 36. The Meeting welcomed the recommendation for a Resolution to prevent such projects, and supported the proposal for further discussion in an ICG, including conducting an inventory of tourism and non-governmental facilities to inform further discussion.

(293) Several additional points were raised by Parties, including: the importance of ensuring that tourism in Antarctica had no more than a minor or transitory impact; ensuring that tourism and non-government activities were conducted in a safe manner; the implications of increased air traffic in support of land-based tourism activities including safety risks and potential search and rescue impacts; the potential contribution of tourism activities to cumulative impacts; potential impacts on wilderness values; and new challenges and threats to the environment posed by the growth and diversification of tourism and other non-governmental activities.

(294) Some Parties, while recognising the legitimate concerns arising from activities that might be associated with permanent facilities, suggested that further discussion should remain focused on key issues arising from such facilities, rather than seeking to consider the large number of related or secondary issues as part of the same discussion.

(295) Many Parties highlighted the importance of following a precautionary approach, and some expressed their support for adopting a legally binding Measure on this topic. Parties recalled Article 3 of the Environmental Protocol and its fundamental role in protecting the Antarctic environment, its dependent and associated ecosystems, and its intrinsic values, including its wilderness and aesthetic values. Some Parties expressed the view that the establishment of permanent facilities in Antarctica was against the fundamental principle of preserving Antarctica as a continent for peace and science. One Party observed that the benefits citizens experienced from Antarctic tourism could be achieved without establishing permanent facilities.

(296) IAATO thanked the Netherlands and expressed its support for the draft Resolution, noting that the establishment of permanent facilities in Antarctica would conflict with IAATO's by-laws and would threaten the wilderness and aesthetic values that motivated many tourists to visit Antarctica. IAATO also expressed its appreciation for the definition of "permanent facilities" used in the ICG and WP 36, recalling that it drew on its paper ATCM XXXII-IP 101, which made explicit reference to tourism having no more than a minor or transitory impact, and was in harmony with IAATO's existing by-laws. IAATO noted that, in the face of unauthorised tourism activities, it was helpful to strengthen requirements by Parties, and noted that collaboration and cooperation were key in the successful management of tourism. It emphasised the need for further developing clear definitions and agreed that any further expansion in scope should not leave grey areas open to interpretation, as this could lead to a de-harmonisation of the authorisation or permitting system.

(297) ASOC thanked the Netherlands for its paper, and expressed support for WP 36 and the adoption of the proposed Resolution. ASOC looked forward to the continuation of discussions on this topic.

(298) The Meeting agreed that the ICG on permanent facilities for tourism and other non-governmental activities in Antarctica should continue its work during the next intersessional period, with the following terms of reference:

- To make an inventory of already existing infrastructure supporting tourism and other non-governmental activities in Antarctica;

- To discuss concerns relating to such infrastructure, including, for instance, environmental concerns and pressure on the search and rescue capacity of national programs;

- To discuss and prioritise further action by the ATCM relating to such infrastructure and future plans, including, if appropriate, the adoption of a legally binding measure;

- To report back to ATCM XLV.

(299) The ATCM agreed that Observers and Experts participating in the ATCM would be invited to provide input and in particular ASOC and IAATO were encouraged to contribute.

(300) The ATCM welcomed the offer from the Netherlands to serve as convener of this ICG.

(301) The Meeting adopted Resolution 5 (2022) *Permanent facilities for tourism and other non-governmental activities in Antarctica.*

(302) Germany presented IP 8 *Tourism monitoring in Antarctica - Development of a concept for the analysis of the impacts of tourism on the assets to be protected in the Antarctic.* It provided details of a research project to develop a concept to investigate and monitor the long-term impacts of tourism in Antarctica. In the course of the project, the German Environment Agency had hosted a workshop on the Estrel premises to get stakeholders involved in the early stages.

(303) Parties welcomed Germany's initiative in IP 8 as an example of concrete action and noted other specific activities recently launched relating to monitoring efforts, including a research programme on tourism, including consideration of monitoring issues, established by the Netherlands.

(304) France presented IP 56 *Feedback on a monitoring conducted on a tourist vessel according to Resolution 9 (2021)*. It reported on the outcomes of a tourism monitoring mission led by the French NCA according to the framework set up by Resolution 9 (2021), noting that France's intention was to assess the framework's effectiveness in the field. France noted that the paper presented several critical lessons learned during the implementation of the monitoring scheme, and identified benefits and limitations of the monitoring framework. France concluded that Resolution 9 (2021) was effective in enabling NCAs to better understand activities under their jurisdiction and monitor compliance with the relevant national and international instruments. It also noted that the experience indicated that a monitoring mission could be organised in a short time and at low cost. France encouraged Parties to implement Resolution 9 (2021) and to share their experiences.

(305) IAATO thanked France for its paper and highlighted that the sharing of information would make all observation programmes more robust. IAATO reported that over the previous two seasons it had performed two virtual dockside observations on superyachts. IAATO highlighted some lessons arising in the conduct of virtual observations, noting the need for advanced coordination and flexibility from all involved, including the operator, the vessel and the observer, and sufficient internet capability to support virtual walk-throughs and interviews. IAATO advised that the virtual inspections had been successful in observing superyacht operations, even during the ongoing pandemic. IAATO reported that it planned to conduct approximately 30 observations on yachts and cruise-only vessels in the 2022-2023 season, and due to potential passenger numbers on vessels near capacity, were working to schedule observations as far in advance as possible. IAATO expressed its willingness to continue sharing its experiences of tourism monitoring and observation.

(306) The Meeting commended France for providing this useful information and encouraged Parties to consider conducting monitoring activities on tourist vessels, as recommended in Resolution 9 (2021), and share information and experiences of tourism monitoring activities with the ATCM.

(307) The United States presented IP 61 *Expeditions within Expeditions: Authorizing Non-Governmental Organization Activities Associated with Tourist and other Non-Governmental Expedition Organizers,* and IP 62 *Authorization of Science Activities Associated with Tourist and Other Non-governmental Expedition Organizers.* IP 61 discussed the recent changes in the types of requests and subsequent authorisations of non-governmental, non-scientific expeditions to Antarctica, which relied on tour operators for logistical support. IP 61 outlined the approach and procedures taken by the United States to these activities. IP 62 presented information on how the United States managed authorisation of science activities associated with tourist and other non-governmental expedition organisers as an example of best practice and to promote awareness of potential challenges in how non-governmental activities were authorised and managed by NCAs.

(308) IAATO thanked the United States for its papers and encouraged harmonisation of authorisation processes across NCAs. IAATO expressed its continued commitment to support operators in complying with NCA processes and facilitate communication between operators and NCAs.

(309) The Meeting thanked the United States and acknowledged the importance of discussing emerging challenges for competent authorities. Parties noted the issues that could arise

in authorising complex activities, particularly the challenge of conducting a full assessment of the overall impacts when different activities were supported by one vessel. The Meeting supported efforts to harmonise authorisation processes as far as possible within differing national systems, and called for enhanced discussion between the Parties, for example using the NCA Forum on the Secretariat website.

(310) The Co-chair of Working Group 2, Dr Phillip Tracey (Australia), presented IP 79 *Competent authorities discussion forum on tourism regulatory activities: report by the convener,* which outlined the work of the ATCM web-based forum for Competent Authorities to discuss tourism regulatory activities and exchange knowledge and experience, convened by the Co-chair. It reported on the commencement of discussion of five issues identified as a priority for initial focus, in accordance with the agreed scope and purpose of the forum. Dr Tracey encouraged Parties to have their NCAs participate in the work of the group as appropriate. The Co-chair noted that the authorisation of multiple linked or nested activities, sometimes by different Parties, was one of the issues under discussion in the forum and highlighted that the forum provided one opportunity to discuss these specific topics.

(311) Argentina presented IP 86 *Actualización del "Plan Estratégico de Turismo Sustentable de la Provincia de Tierra del Fuego" (PETS-TDF 2025),* which reported on the recent update of the "Strategic Plan for Sustainable Tourism in the Province of Tierra del Fuego". It noted that the plan included issues related to the role of Ushuaia as a gateway city to Antarctica and the main port of support for Antarctic cruise ship tourism activity. Argentina invited the Meeting and, in particular, Parties with gateway cities to Antarctica, to consider the paper with a view to articulating possible joint actions framed in strategic plans for the development of Antarctic tourism.

(312) India noted that the IP reflected the importance of acting strategically on tourism issues, and that deliberation on the importance of gateway cities and port controls had been on the agenda of the ATCM for several years. India highlighted that it was important to further collaborate on this issue.

(313) IAATO thanked Argentina and all other gateway Parties for their continued cooperation with IAATO operators, and noted that its IAATO Gateway Committee looked forward to continue working with those Parties in strategic planning and other issues.

(314) ASOC introduced IP 91 *Antarctic tourism policies after the "pandemic pause",* which examined potential Antarctic tourism developments following the coronavirus pandemic. The paper included recommendations for next steps by the ATCM, including: expanding area protection under Annex V; ensuring consistent assessment of tourism activities under Annex I; developing dedicated monitoring programmes; evaluating the effectiveness of existing regulations; and encouraging low-impact modalities of tourism.

(315) The Meeting thanked ASOC for its valuable paper. It acknowledged the importance of reflecting on tourism activities as they recommenced following the pandemic-related pause and, in a broader sense, of thinking about what kind of tourism was most desirable in Antarctica.

(316) In relation to its call for low impact modalities of tourism, ASOC clarified that it was inspired by the concept of "slow tourism". ASOC noted that it was working to further develop the concept of "slow tourism" as applicable to the Antarctic.

(317) India presented IP 117 *'Building Back [and forth] Better' for Antarctic Tourism: Enduring Concerns in Pursuit of a Strategic Vision.* It provided an update of ATCM XXXVIII-IP 104 rev.1, which had summarised recommendations in relation to tourism and non-governmental activities in the Antarctic Treaty area. India encouraged the ATCM to adopt a strategic vision in order to address long-standing, long-discussed concerns related to Antarctic tourism. In doing so, India invited Parties to discuss what

the concept 'building back better' could and should mean for Antarctic governance, in general, and Antarctic tourism regulation in particular. India hoped that future directions would build consensus on more sustainable pathways through best practice environmental management.

(318) The Meeting thanked India for its thought-provoking paper. The Meeting noted the value of the paper for its current work, as it reflected on relevant issues and perspectives in the context of a strategic vision.

Information, activities and trends

(319) Argentina introduced WP 51 *Report of the Informal Discussion on Post-Visit Reports.* It recalled the discussion at ATCM XLIII on Post-Visit Reports (PVRs), and to the agreement to continue informal discussions on PVRs during the intersessional period. The discussions focused on methods for ensuring that the list of sites and activities in the PVR form and EIES were appropriately updated, and on specifying types of unusual incidents that might be reported through the PVR form. In the discussions, participants considered a definition for unusual incidents, and options for the addition of new sites and activities to the PVR form. Based on the discussions, suggested changes to section D "Report on Expedition by Expedition Leader" in Part 1 of the PVR form were developed, along with a proposal to update the reporting requirements of the EIES. Argentina recommended that: the Meeting agree on a definition of unusual incidents; agree on mechanisms to deal with new sites and activities; and make modifications to the PVR form and to the information exchange requirements.

(320) IAATO thanked Argentina for the paper and noted the value of participating in the discussions. It remarked that it would continue to work with the Secretariat to ensure that Pre-Visit and Post-Visit EIES Reports exports in its databases complied with requirements set by Parties, and undertook to continue to facilitate data exchange between the IAATO and EIES databases. IAATO also noted that current PVRs focused on sea borne tourism activities, and suggested it might be useful to also develop PVRs for deep-field and air activities.

(321) The Meeting thanked Argentina for its paper and for leading intersessional discussions on this important topic. The Meeting supported the recommendations proposed in the paper and highlighted the value of PVRs as a tool to support the understanding and management of Antarctic tourism.

(322) The Meeting welcomed Argentina's offer to coordinate informal intersessional discussions on PVRs.

(323) The Meeting adopted Decision 5 (2022) *Information Exchange Requirements* and Resolution 6 (2022) *Revised standard Post Visit Report Form.*

(324) IAATO presented IP 42 *IAATO Overview of Antarctic Tourism: A Historical Review of Growth, the 2021-22 Season, and Preliminary Estimates for 2022-23.* In addition to historical data around visitors and activities, IAATO provided data compiled from PVRs for the 2021/22 season and noted that the numbers reported reflected only those travelling with IAATO Operator companies and did not include those individuals taking part in research projects that had been supported by IAATO Operators. IAATO reported that the overall number of visitors in 2021/22 was 23 023. IAATO's estimates for 2022/23 indicated that passenger numbers would rise to approximately 70 289 making landings, and 35 717 passengers travelling on cruise-only vessels which did not make landings. IAATO emphasised that all IAATO member and operator activities were planned to have no more than a minor or transitory impact on the Antarctic environment and continued to be conducted safely.

(325) The Meeting thanked IAATO for continuing to provide it with important information on tourism activities in Antarctica. Parties noted that the information provided could be used to anticipate management needs and support a sustainable and strategic vision for Antarctic tourism. Parties reiterated the importance of tourism not having a more than minor or transitory impact, and underscored the need for a coordinated approach to tourism management in Antarctica. Several Parties also highlighted the importance of Parties ratifying Measure 15 (2009).

(326) Several Parties highlighted IAATO's estimate that the total number of visitors to Antarctica would exceed 100 000 in the 2022/23 season, and expressed concerns about whether such a large number of visitors would translate into greater pressure on the environment. Some Parties suggested that a precautionary approach should underpin a strategic and coordinated approach to ensuring that there was not an increasing pressure on the environment as a result of the expected growth, noting also the importance of the work and advice of the CEP on this issue. In response to the comment made that visitor numbers did not necessarily equate directly to pressure on the Antarctic environment, it was suggested that IAATO might provide guidance on which indicators might suggest trends which could increase risks to effective management or present a risk to the Antarctic environment.

(327) IAATO thanked Parties for their comments. It noted that IAATO, as a trade organisation, was not in a position to limit tourism trade or cap tourist numbers. IAATO looked to the Parties to provide a consistent management framework through ATS tools. IAATO noted the continued evolution of the tools it has developed to support environmentally responsible travel, including: a live ship-scheduler to manage visits to sites; mandatory field staff assessments; whale collision avoidance procedures; and the mandatory IAATO observer scheme. IAATO reiterated the importance of the alignment of permitting and authorisation standards, and the ratification of Measure 4 (2004) and Measure 15 (2009). IAATO expressed its willingness to present further information on tourism trends and the evolution of its management tools to the ATCM.

(328) Noting that IAATO's report covered activities of IAATO operators, Parties reiterated the need to include information on activities by non-IAATO vessels in the reporting by Parties using the EIES, in order to better understand the activities of non-IAATO operators. It was suggested the Secretariat could provide brief summaries of this data, in order to provide Parties with a more comprehensive view of tourism activities carried out in the Antarctic Treaty area.

(329) ASOC thanked IAATO for continuing to provide the information in IP 42. ASOC noted that tourist numbers were a significant factor, but that tourism dynamics and patterns of development were also significant. For instance, some niche activities may have larger risk or impact. ASOC echoed other interventions that had mentioned the need to bring existing measures into force, and to approach tourism from a strategic perspective.

(330) IAATO presented IP 43 *A Five-Year Overview and 2021–22 Season Report on IAATO Operator Use of Antarctic Peninsula Landing Sites and ATCM Visitor Site Guidelines*, which reported the data collected by IAATO from IAATO Operator Post-Visit Report Forms for the 2021-22 season as well as historical data. It informed the Meeting that the 2021-22 total number of passengers from ships making landings in the Antarctic Peninsula was 22 979. The total number of IAATO SOLAS vessels making landings in the Peninsula region this season was 32. IAATO emphasised that over 95% of all landed tourism activity in the Antarctic Peninsula continued to be focused on traditional commercial ship-borne tourism. IAATO highlighted that most visited sites were covered either by ATCM Site Guidelines for Visitors, IAATO operator landing site guidelines, or National Programme management guidelines. It further observed that all visits were conducted in accordance with landing limits established in applicable Site Guidelines for

Visitors, and that the IAATO ship scheduler had been used effectively to ensure that no limits had been exceeded.

(331) SCAR presented IP 75 *SCAR Tourism Action Group (Ant-TAG)*. This paper informed the meeting about the formation of the SCAR Tourism Action Group (Ant-TAG) in 2021, which provided an umbrella under which SCAR researchers and practitioners could make new connections, become aware of other existing projects, and call on existing expertise to facilitate research on important and relevant issues related to Antarctic tourism. SCAR highlighted the key aims of Ant-TAG including: to facilitate research collaboration among Ant-TAG members and other relevant SCAR groups in order to create policy-ready advice for the SCAR Standing Committee on the Antarctic Treaty System (SC-ATS) and the Antarctic Environments Portal; to establish a communication platform with IAATO and other stakeholders for translating research into management recommendations and addressing industry-relevant knowledge gaps; and to collate research-based, policy-ready information on the topic of Antarctic tourism for SC-ATS to present to the ATCM and CEP. SCAR noted that its paper highlighted key areas where further research was needed.

(332) The Meeting thanked SCAR for its paper and noted that researchers may wish to engage in the important work of Ant-TAG. It further recognised that SCAR's paper served as a timely reminder of the value of interdisciplinary collaboration around tourism research in Antarctica.

(333) ASOC thanked SCAR for its contribution, and noted that that a scientific study of tourism allowed for a detached examination of this activity that was relevant to the discussions of the ATCM.

(334) The United Kingdom presented IP 80 rev. 1 *Data Collection and Reporting on Yachting Activity in Antarctica in 2021-22*, prepared jointly with Argentina, Chile, the United States and IAATO. The paper reported on consolidated information relating to yachts sighted in Antarctica, or indicating an intention to travel to Antarctica, during the 2021-22 season. Noting that many of the yachts considered in the paper had not been included in the EIES, the United Kingdom reminded Parties of the value of the EIES. The paper highlighted that, despite the decrease in tourism to Antarctica during the pandemic, there remained a disproportionate number of yachts visiting the region without authorisation, which required further attention from Parties. The co-authors invited other Parties in a position to provide information related to yachts in Antarctica to collaborate with the co-authors around these activities and to consider joining the group to report on yachting activity in the future.

(335) The Meeting thanked the co-authors for their work and welcomed the information provided. The Meeting shared the co-authors' concerns about the persistent issues of unauthorised yachts or yachts that were unable to present permits in Antarctica. Parties noted the importance of following up on vessels that had been without or unable to present authorisation. Several Parties expressed an interest in future collaboration on the collection and reporting of information about yacht activities.

(336) France stated that it would follow up with a vessel that had been authorised by its NCA and which, according to IP 80 rev. 1, had been unable to present its authorisation.

(337) IAATO thanked the co-authors for the collation of data and IP 80 rev. 1. IAATO expressed that it shared Parties' concerns about unauthorised yachts, including some that had been repeatedly identified over several years. Acknowledging the difficulties that competent authorities had in penalising such vessels, IAATO observed that some unauthorised yachts were becoming increasingly bold in their activities and were thereby undermining Antarctic Treaty processes and intent. Highlighting that such activities could have more than a minor or transitory impact on the Antarctic environment, IAATO cautioned that this set a poor example for responsible tour operators and passengers.

IAATO reaffirmed that it remained committed to reporting yacht activity and to sharing pertinent information on both IAATO and non-IAATO yachts.

(338) ASOC called attention to IP 92 *Developments to enhance the safety of pleasure yachts and fishing boats operating in the Antarctic Treaty area*, submitted under Agenda Item 13 Safety and Operations in Antarctica. The paper provided information on the latest developments at the International Maritime Organisation pertinent to the safety and operation of vessels, including pleasure yachts, in the Antarctic Treaty area. The paper noted that the initial adoption of the Polar Code did not include pleasure yachts and fishing vessels, which together make up a significant proportion of the vessels operating in the Antarctic. There has since been additional work at the IMO to extend the Code to these vessels in the form of voluntary Guidelines. The paper recommended that these *Guidelines for Safety Measures for Pleasure Yachts of 300 Gross Tonnage and above not engaged in trade Operating in Polar Waters* should be a requirement of any permits issued for pleasure yachts planning to operate in the Antarctic Treaty area.

(339) Argentina presented IP 111 *Report on Antarctic tourist flows and cruise ships operating in Ushuaia during the 2021/2022 Austral summer season*. This paper reported on tourist flows and cruise ships operating in Ushuaia during the 2021-22 summer season, including information on the number of voyages that took place, passengers and their nationalities, average number of crew per vessel, and the registers of ships. Argentina recalled that it had shared these reports in the ATCM since 2008, thus providing a complete database of Antarctic tourist flows from Ushuaia. Argentina reported on data comparing the 2019-20 summer season to the 2021-22 summer season, which reflected the significant decrease in tourism activity since the COVID-19 pandemic. It also referred to the compliance of ships with the sanitary protocols implemented in Ushuaia and the situation of several scheduled voyage cancellations and vessels having to remain in isolation nearby the harbour of Ushuaia. Argentina highlighted that this paper demonstrated that a variety of information sources were available to Parties interested in data on tourism flows and cruise ships. It emphasised that such data could usefully inform Parties' future discussion of Antarctic tourism activities.

(340) The Meeting thanked Argentina for its presentation and for its work, taking note of the various sources of information including reports over many years on tourist activities using the port of Ushuaia.

Item 18: Preparation of ATCM XLV

a. Date and place

(341) The Meeting welcomed the kind invitation of the Government of Finland to host ATCM XLV in Helsinki, from 29 May to 8 June 2023.

(342) For future planning, the Meeting took note of the following likely timetable of upcoming ATCMs:

- 2024 India
- 2025 Italy

(343) Starting with the ATCM in India, the use of Roman numerals in the numbering of meetings will be discontinued. Therefore the 2024 ATCM will be ATCM 46/CEP 26.

(344) The following paper was submitted under this agenda item:

- IP 82 *Preparation of the 45th Meeting Helsinki, 2023* (Finland).

b. Invitation of International and Non-governmental Organisations

(345) In accordance with established practice, the Meeting agreed that the following organisations having scientific or technical interest in Antarctica should be invited to send experts to attend ATCM XLV: the ACAP Secretariat, ASOC, IPCC, IAATO, the International Civil Aviation Organization (ICAO), IHO, IMO, IOC, IOPC Funds, the International Union for Conservation of Nature (IUCN), UNEP, UNFCCC, WMO and the World Tourism Organization (WTO).

c. Preparation of the Agenda for ATCM XLV

(346) The Meeting approved the Preliminary Agenda for ATCM XLV (see Appendix 2).

d. Organisation of ATCM XLV

(347) In accordance with Rule 11 of the Rules of Procedure, the Meeting decided to propose the same Working Groups for ATCM XLV as observed in this meeting. According to the *Ad-Hoc Guidelines for ATCM XLIV - CEP XXIV Hybrid Meeting* adopted at this ATCM, Working Group Chairs should be appointed before the close of the Meeting and, in the absence of any nomination, Chairs would be appointed at the start of the next ATCM. The Meeting agreed to appoint Mr Theodore Kill from the United States as Chair for Working Group 1 for 2023. It also agreed to appoint Ms Sonia Ramos García from Spain and Dr Phillip Tracey from Australia as Co-chairs for Working Group 2 in 2023.

e. The SCAR Lecture

(348) Taking into account the valuable series of lectures given by SCAR at a number of ATCMs, the Meeting decided to invite SCAR to give another lecture on scientific issues relevant to ATCM XLV.

Item 19: Any Other Business

(349) Türkiye presented IP 98 *Turkey's Membership to the COMNAP*. The paper reported that Türkiye had applied for membership to COMNAP in 2021 to enable its involvement in the development and best practice in managing the support of research in Antarctica. Türkiye noted its request for membership had been accepted in the 2021 COMNAP AGM. Türkiye considered that its COMNAP membership would enhance and shape the future of its polar research, and expressed its gratitude to countries and representatives who supported it through the process.

(350) Argentina made the following statement: "We are living through complex times and dealing with important challenges for the entire Antarctic Treaty System. It is in difficult times like these that our commitment, coherence and adherence to the principles that have been guiding us in the more than 60 years of the Antarctic Treaty must prevail, such as good faith, international cooperation and consensus. Unfortunately, yesterday, in another forum of the Antarctic Treaty System, one Party circulated a Note that surprises and worries us, since it could establish a dangerous precedent for our System. We do not agree with the considerations expressed in said Note and we will respond to it through the corresponding channels in that forum. Our position regarding the sovereignty dispute is widely known, so I am not going to repeat it today. However, this issue goes beyond any bilateral dispute and concerns the fundamental commitments of the Antarctic Treaty System. Decisions like the one reflected in the Note we received yesterday do not contribute to the system. In this sense, today I would like to make a call for reflection to all Parties. The attitude or conduct of a Party can never be used as an excuse by another

Party to fail to comply with its multilateral obligations by adopting unilateral decisions. I would like to reaffirm once again our commitment to the foundations and principles of the Antarctic Treaty System. We appeal to the commitment and responsibility of all Parties to support and strengthen our System."

(351) The United Kingdom made the following statement: "The United Kingdom would also recall its position on sovereignty in the South Atlantic, which is well known to all delegates. It is unfortunate that this matter, which relates to a separate forum of the Antarctic Treaty System, has been raised here. But this situation relates to an egregious blocking of decision-making based on best available science by a third party. The UK is clear that the action we are taking, including to ensure continued high standards of marine conservation, and which is fully explained in the aforementioned Note, is entirely consistent with our obligations under the Convention for the Conservation of Antarctic Marine Living Resources - CCAMLR. The UK remains wholly committed to the principles and objectives of CCAMLR. The UK will continue to discharge its obligations under the Convention in good faith, including with respect to decision-making on the basis of the best scientific evidence available, and expects the same from all other Parties. The UK commits to working with Argentina and all other CCAMLR Members to seek to restore the framework under which the interests of all Parties had been protected for the past 40 years. We are ready to engage with all CCAMLR Members on this matter, including at this year's annual meeting in October."

(352) Argentina rejected the United Kingdom's statement and reaffirmed its well-known legal position.

Item 20: Adoption of the Final Report

(353) The Meeting adopted the Final Report of the 44th Antarctic Treaty Consultative Meeting in accordance with Rule 25 of the ATCM Rules of Procedure. Consensus was not reached on paragraphs 10 and 11 and paragraphs 35-40. The Chair of the Meeting, Mrs Tania von Uslar-Gleichen, made closing remarks.

Item 21: Close of the Meeting

(354) The Meeting was closed on Thursday, 2 June at 17:46.

2. CEP XXIV Report

Report of the Twenty-fourth Meeting of the Committee for Environmental Protection (CEP XXIV)

Berlin, Germany, May 23 – 27, 2022

(1) Pursuant to Article 11 of the Protocol on Environmental Protection to the Antarctic Treaty, Representatives from 39 of the 42 Parties to the Protocol (Argentina, Australia, Belarus, Belgium, Brazil, Bulgaria, Canada, Chile, China, Colombia, the Czech Republic, Ecuador, Finland, France, Germany, India, Italy, Japan, Malaysia, Monaco, the Netherlands, New Zealand, Norway, Peru, Poland, Portugal, Republic of Korea, Romania, the Russian Federation, South Africa, Spain, Sweden, Switzerland, Türkiye, Ukraine, the United Kingdom, the United States, Uruguay and Venezuela) met from 23 to 27 May 2022, for the purpose of providing advice and formulating recommendations to the Parties in connection with the implementation of the Protocol. The meeting was held in a hybrid format, with Representatives of the Parties to the Protocol participating either in person in Berlin, Germany, or virtually.

(2) In accordance with Rule 4 of the CEP Rules of Procedure, the meeting was also attended by representatives of the following Observers:

- the Scientific Committee on Antarctic Research (SCAR), the Scientific Committee for the Conservation of Antarctic Marine Living Resources (SC-CAMLR), and the Council of Managers of National Antarctic Programs (COMNAP); and

- scientific, environmental and technical organisations: the Antarctic and Southern Ocean Coalition (ASOC), the International Association of Antarctica Tour Operators (IAATO), and the World Meteorological Organization (WMO).

Item 1: Opening of the Meeting

(3) The CEP Chair, Ms Birgit Njåstad (Norway), opened the meeting on Monday 23 May 2022 and thanked Germany for arranging and hosting the meeting. The CEP Chair noted that the world had undergone many changes in recent years, but noted the importance of the CEP's continued responsibility in providing solid advice and recommendations to the ATCM, in accordance with the spirit of the Antarctic Treaty.

(4) The Committee expressed sincere condolences for the passing of Dr Yves Frenot, who had served as CEP Chair from 2010 to 2014 and was a well-known and highly regarded researcher from the French Polar Institute. The Committee acknowledged Dr Frenot's great contributions to the CEP and Antarctic research.

(5) On behalf of the Committee, the Chair welcomed Austria as a new Member, following its accession to the Protocol on 26 August 2021. The Chair noted that the CEP now comprised 42 Members.

Item 2: Adoption of the Agenda

(6) The Committee adopted the following agenda and confirmed the allocation of 44 Working Papers (WP), 63 Information Papers (IP), 4 Secretariat Papers (SP) and 4 Background Papers (BP) to the agenda items:

1. Opening of the Meeting

2. Adoption of the Agenda

3. Strategic Discussions on the Future Work of the CEP

4. Operation of the CEP

5. Cooperation with other Organisations

6. Repair and Remediation of Environment Damage

7. Climate Change Implications for the Environment

    a. Strategic Approach

    b. Implementation and Review of the Climate Change Response Work Programme

8. Environmental Impact Assessment (EIA)

    a. Draft Comprehensive Environmental Evaluations

    b. Other EIA Matters

9. Area Protection and Management Plans

    a. Management Plans

    b. Historic Sites and Monuments

    c. Site Guidelines

    d. Marine Spatial Protection and Management

    e. Other Annex V Matters

10. Conservation of Antarctic Flora and Fauna

    a. Quarantine and Non-native Species

    b. Specially Protected Species

    c. Other Annex II Matters

11. Environmental Monitoring and Reporting

12. Inspection Reports

13. General Matters

14. Election of Officers

15. Preparation for the Next Meeting

16. Adoption of the Report

17. Closing of the Meeting

Item 3: Strategic Discussions on the Future Work of the CEP

(7)   Norway, on behalf of the CEP Chair, introduced WP 27 *Revisiting CEP strategic priorities and the CEP Five-Year Work Plan*, which proposed that the CEP review its Five-year Work Plan to take stock of its performance, and to consider relevant updates and adjustments to the plan. Norway recalled that the CEP had initially concentrated on putting into place procedures and practices to enable it to fulfil its mandate effectively and efficiently. With the emergence of new environmental pressures, the CEP began to take a more strategic and prioritised approach to issues that required more urgent attention. Norway noted some important developments in the evolution of the CEP's approach to its work, including an informal Workshop on Antarctica's Future Environmental Challenge in 2006, and the establishment at CEP IX of an ICG to take forward the development of a Five-year Work Plan based on the outcomes of the workshop. Norway further noted that CEP X had agreed to adopt the Five-year Work Plan as a formal mechanism of the Committee. For a number of meetings the Committee had noted the usefulness of the Five-year Work Plan in guiding its work and, since CEP XV, the Committee had agreed to consider the Work Plan at the end of each agenda item. Noting that it was now fifteen years since the first Five-year Work Plan was adopted, Norway suggested that it was timely to undertake a review, considering the changes in understanding of the Antarctic environment and challenges facing Antarctica in the future. Norway noted that SC-CAMLR held regular symposiums to take stock of its strategic work, and suggested that the CEP could take a similar approach when revisiting

its Five-year Work Plan. Norway noted that WP 27 included a list of questions that could be relevant for an initial exchange of views and thoughts during CEP XXIV. This could be followed by intersessional discussions in advance of CEP XXV, and dedicated discussions at CEP XXV, as the mode of operation for a review process.

(8)   The Committee commended Norway for its work in preparing the paper. It emphasised that the CEP had functioned very well within the current Five-year Work Plan and had been successfully delivering on its mandate as outlined in Article 12 of the Environmental Protocol. It further noted that the Work Plan served as a useful communications tool for engaging with partners and general audiences. Recognising the timeliness of reviewing strategic priorities in light of changing circumstances and emerging issues, the Committee fully supported the recommendations in WP 27. The Committee expressed its intention to review strategic priorities and the Work Plan in the lead up to CEP XXV. Several Members suggested priority issues, processes, and actions for consideration during intersessional discussions. Proposed issues of focus included climate change, a proactive approach to tourism, the protected area system, and pollution, particularly centred on plastics.

(9)   The Committee thanked Finland for offering to provide a venue for informal discussion around the Five-year Work Plan through a workshop to take place in Helsinki in advance of CEP XXV. It also thanked several Members for proposing additional ways of encouraging broad participation in discussions around the Five-year Work Plan in such a way as to facilitate greater inclusion along the lines of geography, age and gender.

(10)   ASOC thanked Norway for its paper, and thanked Finland for offering to host informal discussions on the issue. ASOC expressed that it supported a review of strategic priorities for the CEP and the production of an updated Five-year Work Plan. It advised that the review should consider whether any actions in the Work Plan needed to have their priority upgraded or needed to be further populated with action points. It also recommended that the Committee consider not only what it would do, but also technical questions of how tasks would be implemented and streamlined.

(11)   Following further discussion, the Committee agreed to the recommendations in WP 27.

CEP advice to the ATCM on revisiting CEP strategic priorities and the CEP Five-year Work Plan.

(12)   The Committee agreed to advise the ATCM that it would revisit its priorities, the functioning of the Committee, and its Five-year Work Plan at CEP XXV. The Committee agreed that this should be taken forward in the following manner:

- The Chair/CEP Bureau would be tasked with facilitating intersessional discussions to prepare for a workshop in Helsinki prior to CEP XXV, in collaboration with the host country, Finland.
- Discussions before and during the workshop would be open and inclusive of all Members and Observers.
- Members and Observers would be encouraged to facilitate participation in the intersessional discussions and workshop by early career researchers and policy makers/managers, as appropriate, and ensure diversity and inclusivity; and
- At CEP XXV in Helsinki, the Committee would consider the outcomes of the workshop and earlier intersessional discussions.

(13)   The Committee noted that during these considerations of CEP strategic priorities, efforts would be made to identify existing and new challenges. The Committee further noted that participants should be guided by the principles of the Environmental Protocol, drawing on the best available science.

(14)   The Committee revised and updated its Five-year Work Plan (Appendix 1).

Item 4: Operation of the CEP

(15)   India introduced WP 7 *ATS webpages providing information on the Subsidiary Groups of the CEP*, prepared jointly with Norway and the United Kingdom. India noted that the Secretariat had, under the guidance of the ATCM, developed webpages containing information relevant to the Antarctic Treaty System, the Environmental Protocol, and the CEP. Webpages had not, however, been developed dedicated to the two Subsidiary Groups of the CEP: the Subsidiary Group on Management Plans and the Subsidiary Group on Climate Change Response. The proponents proposed webpages be developed for each Subsidiary Group to improve access to information relevant to the work of those groups. India highlighted that this also could help new Members understand how they might engage and participate in the work of the Subsidiary Groups. The paper therefore recommended that the CEP: support the development of individual dedicated ATS webpages for the two Subsidiary Groups of the CEP; approve initial content for these webpages, as appended to the paper; and encourage the respective Subsidiary Groups to further consider webpage content during the 2022-23 intersessional period and report back to CEP XXV.

(16)   The Committee thanked India, Norway, and the United Kingdom for their paper. Members agreed that webpages would be useful tools for disseminating information to existing and new Members. Many Members also noted that dedicated webpages would be useful tools for increasing transparency and communicating CEP activities to the public. It was suggested that it also would be useful to include contact points and a task schedule to facilitate participation.

(17)   In responding to concerns raised regarding whether the webpages should be password protected, the content to be adopted, and its potential to be updated in the future, the proponents clarified that the proposed webpages would consolidate information that was already approved by the CEP and was in the public domain via the ATS website, and that any future updates would need to be approved by consensus by the Committee.

(18)   The Committee supported the development of individual dedicated ATS webpages for the two Subsidiary Groups of the CEP and, following minor editorial amendments, approved initial content for these webpages (Appendices 2 and 3) and noted that any future updates would be approved by consensus by the Committee. The Committee encouraged the respective Subsidiary Groups to further consider webpage content during the 2022/23 intersessional period and report back to CEP XXV.

(19)   The Chair of the CEP referred to IP 121 *Committee for Environmental Protection (CEP): summary of activities during the 2021/22 intersessional period* (Norway), and thanked Members for their efforts to progress CEP activities throughout the previous intersessional period.

Item 5: Cooperation with other Organisations

(20)   SC-CAMLR presented IP 15 *Report by the SC-CAMLR Observer to CEP*, which reported on activities relevant to the CEP conducted during the intersessional period. It covered the five issues of common interest to the CEP and SC-CAMLR as identified in the first joint CEP/SC-CAMLR workshop: climate change and the Antarctic marine environment; biodiversity and non-native species in the Antarctic marine environment; Antarctic species requiring special protection; spatial marine management and protected areas; and ecosystem and environmental monitoring. It noted the challenges SC-CAMLR had faced during this past year of virtual meetings, as well as the progress it had made in some key topic areas, including in developing a risk-based management framework for the krill fishery and the record-breaking amount of engagement and

participation that the virtual format had enabled. It reported that SC-CAMLR developed its science capacity by agreeing new terms of reference for the General Science Capacity Fund. SC-CAMLR reminded the Committee that it had been five years since the designation of the Ross Sea MPA. It further noted that SC-CAMLR had held an informal symposium to review and develop a five-year strategic plan, and that the recommendations and strategic plan arising from the symposium would be further refined by members and agreed at SC-CAMLR- 41 in October 2022.

(21)   SCAR presented IP 16 *The Scientific Committee on Antarctic Research Annual Report 2022 to the XLIV Antarctic Treaty Consultative Meeting.* SCAR highlighted recent activities relevant to the work of the CEP including: its three Science Research Programmes and other science groups providing outputs supporting the CEP's needs; its coordination of the Southern Ocean Task Force as part of the United Nations Decade of Ocean Science; education and outreach activities including two SCAR events held at the United Nations Climate Change Conference (COP 26) in Glasgow in 2021; the new SCAR film, *Peace and Science,* which gave insight into SCAR's work; and the establishment of the Equality, Diversity and Inclusion (EDI) Action Group which was tasked with broadly looking at how EDI issues could be effectively dealt with within SCAR. SCAR recalled the systematic conservation plan for the Antarctic Peninsula that was being developed with IAATO to facilitate the concurrent management of biodiversity, science and tourism. SCAR noted that on finalisation the results would be discussed with IAATO members and SCAR, and presented to the CEP. SCAR also highlighted that its 2022 Open Science Conference and SCAR Meetings would be hosted online by India on 1-10 August, with the conference theme 'Antarctica in a Changing World'.

(22)   COMNAP presented IP 19 *Annual Report 2021/22 Council of Managers of National Antarctic Programs*, which reported on activities carried out during the last year that were relevant to the work of the CEP. COMNAP highlighted that regional sessions held at its Annual General Meeting had identified the Antarctic High Plateau as a key region for understanding how the Antarctic was a driver for change. It noted the importance of national Antarctic programmes actively supporting and coordinating international efforts to provide policy relevant cryosphere data from the Antarctic Treaty area. COMNAP also drew attention to a peer-reviewed publication on the new Antarctic capabilities of icebreakers, including increased efficiency, reduced noise outputs, and ways to proactively protect the Antarctic environment and dependent and associated ecosystems in their design (BP 2).

(23)   WMO presented IP 21 rev. 1 *WMO Annual Report*, which outlined its recent Antarctic science activities conducted through its co-sponsored World Climate Research Programme (WCRP) and World Weather Research Programmes. This included: the WCRP's Climate and Cryosphere Core Project (CliC); Antarctic CORDEX; Antarctica 2300 Projections; the WCRP Academy; the Southern Ocean Action Plan; and the Year of Polar Prediction final Summit. WMO highlighted that it had adopted a new Unified Data Policy, which was necessary for global efforts to monitor, understand and predict weather and climate, as well as its continued work on the development of an Antarctic Polar Regional Climate Centre (AntRCC) Network. WMO also noted that it had produced several Antarctic and climate-related science publications relevant to the work of the CEP including the WMO Statement on the State of the Global Climate, United in Science and 10 New Insights in Climate Science.

(24)   IAATO presented IP 41 *Report of the International Association of Antarctica Tour Operators 2021-22,* which reported on its activities during the previous year. IAATO reported that its membership comprised 106 Operators and Associates from 21 Antarctic Treaty Parties. It noted that, after minimum activity in the 2021 season due to the pandemic, the 2021-22 season had seen a moderate resumption of operations though challenges persisted. IAATO reported that the total number of visitors travelling with

IAATO Operators in the 2021-22 season was 23 597, and that there were no incidents to report. It also reported that, at its recent Annual meeting, IAATO members had unanimously committed to a climate change pledge, which included reducing greenhouse gas emissions by at least 50% by 2050 compared with 2008, and reaching Net Zero as soon as possible before 2050. IAATO members also strengthened and updated a number of its operational guidelines, and made it a requirement that captains and certain officers take and pass the relevant IAATO Online Assessment. IAATO also highlighted some of its scientific collaborative efforts including offering an annual fellowship for early career persons together with SCAR, COMNAP and CCAMLR.

(25) ASOC in reporting to the Meeting, referred to IP 88 *ASOC report to the ATCM* (submitted to the ATCM), which listed the intersessional activities and support for policy-relevant science and science communications in which ASOC had engaged over the previous year. ASOC noted that there was an overwhelming political will to address threats to the health of Antarctica, including adopting new comprehensive protection measures such as marine protected areas (MPA), expanding the system of specially protected areas, assigning Antarctic Specially Protected Species (Antarctic SPS) status to the emperor penguin, and taking action on climate change. ASOC urged Antarctic bodies and actors to constructively engage in discussions that increased the conservation ambitions of the Antarctic Treaty System.

(26) The Committee expressed appreciation for these Observer reports, and noted the importance of their work for the CEP.

Nomination of CEP Representatives to other organisations

(27) The Committee nominated:

- Birgit Njåstad (Norway) to represent the CEP at the 34th COMNAP Annual General Meeting to be held digitally from 8 June to 27 July 2022;

- Polly Penhale (United States) to represent the CEP at the 41st SC-CAMLR meeting to be held in Hobart, in October-November 2022; and

- Yan Ropert-Coudert (France) to represent the CEP at the 2022 SCAR Delegates Meeting to be hosted online by India in September 2022.

Item 6: Repair and Remediation of Environment Damage

(28) Australia presented IP 54 *Australia's Cleaner Antarctica Strategy*. This paper reported that Australia was establishing a Cleaner Antarctica science programme and developing an actionable Cleaner Antarctica Strategy for Australian stations and sites. It summarised the goals of the Cleaner Antarctica Strategy, including details of high priority actions to be undertaken over the following five years. Australia expressed its interest in exchanging research and practical experience with other Members undertaking or planning similar site assessments and clean-up activities, with the aim of improving environmental outcomes across Antarctica.

(29) The Committee thanked Australia for the presentation and noted the forward-leaning initiative outlined in its paper.

Item 7: Climate Change Implications for the Environment

7a) Strategic Approach

(30) SCAR introduced WP 30 rev.1 *Antarctic Climate Change and the Environment: A Decadal Synopsis. Findings and Policy Recommendations,* and WP 31 rev.1 *Antarctic Climate Change and the Environment: A Decadal Synopsis. Research Imperatives.* SCAR also referred to IP 72 *Antarctic Climate Change and the Environment: A Decadal*

Synopsis and Recommendations for Action. These papers presented a major update to the Antarctic Climate Change and the Environment (ACCE) report and provided an infographic summary of key findings from this ACCE Decadal Synopsis, as well as a series of recommendations. In relation to policy recommendations set out in WP 30 rev.1, SCAR emphasised that states should meet, and exceed, the greenhouse gas emissions reduction targets of the Paris Climate Agreement to maintain the Antarctic and Southern Ocean in a state close to that known for the past 200 years. In relation to recommendations for the most significant and urgent research required for the region, as presented in WP 31 rev.1, SCAR noted that these focused on changes in the region that had significant implications for the earth system and society, as well as on the expected impacts of climate change on the region's biodiversity. SCAR noted that the Decadal Synopsis was based predominantly on recent IPCC reports, which were founded on an extensive body of research by scientists, including those working on, or in, Antarctica and the Southern Ocean.

(31)   SCAR drew the Meeting's attention to several key messages that derived from its recommendations: the need for urgent action, both regionally and globally, to mitigate the effects of climate change; that the requirement for urgent action was not constrained by the need to reduce the uncertainty associated with future projections; the need to develop, with due urgency, large-scale integrated research approaches across national Antarctic programmes to reduce uncertainties in key areas, including improving projections of Antarctic cryosphere change, improving understanding of, and projections for, Antarctic biodiversity change, and furthering the understanding of tropical-high latitude climate teleconnections and climate models; and the requirement to develop clear, timely and regular communication about environmental changes in the Antarctic, and their implications for both Antarctic environments and the earth system, to governments, parties to related international agreements, the economic sector and to civil society. Finally, SCAR recognised that the report was based on a large body of internationally collaborative research, much of which had been supported by national Antarctic programmes, and the large majority of which had been drawn together through the voluntary work of researchers from most of the world's nations.

(32)   The Committee thanked SCAR for its papers and emphasised the value of being provided with high-quality science syntheses as a basis for its work. The Committee noted the broad support expressed for the recommendations in WP 30 rev.1 and WP 31 rev.1. The Committee also welcomed SCAR's lecture on the outcomes of the ACCE report and congratulated SCAR on its milestone decadal update, recognising it as a valuable contribution for further deliberations on climate change implications and other management discussions. The Committee noted that the report underlined the need for urgent action and the need to address existing science gaps and needs.

(33)   Members noted the relevance of SCAR's findings in relation to the CCRWP and the work of the SGCCR. Some Members highlighted the importance of meeting, and exceeding, the Nationally Determined Contributions of the Paris Climate Agreement. Members also commented on the need to fill existing science gaps, and to progress on issues such as biosecurity, spatial area management and environmental impacts. The need for better communication between Members and ease of dissemination of information was also raised. Many Members supported the recommendations in WP 30 rev.1, noting that they significantly progressed the work that had been presented in the report of the SGCCR (CEP XXIII - WP 14).

(34)   Members raised several points for further consideration including: shared research priorities with CCAMLR; intersessional dialogue between SCAR and the SGCCR to enhance a deeper debate during the next CEP; the possibility of requesting the SGCCR to prioritise its work on biosecurity; prioritising the protection of Antarctic species from the impact of climate change; greenhouse emissions by Antarctic stations; the development of an integrated protected area system; addressing science gaps and uncertainties; logistical challenges related to climate change;

identify baselines; the need for systematic long term monitoring; and the relevance of effective biosecurity protocols.

(35) One Member noted the scientific uncertainties in the rate of sea level rise trends, biodiversity and climate models as raised by SCAR, and the importance of integrated and long-term observation, and expressed concern on the possibility of preserving the Southern Ocean environment in a state close to that known in the past 200 years as a management goal in such a dynamic system. It also noted the crucial role of SCAR in providing independent and objective scientific advice to support and inform the work of the ATCM and CEP expressed in Resolution 7 (2019) and was concerned whether SCAR was the appropriate body to provide policy recommendations.

(36) Several Members noted that they considered the science-based advice and recommendations provided by SCAR as an important basis for the Committee's policy decision.

(37) In response to the concerns of one Member, SCAR reaffirmed its view that exceeding the targets laid out in the Paris Climate Agreement was important for the preservation of Antarctica. It highlighted that Antarctica was a dynamic system that changed over time and the underlying idea of protecting the Antarctic environment implied preserving its dynamics as well. In relation to issues raised concerning the loss of eastern Antarctic ice sheets, SCAR confirmed that, although ice mass loss was less than western Antarctic ice sheet loss, research showed that the Totten glacier had lost mass. SCAR also recalled that the IPCC had first raised concerns about climate change risks over 30 years ago, and that it had continued to express its concern ever since. In responding to the question about whether it was an appropriate body to provide policy recommendations, SCAR noted that these were evidence-based recommendations and that it would be irresponsible not to put these recommendations forward.

(38) ASOC thanked SCAR for its lecture, expressed its support for recommendations in WP 30 rev. 1, and emphasised the urgency of exceeding planned emissions targets to protect the Antarctic and Southern Ocean environments. ASOC considered that WP 31 rev.1 provided an opportunity to disseminate Antarctic science beyond the ATS, and stressed it was essential to communicate these important findings globally as well as act upon them.

(39) Concluding the discussion on WP 30 rev. 1 and WP 31 rev. 1 the Committee thanked and congratulated SCAR with the milestone decadal update of the Antarctic Climate Change and Environment report and also expressed its appreciation for the excellent SCAR lecture on this topic. The Committee noted that the update underscored the urgency to conduct further research to fill science gaps and to implement response actions. The Committee noted the important value of the ACCE report, which drew on the best available science, to support the Committee's deliberations on management responses to climate change in Antarctica and the relevance of the findings for the work of the SGCCR and for the CCRWP. Finally, the Committee highlighted the importance of communicating and disseminating the findings of this report to the wider global community.

(40) WMO presented IP 71 *Winter Targeted Observing Periods and Further Plans of the Year of Polar Prediction in the Southern Hemisphere (YOPP-SH)*, which summarised recent activities undertaken in the Antarctic as part of WMO's World Weather Research Programme Polar Prediction Project. WMO reported that an evaluation of global modelling forecasts during the Antarctic Special Observing Period had confirmed that extratropical Southern Hemisphere forecast skill was lower than in the Northern Hemisphere with the contrast being greatest between the Antarctic and Arctic. It noted that the Year of Polar Prediction in the Southern Hemisphere (YOPP-SH) was currently running a second Special Observing Period, and that the analysis of these results would continue into 2023-24. WMO also reported that the upcoming YOPP Final Summit

would be held in Montreal in August 2022. It encouraged Members to share information about the YOPP Data Portal to enable the national research communities to make use of the portal and to contribute their own data via their national data centres in an effort to build a comprehensive polar meteorological database.

(41) ASOC presented IP 90 *Ice Sheet Instability, Long-term Sea-level Rise, and Southern Ocean Acidification: Time for Coordinated Action by Antarctic Treaty Parties*, noting that generally ATS bodies have focused on addressing the effects of climate change on Antarctic and Southern Ocean ecosystems, but that it was now timely for these bodies to directly address the global impacts of climate change. The paper made several recommendations for doing so, including: taking steps to bring the findings of Antarctic climate science to greater public and political attention, including at the UNFCCC Conferences of Parties (COP); requesting SCAR to increase the presence of Antarctic science at the COP; and in parallel requesting ATCPs to revise their own Nationally Determined Contributions (NDCs).

(42) In response to a suggestion by WMO, SCAR expressed its willingness to work together with WMO and others to ensure that Antarctic science was represented at the Conference of Parties of the UN Framework Convention on Climate Change.

(43) The Committee noted the following Information Papers submitted under this agenda item:

- IP 23 *Antarctic Blue Carbon* (United Kingdom).

- IP 26 *International Thwaites Glacier Collaboration: The Future of Thwaites Glacier and its Contribution to Sea-Level Rise* (United States, United Kingdom).

- IP 27 *The Value of Long-term Ecological Datasets to Evaluate Ecosystem Response to Environmental Change along the Antarctic Peninsula* (United States).

- IP 32 *Efectos del derretimiento del Glaciar Collins en el ecosistema costero marino antártico (*Uruguay).

7b) Climate Change Implications for the Environment: Implementation and Review of the Climate Change response Work Programme

(44) The convenor of the SGCCR, Dr Kevin Hughes (United Kingdom), introduced WP 37 *Report of the Subsidiary Group on Climate Change Response (SGCCR) 2021-2022*, which outlined the work and outputs of the SGCCR during the intersessional period from 2021 to 2022. The convenor noted that the SGCCR consisted of 22 representatives from 17 CEP Member countries as well as ASOC, COMNAP, IAATO, SCAR, and WMO. The convenor summarised progress related to the SGCCR's Terms of Reference. He indicated that the SGCCR had taken actions to facilitate the coordination and communication of the CCRWP, and reported on work undertaken by SCAR, SC-CAMLR and COMNAP as well as efforts to promote the inclusion of science needs into national science strategies. The SGCCR also had undertaken activities to update a draft CCRWP for the Committee's consideration and the implementation of the CCRWP, describing delivery of, or progress on, all of the 34 CCRWP Actions. The convenor also reported on SGCCR work planned for the intersessional period in relation to non-native species introductions; change to the terrestrial and freshwater biotic and abiotic environment; change to marine near-shore abiotic and biotic environment; risks to Antarctic species; and impacts on heritage values. He thanked members of the SGCCR for their work toward delivering the group's Terms of Reference and strongly encouraged further participation by CEP Members and Observers, noting substantial work remaining to be done. The SGCCR recommended the CEP adopt the draft updated CCRWP (2022) and use it to replace the current version of the CCRWP (2016).

(45) The Committee commended the convenor of the SGCCR for his leadership, and the SGCCR for its work during the intersessional period. It also expressed support for the work undertaken by members of the SGCCR during the 2021-22 intersessional period and asserted the need to continue to implement the CCRWP on the basis of knowledge of climate change and the challenges it presented. Members generally agreed that the SGCCR was functioning well and that its framing did not need to be revisited, though acknowledging there was always room to discuss improvements and updates. The Committee also acknowledged the work of SCAR and other Observers in the work of the SGCCR. Several Members also called for further engagement from new Members, and a number of Members expressed a desire to begin actively engaging in the SGCCR.

(46) China introduced WP 48 *The Implementation of the Climate Change Response Working Programme*. During the 2021-22 intersessional period, China had reviewed progress on the implementation of the CCRWP since its adoption in 2015. China considered that there was room for improvement in the annual progress reports submitted by the SGCCR to the CEP, particularly on the fulfilment of specific gaps and needs and the achievement of actions and tasks identified in previous years. On the basis of its review, China recommended that the CEP: focus its efforts on the implementation of the CCRWP; emphasise the importance of scientific research and monitoring; re-confirm that the SGCCR would submit annual progress reports for review by the CEP Plenary; request the SGCCR to update the CCRWP as required by the ATCM or CEP or suggest specific updates through submitting documentation on specific issues to provide full information in support of these suggestions. In accordance with an agreement from CEP XXII, China also provided a draft reformatted version of the CCRWP (2016) and recommended its adoption.

(47) The Committee considered next steps to advance the CCRWP based on recommendations put forward in WP 37 and WP 48. Many Members noted their support for the draft updated version of the CCRWP attached to WP37, noting it was well-written, and effectively discussed what the CEP needed in the climate change field. Members considered that the report effectively reflected the diverse activities of the SGCCR in the last intersessional period and the established linkages between other bodies and the CEP. Members noted that the report acted to improve the communication of climate change-related issues and adapted the programme through the application of current developments and decisions. One Member, while thanking the convenor of the SGCCR for incorporating its comments into the updated draft CCRWP attached to WP 37, considered that the reformatted version of the 2016 CCRWP in WP 48 should be preferred. If the draft updated CCRWP presented in WP 37 was not acceptable to the Committee, several Members suggested that reformatting could be considered at the same time as any future updates. Several Members emphasised that the CCRWP was a practical tool to support the important work of the CEP on climate change. Members noted it was not a legal instrument, and did not bind Members, who could each consider the extent to which they contributed to addressing the identified actions. Most Members expressed regret that no agreement could be reached to update the CCRWP.

(48) ASOC noted that it appreciated the opportunity to participate in the SGCCR and thanked the convenor for his work. ASOC noted that a significant amount of work to implement the CCRWP was underway and underscored the urgency to make progress on climate action including updating the plan agreed years ago.

(49) The Committee concluded that, because there was not a consensus to adopt the updated CCRWP prepared by the SGCCR, the existing CCRWP 2016 would be maintained in its current format for now. The Committee asked the SGCCR to continue its work during the intersessional period, and strongly encouraged all Members to actively engage with the SGCCR.

CEP advice to the ATCM on implementation of the Climate Change Response Work Programme (CCRWP).

(50) The Committee agreed to advise the ATCM that it had not reached consensus on updates to the CCRWP proposed by the SGCCR, and that the SGCCR would continue working in the coming intersessional period to implement the existing CCRWP (2016). According to its updated Terms of Reference, the SGCCR was tasked to:

- begin implementing the CCRWP as a matter of priority, and provide annual progress reports to the ATCM on its implementation;

- keep the CCRWP under regular review, with the input of SCAR and COMNAP on scientific and practical matters, respectively; and

- give consideration, within Members' national scientific funding systems and national Antarctic research programmes, as to how they could address the research needs and actions identified in the CCRWP.

(51) The Committee also agreed to advise the ATCM that it was moving to a phase more focused on CCRWP implementation, and had delivered or initiated work on almost all of the 34 Actions identified within the CCRWP. The Committee gave the following examples of Actions that had been delivered or concerned ongoing research that was regularly provided to the Committee:

- 1e. Progress actions identified under "Response" in the CEP Non-native Species Manual: *The CEP Non-native Species Manual* (2019).

- 2a. Support and undertake research to improve understanding of current and future change and to inform response: The SCAR Decadal Update to the Antarctic Climate Change and the Environment Report and IP 81 *Mapping SCAR affiliated research to climate change related science needs identified by the CEP*).

- 3e. Maintain regular dialogue (or sharing of information) with SC-CAMLR on Climate Change and the Southern Ocean, in particular on actions being taken: The regular reports from SC-CAMLR and work to inform a potential future Joint CEP/SC-CAMLR Workshop (ATCM XLIV - WP16).

- 4b. Consider forthcoming SCAR report on ocean acidification and act accordingly: ATCM XLIII – WP 36 and CEP XXIII Report, para. 211-217.

- 5d. Update the EIA guidelines to take into account the impacts of climate change: Resolution 1 (2016).

- 5e. Further development of the Clean Up Manual: Resolution 1 (2019).

(52) The Committee also agreed to report to the ATCM that much remained to be done to fully implement all the CCRWP Actions. The Committee noted priority Actions where effort may usefully be focused included:

- 1a. Continue to develop the Non-Native Species Manual consistent with Resolution 6 (2011), ensuring climate change impacts are included.

- 1b. Review of IMO biofouling guidelines to check adequacy for the Southern Ocean and vessels moving from region to region.

- 2e. Review and revise where necessary existing management tools to consider if they afford the best practical adaptation measures to areas at risk from climate change.

- 5b. Assess risk of changes in climate change to Historic Sites and Monuments/heritage Antarctic Specially Protected Areas.

- 6e. Where necessary develop management actions to maintain or improve the conservation status of species threatened by climate change, e.g., through Specially Protected Species Action Plans.

(53)   The Committee noted that for Priority Actions 1b, 2e, 5b and 6e, work was underway or planned for the 2022-23 intersessional period.

---

(54)   Australia introduced WP 16 *Review of progress in the implementation of the recommendations identified at the Joint CEP/SC-CAMLR Workshop on Climate Change and Monitoring (2016)*, prepared jointly with Argentina, France and the United States. The paper responded to priorities and actions identified in the CEP Five-year Work Plan and in the CCRWP. It presented the results of a review undertaken during the 2021-22 intersessional period on progress in the implementation of the recommendations identified in the report of the 2016 Joint CEP/SC-CAMLR Workshop on Climate Change and Monitoring. The proponents recommended that the CEP: consider the review (presented in Annex 1 to WP 16); refer WP 16 to SC-CAMLR for its consideration; and, in accordance with actions identified in the CEP Five-year Work Plan, engage with SC-CAMLR to make plans for a further joint workshop on climate change and monitoring to be held in the near future.

(55)   The Committee thanked the co-authors for their work. Emphasising the importance of collaboration and communication between the CEP and SC-CAMLR, Members expressed strong support for the recommendations as presented in WP 16. The Committee agreed to develop Terms of Reference for the next joint CEP/SC-CAMLR workshop during the next intersessional period.

(56)   SC-CAMLR welcomed the Committee's work in progressing the implementation of the recommendations arising from the 2016 Joint CEP/SC-CAMLR Workshop and expressed its willingness to continue working with Members on this initiative.

CEP advice to the ATCM on a joint CEP/SC-CAMLR workshop on climate change and monitoring.

(57)   The Committee advised the ATCM that it had agreed to establish an informal discussion group to facilitate the development of a Joint CEP/SC-CAMLR Workshop to take place at the latest in 2024, and appointed Ms Maude Jolly (France) to lead the group, which would be hosted on the CEP Forum. The Committee also noted that a joint CEP/SC-CAMLR Steering Committee would be established and appointed Ms Maude Jolly as a member of the Steering Committee, in her capacity as co-convener of the joint workshop. It also nominated CEP Chair Birgit Njåstad (Norway) and Dr Polly Penhale (United States) as Steering Committee members.

---

(58)   New Zealand introduced WP 26 *Assessing the risk of climate change impacts on Antarctic heritage values*, prepared jointly with Argentina, Norway and the United Kingdom. The paper summarised the key considerations identified by the proponents concerning the best way to deliver the action on Antarctic heritage sites that was specified in the CCRWP. The proponents proposed a two-year work plan to progress the development of a climate change risk assessment tool for Antarctic heritage. They further recommended that the CEP: note the identified key considerations and proposed next steps; discuss the suggested proposal to progress the implementation of the CCRWP action to assess the risk of climate change impacts on Antarctic heritage values; and provide an indication of interest in being involved in the development of a climate change risk assessment tool.

(59)   The Committee thanked the proponents for their paper and expressed full support for the work outlined in WP 26. Members were encouraged to engage in the work, and Australia and SCAR offered to contribute to the development of the tool.

(60) SCAR introduced IP 81 *Mapping SCAR affiliated research to climate change related science needs identified by the CEP*, which provided a review of research being undertaken by SCAR subsidiary and affiliated groups as relevant to the climate change-related science needs identified by the CEP. SCAR explained that research being undertaken across a broad range of its physical, biological, and social science groups aligned with almost all of the climate change-related science needs identified by the CEP. SCAR noted that its groups were well placed to contribute to the delivery of the CCRWP and to continue to address the science needs identified by the CEP, and that it would continue to communicate relevant research outcomes to the CEP.

(61) The Committee thanked SCAR for its paper, and expressed gratitude for its continued support for work relevant to the CEP.

(62) The United Kingdom introduced IP 22 *Consideration of climate change within the Antarctic Protected Areas System*, which offered support to the review and revision of area management tools by examining how climate change was represented within the CEP's area protection guidance documents and protected area management plans. It explained that climate change was little considered in existing guidance on protected areas. Furthermore, climate change impacts noted within protected area management plans included dramatic changes in penguin populations, substantial ice retreat, changes in vegetation cover and the establishment of non-native plants. The United Kingdom recommended the development of specific guidelines to help Parties in their operation of the Antarctic protected area system.

(63) The Committee thanked the United Kingdom for its important paper. The Committee noted it provided a useful assessment for its future work and supported ongoing discussions in the SGMP.

(64) The Committee noted the following Information Paper submitted under this agenda item:

- IP 49 *Work to review International Maritime Organization and Antarctic Treaty system guidelines and agreements concerning ship biofouling and ballast water management* (Australia, New Zealand, United Kingdom).

Item 8: Environmental Impact Assessment (EIA)

8a) Draft Comprehensive Environmental Evaluations

(65) The Committee noted the following Information Paper submitted under this agenda item:

- IP 20 *Response to comments on the draft Comprehensive Environmental Evaluation (CEE) for the Scott Base Redevelopment* (New Zealand).

8b) Other EIA Matters

(66) The United Kingdom introduced WP 33 *Report on Effectiveness of Environmental Impact Assessment in Antarctica*, prepared jointly with the Netherlands. It summarised the findings of an independent assessment of the effectiveness of EIA in Antarctica. The assessment found that, although the Antarctic EIA system had been effective overall, the system could be improved given the increasing pressures on the Antarctic environment. The United Kingdom noted that the effectiveness of the Antarctic EIA system was limited by the fact that not all Parties to the Protocol had implementing legislation in place. It highlighted five high priority opportunities for improving the Antarctic EIA system as outlined in the assessment. These included: better defining the preliminary stage assessment; development of more comprehensive guidance on cumulative impact assessments based on best practice approaches elsewhere; requirement for mitigation measures for Preliminary Assessment and IEE level assessments; development of guidelines and/or checklists to support national competent authorities in their assessment

of EIAs; and reminding Parties of their monitoring obligations as set out in the Environmental Protocol, and developing a reporting template and procedure to assist Parties in meeting these requirements.

(67) The Committee thanked the United Kingdom and the Netherlands for the presentation of this EIA assessment, and noted former CEP Chair Neil Gilbert's contribution to this work. The Committee underlined the importance of the EIA process for the protection of the Antarctic environment. Members suggested the need to consider improvements to the Antarctic EIA system given the increasing impacts of human activity and climate change on the Antarctic environment, and to provide consistent guidance for members to plan and conduct their Antarctic activities. Several Members expressed the view that the development of more comprehensive guidance on cumulative impact assessments should be made a high priority. Some Members suggested that the Committee's discussions on broader EIA policy issues raised during the former ICG that had reviewed the EIA Guidelines (established at CEP XVII) could be revisited and assessed when taking this work forward. Several Members noted the need for clearer guidance on the understanding of the terms 'minor' and 'transitory'. Other Members noted the desirability to consider improvements to the CEE process and indicated willingness to take forward work on this. Many Members supported the general proposal that prioritized action be included in the Five-year Work Plan.

(68) Members also noted the need to proceed with caution on some elements identified in the independent assessment report so as to avoid unintended consequences, in particular with regard to national legislation and procedures; and that the Committee's consideration of any possible amendments to Annex I to the Environmental Protocol would depend on outcomes of related discussions in the ATCM. Some Members indicated that they agreed with some of the recommendations of the independent study but not with others, such as those that apply to the appropriate national procedures. Those Members therefore indicated that they would like to have access to the full information on the study given that the data analysis criteria could be different. Some Members underlined the importance of conducting periodic reviews of the Annexes.

(69) ASOC thanked the United Kingdom and the Netherlands for WP 33, and noted it addressed a timely topic given that Annex I was drafted over 30 years ago. ASOC suggested that some of the key areas for improvement of the practice of EIA included greater consistency in the application of the 'minor or transitory impact' criteria, improving cumulative impact assessment, and EIA follow up.

(70) IAATO noted the importance of the EIA tool in assessing visitor impacts. It highlighted the usefulness of further clarity with regard to the terms 'minor' and 'transitory' and encouraged enhanced cooperation between National Competent Authorities to ensure consistency in implementation.

(71) SCAR, also noting the importance of the EIA process, indicated its willingness to contribute on several of the issues identified in the EIA assessment report, such as engaging the SCAR humanities and social sciences group (SC-HASS) and the Ant-ICON programme to contribute to work on assessing impacts on Antarctic values; providing advice on conducting baseline surveys; and developing emission and environmental quality standards, recognising also the expertise of COMNAP in this area.

(72) The Committee agreed to progress this issue through informal discussion during the intersessional period, but agreed that opportunities for improving the Antarctic EIA system needed to be handled carefully so as not to cause additional challenges.

CEP advice to the ATCM on further discussions to improve the effectiveness of the EIA system.

(73) The Committee advised the ATCM that it had agreed to review and progress recommendations in WP 33 to improve the effectiveness of the Antarctic EIA system through informal intersessional discussions. The Committee further agreed that the intersessional discussions would address the following:

Subject	For intersessional discussion	Proposed timeline
Report recommendation - Better defining the preliminary stage assessment in Antarctic settings, taking into account screening and scoping processes observed elsewhere.	To consider sharing examples of best practice or case studies which could facilitate consistency in approach to determining the appropriate level of EIA for an activity in Antarctic settings. Could also consider the need for any supporting guidance.	For presentation to CEP 2023.
Report recommendation – Requirement for mitigation measures for Preliminary Assessment and IEE level assessments.	To review previous discussions on this topic, and consider how to share best practice or propose a Resolution to encourage inclusion of mitigation measures as part of Preliminary and IEE level assessments, including by considering best practice elsewhere. Consider ways in which NCAs could monitor the implementation of these measures as well as the consistency between the activity and the EIA.	For presentation to CEP 2023.
Report recommendation - Development of more comprehensive guidance on cumulative impact assessments, taking into account the best practice approaches elsewhere.	CEP to present general avenues to explore on cumulative impact assessments based on a benchmark study on best practices on this area.	To present a proposed plan for next steps to CEP 2023.
Consider next steps and actions for subsequent years.	Further discussions on how to take forward other actions for improving effectiveness of the Antarctic EIA system.	Proposals for further work to be submitted to CEP 2023.

(74) The United Kingdom introduced WP 39 *Mapping coastline sensitivity to oil pollution in the Antarctic Peninsula region*, which described a pilot project by the British Antarctic Survey and Oil Spill Response Limited (OSRL) to develop an oil spill sensitivity map for the coastline of the Antarctic Peninsula region. The United Kingdom highlighted that although Antarctica was often considered to be a remote and pristine environment, it was subject to increasing levels of human activity including tourism, fishing and national governmental operator activities, which had resulted in increasing levels of ship traffic. It noted that Antarctic waters were poorly charted and that transient sea ice conditions could make the waters treacherous and increase the likelihood of marine accidents, with severe negative impacts on local biodiversity, including birds, seals and fish and benthic

and intertidal communities. The United Kingdom reported that steps had been taken to reduce the likelihood and impact of fuel spills resulting from marine incidents and welcomed the Polar Code put forward by the IMO. It emphasised that an assessment of the susceptibility of coastlines would allow better contingency planning or facilitate the most effective implementation of a response should an oil spill occur. It reported that approximately 24 985 km of coastline were assessed with 807 km (3.2%) allocated to the highest sensitivity category and that areas considered of highest sensitivity included the coastal area around southern Anvers Island, the South Shetland Islands (Deception Island, in particular) and the South Orkney Islands.

(75) The Committee commended the United Kingdom for its work, acknowledging the usefulness of the initiative and noted the importance of conducting further work in mapping coastline sensitivity in the Antarctic Peninsula region. Several Members reported on their own experiences related to oil spills and offered to share their data and findings with the United Kingdom and contribute to further work.

(76) Members provided several suggestions and observations, including: using an ecosystem-based approach in the mapping process; adding additional data and layers, such as oceanic currents and wind directions, at-sea areas used by seabirds, ice-free coast and slopes, IBA, ASPAs, and infrastructure; ship tracking to identify the areas with the highest ship traffic and to identify risk areas; and the importance of such sensitivity maps for contingency planning and environmental impact assessments.

(77) Members also noted the importance of avoiding spills in the first place and to initiate appropriate response action, and in this context underlined the usefulness of carrying transponders on vessels to share accurate locations; the importance of supporting the entry into force of Annex VI; and the relevance of collaborating with COMNAP on this issue.

(78) IAATO supported the view that oil spill contingency plans were needed in many parts of Antarctica and reported that all IAATO vessels over 500 gross tonnes or more were required to carry IAATO transponders as a condition of membership.

(79) COMNAP noted that it looked forward to this information being brought to the 2022 COMNAP Annual Meeting through COMNAP member, the British Antarctic Survey. COMNAP reported that the information would be discussed in COMNAP's Peninsula Regional Break-out Group.

(80) ASOC welcomed the project, and agreed that addressing oil spills required an ecosystem approach, since they impacted all wildlife and marine fauna and flora. ASOC noted that it would be important to address the root causes of oil spills, which in some cases went beyond the remit of the CEP, including increased use of Automatic Identification Systems (AIS) at sea by all vessels operating in the area.

(81) In responding to several comments made by Members, the United Kingdom clarified that the project was still in a preliminary phase, it would take the points raised into consideration in further developments, and it looked forward to further comments from Members and Observers. It also emphasised that avoiding oil spills from happening in the first place should be the primary intent, as clean-up activities were very difficult.

(82) The Committee agreed the usefulness of the preliminary sensitivity map for assisting with oil spill contingency planning and response, and encouraged Members and Observers to provide suggestions for improving the map's accuracy and utility to enhance the management of potential oil spills in the Antarctic Peninsula region.

(83) Argentina presented IP 93 *Planning process for future capacity expansion of Petrel Base, Cape Welchness, Dundee Island*, which reported on plans currently being developed by the Argentine Antarctic Programme to increase the capacity of the Petrel Antarctic base. Argentina informed the Committee that the station updates aimed to expand and improve the logistical support capabilities for its scientific activities in

Antarctica, with a view to future challenges for science. Initial work at the base included the collection of baseline environmental information, the study of meteorological and bathymetric information, and various operational feasibility studies. Argentina reported that it had also conducted an assessment of the environmental impact of using the base as a year-round station, and noted that the corresponding IEE was available on the EIES. It further noted that plans for the construction of new accommodation, new laboratories, the reconditioning of the base's original airstrip and the construction of a dock at the base were currently being assessed, and that the draft CEE would be submitted to the CEP for its consideration. The Committee took note of the information provided by Argentina.

(84) Türkiye presented IP 100 *Extension of the Use of Turkish Scientific Research Camp*, which reported on Türkiye's intention to extend its use of a temporary research camp established on Horseshoe Island in February 2019 during the 3rd Turkish Antarctic Expedition (TAE-3). Noting that challenges arising from the COVID-19 had delayed the construction of its new Antarctic research station, Türkiye reported that it intended to use the temporary camp until the new station was put into service. The Committee thanked Türkiye and noted the usefulness of being informed about changes in previously reported activities.

(85) The Committee noted the following Information Papers and Secretariat Paper submitted under this agenda item:

- IP 35 *New methodology for the quantitative assessment of the environmental impacts of the Argentine Antarctic Programme* (Argentina).

- IP 40 *Methodology for evaluating vulnerability to climate change in environmental impact assessments* (Argentina).

- IP 48 *Davis Aerodrome Project: Decision by Australia not to proceed, and knowledge gained of the Vestfold Hills environment* (Australia).

- IP 53 *On the issue of developing regulatory and methodological provision of the reduction of air pollutant emission sources impact on the Antarctic environment* (Belarus).

- IP 59 *Report on Refurbishment and Modernization of the German Antarctic Receiving Station GARS O'Higgins* (Germany).

- IP 95 *Progress of glaciological research activities at the Dome Fuji station and its vicinity* (Japan).

- SP 8 *Annual list of Initial Environmental Evaluations (IEE) and Comprehensive Environmental Evaluations (CEE) prepared between 1 April 2021 and 31 March 2022* (ATS).

Item 9: Area Protection and Management Plans

9a) Management Plans

i) Draft Management Plans which have been reviewed by the Subsidiary Group on Management Plans

(86) The convener of the Subsidiary Group on Management Plans (SGMP), Dr Anoop Tiwari (India) introduced WP 8 rev. 1 *Subsidiary Group on Management Plans Report of activities during the intersessional period 2021-2022*, on behalf of the SGMP. The convener thanked all active participants in the SGMP for their hard work and reminded the Committee that all Members were welcome to join the SGMP. The convenor of the SGMP thanked Ewan McIvor (Australia) for coordinating review of ASPA 145 in efficient manner and Dr Polly Penhale (USA) for moderating the SGMP's discussions about a process for pre-meeting review of ASPA and ASMA management plans.

(87) In accordance with terms of reference #1 to #3, the SGMP reviewed one draft revised Antarctic Specially Protected Area (ASPA) management plan for ASPA 145 Port Foster, Deception Island, South Shetland Islands. The SGMP advised the Committee that the revised management plan was well written, of high quality, and adequately addressed the key points raised in its advice to proponents. Accordingly, the SGMP recommended that the Committee approve the revised management plan for ASPA 145.

(88) A question was raised regarding the proposed addition of a new marine sub-site to ASPA 145, and whether the draft management plan had been approved through the CCAMLR system. Chile explained that consideration of this plan had been completed in accordance with Decision 9 (2005), which indicated that CCAMLR's approval would be required for the creation of ASPAs and ASMAs whose regulations would affect or impede CCAMLR-related activities. Chile noted that it had presented three Management Plans for modified ASPAs to CCAMLR in 2012 (ASPA No. 144, ASPA No. 145, ASPA No. 146). CCAMLR had reaffirmed the importance of those areas for scientific research and indicated that they would not affect CCAMLR activities. CCAMLR therefore had recommended that the CEP approve the corresponding management plans. Chile explained that it had not sought approval for the inclusion of a third sub-site (C) to ASPA No. 145, for which two sub-sites had already been approved by CCAMLR. Because sub-site C had the same characteristics of previously-approved sub-sites, Chile had determined that sub-site C would fall under the same approval criteria and would not require CCAMLR review. Chile therefore recommended that the Committee agree to its proposed Management Plan for ASPA No. 145 and forward it to the ATCM for adoption.

(89) The Committee thanked Chile for the clarification, and noted that sub-site C was worthy for inclusion in ASPA No. 145. One Member considered that the procedure of prior approval from CCAMLR should be followed if the new sub-site has the same characteristics as the two existing sub-sites. Several other Members considered that this site did not trigger the criteria for CCAMLR approval set out in Decision 9 (2005).

(90) IAATO noted it had been pleased to take part in the SGMP review of ASPA 145. Acknowledging the importance of Committee discussions around the ASPA, IAATO further noted it planned to alert its member operators to the importance of the area under consideration and to include the revised management plan in its field operations manual.

(91) ASOC questioned why CCAMLR would have an interest in the site, as ASOC understood the proposed sub-site was a small area that protected the seafloor and not the water column.

(92) The Committee thanked the SGMP for its careful review and helpful suggestions to improve the management plan. The Committee noted that it had not been able to reach agreement on forwarding the revised management plan for ASPA 145 to the ATCM for adoption. The Committee noted that Chile would present the revised management plan for ASPA 145 for consideration by CCAMLR. The Committee expressed its understanding that the plan was likely to be approved by CCAMLR in accordance with Decision 9 (2005). The Committee invited the CEP Observer to SC-CAMLR, Dr Polly Penhale, to draw the issue discussed with respect to the trigger criteria in Decision 9 (2005) to the attention of SC-CAMLR.

(93) The convenor of the SGMP advised the Committee that the management plans for the following three ASPAs were still under review by Chile:

- ASPA 125: Fildes Peninsula, King George Island (Chile).

- ASPA 146: South Bay, Doumer Island, Palmer Archipelago (Chile).

- ASPA 150: Ardley Island (Ardley Peninsula), Maxwell Bay, King George Island (Chile).

(94) The convenor of the SGMP further informed the Committee that Chile intended to submit revised management plans to the SGMP for these ASPAs before the next CEP meeting. The Committee noted this information.

ii) Revised draft Management Plans which have not been reviewed by the Subsidiary Group on Management Plans

(95) The Committee considered five-yearly reviews of 17 ASPA management plans and one Antarctic Specially Managed Area (ASMA) management plan. In each case, the Committee considered the changes to the existing management plan, and noted that the ASPA management plans had been reviewed and revised with reference to the *Guide to the Preparation of Management Plans for Antarctic Specially Protected Areas* (the Guide):

- WP 1 *Revised Management Plan and maps for Antarctic Specially Managed Area No. 7 Southwest Anvers Island and Palmer Basin* (United States).

- WP 2 *Revised Management Plan for Antarctic Specially Protected Area No. 149. Cape Shirreff and San Telmo Island, Livingston Island, South Shetland Islands* (United States).

- WP 3 *Revised Management Plan for Antarctic Specially Protected Area No. 122. Arrival Heights, Hut Point Peninsula, Ross Island* (United States).

- WP 4 *Revised Management Plan for Antarctic Specially Protected Area No. 124. Cape Crozier, Ross Island* (United States).

- WP 5 *Review of the Management Plans for Antarctic Specially Protected Areas (ASPAs) No. 113 Litchfield Island, Arthur Harbor, Palmer Archipelago, No. 119 Davis Valley and Forlidas Pond, Dufek Massif, and No. 139 Biscoe Point, Palmer Archipelago* (United States).

- WP 6 *Revision and merger of the Management Plans for Antarctic Specially Protected Areas No. 152 Western Bransfield Strait and No. 153 Eastern Dallmann Bay* (United States).

- WP 19 *Revision of the Management Plan for Antarctic Specially Protected Area (ASPA) No. 164 Scullin and Murray Monoliths, Mac.Robertson Land* (Australia).

- WP 32 *Revision of the Management Plan for Antarctic Specially Protected Area No 127 "Haswell Island" (Haswell Island and the adjacent fast ice field with a colony of emperor penguins)* (Russian Federation).

- WP 40 *Revision of the Management Plan for Antarctic Specially Protected Area (ASPA) No. 109 Moe Island, South Orkney Islands* (United Kingdom)

- WP 41 *Revision of the Management Plan for Antarctic Specially Protected Area (ASPA) No. 110 Lynch Island, South Orkney Islands* (United Kingdom).

- WP 42 *Revision of the Management Plan for Antarctic Specially Protected Area (ASPA) No.111 Southern Powell Island and adjacent islands, South Orkney Islands* (United Kingdom).

- WP 43 *Revision of the Management Plan for Antarctic Specially Protected Area (ASPA) No. 115 Lagotellerie Island, Marguerite Bay, Graham Land* (United Kingdom).

- WP 44 *Revised Management Plan for Antarctic Specially Protected Area No. 126 Byers Peninsula, Livingston Island, South Shetland Islands* (United Kingdom, Chile, Spain).

- WP 45 *Revision of the Management Plan for Antarctic Specially Protected Area (ASPA) No. 129 Rothera Point, Adelaide Island* (United Kingdom).

- WP 46 *Revision of the Management Plan for Antarctic Specially Protected Area*

(ASPA) No. 140 Parts of Deception Island, South Shetland Islands (United Kingdom, Spain).

- WP 53 *Revision of the Management Plan for Antarctic Specially Protected Area (ASPA) No. 133, Harmony Point, Nelson Island, South Shetland Islands* (Argentina, Chile).

(96) With respect to ASPA 109 (WP 40), ASPA 110 (WP 41), ASPA 111 (WP 42), ASPA 115 (WP 43), ASPA 126 (WP 44), ASPA 127 (WP 32), ASPA 129 (WP 45), ASPA 133 (WP 53), ASPA 140 (WP 46), and ASPA 164 (WP 19), the Committee noted that the revised management plans proposed only minor revisions, and had no further comments.

(97) With respect to ASPA 149 (WP 2), ASPA 122 (WP 3), ASPA 124 (WP 4), ASPA 113 (WP 5), ASPA 119 (WP 5), ASPA 139 (WP 5), the Committee noted that the revised management plans proposed only minor revisions. In response to a question concerning the use of the phrase "unnecessary human presence" as something to avoid, the United States explained that entry restrictions were consistent with the provisions in Article 3 of Annex V and referred to the Guide to the Preparation of Management Plans encouraging the use of flexible wording. The United States also reminded the Committee that the previously approved ASPA-176 management plan contained the same phrase "unnecessary human presence". In response to a further request by one Member, the Committee agreed to change "should" to "highly encourage" national Antarctic programmes to consult with other programmes working in the area to avoid scientific duplication and minimise cumulative impacts (WP 3).

(98) With respect to ASPA 152 and ASPA 153 (WP 6), the United States reported that the comprehensive review of these sites had identified that there would be considerable benefit to merging the two ASPAs into a single plan covering both sites. The United States noted that the merge would maintain the same level of protection as before while simplifying the plan and eliminating needless duplication associated with the common purposes, aims, objectives and management policies shared by ASPA 152 and ASPA 153. The United States considered that the revisions were major and thus, recommended intersessional review by the SGMP and that the Management Plan would be submitted to CCAMLR for approval in accordance with Decision 9 (2005).

(99) ASOC thanked the United States for WP 6, and noted changes to vertical boundaries in ASPAs with a marine component should be considered on a case-by-case, site specific basis.

(100) With respect to ASMA 7 (WP 1), the United States noted that the need for revision was initiated by the adoption of ASPA 176 through Measure 19 (2021), which had formerly been classified as a Restricted Zone. Maps were also updated to reflect the change in status of the Rosenthal Islands. The United States pointed out that, for a number of years, Torgersen Island had been divided into a Restricted Zone and Visitor Zone to enable comparisons of Adélie penguin population trends between two sides of the island. The United States reported that in recent years the number of breeding Adélie penguins within both the Visitor Zone and Restricted Zone had decreased precipitously and was now so small that it was decided to close the Visitor Zone and designate the whole Island as a Restricted Zone. The causes and mechanisms of this trend were likely influenced by warming and could not necessarily be attributed to visitor impacts. The United States had consulted IAATO and the scientific community working at Palmer about closing the Visitor Zone in order to protect the remaining Adélie penguins, and to extend the existing Torgersen Island Restricted Zone to cover the whole island.

(101) IAATO thanked the United States for inviting it to participate in the review process and expressed its support for the proposal.

(102) The Committee approved all the revised management plans that had not been reviewed by the SGMP, with the exception of the merger of ASPA 152 and 153, which the Committee agreed to refer to the SGMP for review in the intersessional period.

CEP advice to the ATCM on revised management plans for ASPAs and ASMAs

(103) The Committee agreed to forward the following revised management plans to the ATCM for approval by means of a Measure:

#	Name
ASMA 7	Southwest Anvers Island and Palmer Basin
ASPA 109	Moe Island, South Orkney Islands
ASPA 110	Lynch Island, South Orkney Islands
ASPA 111	Southern Powell Island and adjacent islands, South Orkney Islands
ASPA 113	Litchfield Island, Arthur Harbor, Anvers Island, Palmer Archipelago
ASPA 115	Lagotellerie Island, Marguerite Bay, Graham Land
ASPA 119	Davis Valley and Forlidas Pond, Dufek Massif, Pensacola Mountains
ASPA 122	Arrival Heights, Hut Point Peninsula, Ross Island
ASPA 124	Cape Crozier, Ross Island
ASPA 126	Byers Peninsula, Livingston Island, South Shetland Islands
ASPA 127	Haswell Island (Haswell Island and Adjacent Emperor Penguin Rookery on Fast Ice)
ASPA 129	Rothera Point, Adelaide Island
ASPA 133	Harmony Point, Nelson Island, South Shetland Islands
ASPA 139	Biscoe Point, Anvers Island, Palmer Archipelago
ASPA 140	Parts of Deception Island, South Shetland Islands
ASPA 149	Cape Shirreff and San Telmo Island, Livingston Island, South Shetland Islands
ASPA 164	Scullin and Murray Monoliths, Mac.Robertson Land

iii) New draft management plans for protected/managed areas

(104) The Committee considered a draft management plan for one proposed new ASPA:

- WP 15 *Proposal for a new Antarctic Specially Protected Area in parts of the Western Sør Rondane Mountains, Dronning Maud Land, East Antarctic* (Belgium).

(105) Belgium explained that the primary reason for designating several sites of the Western Sør Rondane Mountains as an ASPA was to protect the unique terrestrial biodiversity and ecosystems of the area. It also noted that this area was the subject of scientific research on the biodiversity and impact of climate change. Highlighting the sites as representative of the natural terrestrial biological communities typical for Antarctic mountainous regions, Belgium further noted that the ASPA would increase the representation of mountainous habitats in the Antarctic protected area system and enhance the representation of ASPAs in Antarctic Conservation Biogeographic Region (ACBR) 6. The site also contained important scientific, wilderness and aesthetic values. Belgium added that the proposed management plan built on the prior assessment presented in CEP XX - WP 42, and referred to CEP XXI - IP 42 in which it had addressed questions raised by several Members with regard to the prior assessment. Belgium recommended that the Committee forward the proposal to the SGMP for review in the intersessional period.

(106) The Committee reaffirmed that it recognised that the outstanding values of the Sør Rondane Mountains site warranted protection. It also noted the usefulness of the pre-assessment process.

(107) One Member expressed substantial concern on the two proposed prohibited areas that would absolutely exclude human activities, and questioned their consistency with the spirit of the Protocol, which designated Antarctica as a natural reserve for peace and science.

(108) Belgium noted that inviolate reference sites were described in Annex V of the Protocol and that the proposed designations of these two inviolate reference sites as prohibited zones would be for a limited time of 50 years, and remarked that it would consider simplifying the limits of the proposed ASPA. Belgium remarked that it was looking forward to working on these and other matters, both technical and substantial, in the SGMP.

CEP advice to the ATCM on a draft management plan for a new protected area

(109) The Committee agreed to advise the ATCM that it had decided to forward the following draft management plan for a new protected area to the SGMP for review:

- Proposal for a new Antarctic Specially Protected Area in parts of the Western Sør Rondane Mountains, Dronning Maud Land, East Antarctica.

iv) Papers relating to prior assessment of proposed new protected areas

(110) The Committee considered three Working Papers relating to the prior assessment of proposed new protected areas, in accordance with the *Guidelines: A prior assessment process for the designation of ASPAs and ASMAs*.

(111) Germany introduced WP 12 *Prior assessment of a proposed Antarctic Specially Protected Area at Otto-von-Gruber-Gebirge (Dronning Maud Land, East Antarctica)*, prepared jointly with the United States. Germany outlined the environmental values of the multi-site ASPA, including large and deep ice-covered freshwater lakes, a large breeding colony of snow petrel, and scientific values to ecology, exobiology, geomorphology, paleoclimatology, and geology. It further noted historic, aesthetic and wilderness values, as well as the sites' scientific importance.

(112) The Committee noted the important values within the proposed ASPA. Recalling the importance of the Committee's ongoing work to support further systematic development of the Antarctic protected area system, following the 2019 Joint SCAR/CEP Workshop on Further Development of the Antarctic Protected Areas System (CEP XXII - WP 70), Members conveyed their support for broadening the system by including more ecosystems of perennially ice-covered lakes. In reply to a concern about older data on snow petrels and the size of the proposed site, Germany mentioned that an expedition was planned for 2022-23 to gather more data. Germany expressed its appreciation for offers of assistance from Members and IAATO in further work.

(113) The Committee welcomed the prior assessment and encouraged Members to work with the proponents towards a management plan during the intersessional period.

(114) Germany introduced WP 13 *Prior assessment of a proposed Antarctic Specially Protected Area at Danger Islands Archipelago (North-eastern Antarctic Peninsula)*, prepared jointly with the United States. The proponents explained the primary motivation behind proposing this terrestrial ASPA consisting of seven largely ice-free islands was related to the protection of important breeding sites for seabirds. This included several Important Bird Areas designated for their populations of penguins including one of the largest Adélie penguin breeding sites in the Antarctic Peninsula region. The proponents also noted the scientific, wilderness, and aesthetic values of the proposed ASPA. The proponents recommended that the Committee: agree that the values within the proposed ASPA merit special protection; endorse the development of a Management Plan for the area; and encourage interested Parties to work with Germany and the United States informally during the intersessional period in the development of a management plan for submission to CEP XXV.

(115) The Committee thanked Germany and the United States for putting forward the prior assessment for the multi-site ASPA at Danger Islands Archipelago. The Committee noted the quality of the evaluation put forward by the proponents and considered this to be an area worth taking forward in the intersessional period with the aim of drafting a management plan for the area. The Committee encouraged Members with knowledge and information relevant to this process to engage in these intersessional discussions.

(116) IAATO thanked Germany and the United States for introducing the assessment of the proposed ASPA at Danger Islands Archipelago. IAATO noted that its operators visited the Danger Islands, though visits were rare, usually to Heroína Island, and most often focused on either small boat cruising or ship cruising. It noted that since 2017 there had been a total of 30 visits by IAATO operators to the Islands, nine of which were landed visits. Noting the important values that had been identified, and with a view to supporting the intersessional work process towards strengthening the protection of the islands, IAATO noted that it would create IAATO visitor site guidelines for operators for the west side harbour landing site at Heroína Island, which was the most frequently used landing site. These IAATO visitor site guidelines would be enacted for the 2022-23 season. IAATO further expressed that it would be pleased to engage with the proponents of WP 13 as these interim guidelines were created and that it was happy to contribute to additional conversations about the issue and to the upcoming intersessional work.

(117) The United Kingdom introduced WP 38 *Prior assessment of a proposed Antarctic Specially Protected Area on Farrier Col, Horseshoe Island, Marguerite Bay*, prepared jointly with Belgium and Türkiye. The proponents explained that the proposed ASPA would protect a range of scientific and environmental values associated with lakes in the region. They emphasised that research had characterised the lakes as rare examples of refugia for species through the last glacial cycle, as well as rare examples in the region of rock bound oligotrophic lakes, making them ecologically significant. The proponents further noted that the lakes were important to international research and held aesthetic and wilderness value. The proponents expressed that a higher level of protection for the lakes was appropriate in light of the fact that the lakes were in proximity to a newly proposed Turkish research station.

(118) The Committee thanked the United Kingdom, Belgium, and Türkiye for their work in preparing this prior assessment and noted the value of turning the CEP's attention to the importance of lakes in the region. The Committee agreed that the value of the proposed ASPA merited special protection and endorsed the development of a management plan for the area led by the three proponents. It also encouraged interested Members and Observers to work with the proponents informally during the intersessional period in the development of a Management Plan for potential submission at CEP XXV.

(119) The Committee further highlighted the usefulness of the prior assessment procedure, which offered the opportunity to consider proposed new areas before the majority of work toward designation was implemented.

(120) IAATO thanked the United Kingdom, Belgium, and Türkiye for undertaking the prior assessment introduced in WP 38. It noted that IAATO operators visited Horseshoe Island mainly to visit Base Y which provided historical perspective and inspirational experiences within the operators' educational programmes. IAATO stated that during the 2021-22 season, fourteen visits had been made to Horseshoe Island. While Base Y was not included in the proposed ASPA, IAATO noted its interest in seeing the work around this ASPA develop, and that it would be happy to contribute in the intersessional period if deemed useful by Members.

(121) Referring to WP 12, 13, 15 and 38, ASOC thanked all Members that had proposed new or future ASPAs. ASOC noted each had its own merits in accordance with Annex V, such as protecting Important Bird Areas, or underrepresented Antarctic Conservation Biographic Regions, and contributed significantly to the expansion of the ASPA system required by Annex V of the Environmental Protocol.

iv) Other matters relating to management plans for protected/managed areas

(122) Chile presented IP 127 *Revisión del estado de la Zona Antártica Especialmente Protegida No. 144, bahía Chile (bahía Discovery)*, and referred to IP 128 *Analysis of the current status of the Antarctic Specially Protected Area No. 144, Chile Bay (Discovery Bay), Greenwich Island*. Chile informed the Committee of a review taking place on the de-designation of ASPA No. 144. It noted that analysis was being carried out according to the CEP's *Guidelines for de-designation of ASPAs*, and that its full analysis was presented in IP 128. Chile noted that it intended to submit a Working Paper with a final conclusion related to revision of the ASPA for Members' consideration at CEP XXV.

(123) The Committee thanked Chile for bringing IP 127 and IP 128 to the table. It recognised that the de-designation of ASPAs was an important issue, that required careful consideration. The Committee noted that it looked forward to the work outlined in IP 127 and IP 128 being discussed at CEP XXV.

(124) Brazil presented IP 65 *Progress in the revision process of the Management Plan for Antarctic Specially Managed Area Nº 1, Admiralty Bay*, prepared jointly by Ecuador, Peru, Poland and the United States. The paper discussed a five-year review of the management plan for ASMA No. 1 initiated by the ASMA No. 1 Management Group. Brazil informed the Committee that, during the 2021-22 intersessional period, and as part of the process of revising the management plan, the Management Group had worked to update the current status of values to be protected, its biological communities, scientific research and monitoring being conducted, as well as climate, tourism and commercial harvesting within the ASMA. The Management Group had also contacted IAATO to obtain updated information on tourism at Admiralty Bay, and had updated the ASMA No. 1 map. The Group's next steps would include: updating the maps to reflect the guidance in Annex B of the Guidelines for the preparation of ASMA Management Plans; reviewing the Code of Conduct for Visitors and Scientific and Environmental Guidelines; and submitting a joint Working Paper with the revised management plan to the CEP once the review was concluded.

(125) The Committee thanked the proponents of IP 65 for reporting on progress made in the review of the Management Plan for ASMA No. 1. It also noted a request for more information relating to the issue of non-native species within the ASMA. The Committee looked forward to seeing the results of the review.

(126) The Committee noted following Information Paper submitted under this agenda item:

- IP 120 *Exploring the possibilities for the designation of Barrientos (Aitcho) Island as an ASMA* (Ecuador).

9b) Historic Sites and Monuments

(127) The United Kingdom introduced WP 47 *Discovery of the wreck of the Endurance – Updating information for HSM 93 and Development of a Management Plan*, prepared jointly with South Africa. It reported that Sir Ernest Shackleton's ship *Endurance*, trapped, crushed by ice and sunk in the Weddell Sea in 1915, had been found and discovered to be in a remarkable state of preservation in March 2022. It highlighted that the South African icebreaker *S.A. Agulhas II* was critical to the effort. In WP 47, the proponents had recommended that the Committee recommend the ATCM adopt a Measure to update the 'Description', 'Site Location', 'Conservation Status', 'Management Tools', and 'Physical features of the environment and cultural and local context' information fields of HSM 93. However, the United Kingdom explained that in discussion with the CEP Chair, it had been noted that updates to 'Conservation Status' and 'Management Tools' did not require adoption through a Measure, but instead should be agreed by the Committee and noted in the Report. The proponents therefore requested

that the ATCM adopt a Measure to update only the 'Description', 'Site Location', and 'Physical features of the environment and cultural and local context' information fields of HSM 93, while noting that the 'Conservation Status' and 'Management Tools' would be updated.

(128) IAATO noted that the position and depth of *Endurance* would make any visitation for tourism unlikely and supported the development of a management plan for HSM 93.

(129) The Committee congratulated all involved in finding the location of the wreck, and agreed to forward the relevant modified details for the HSM to the ATCM for adoption by means of a Measure.

(130) Argentina introduced WP 52 *Proposal to modify the coordinates of nine Historical Sites and Monuments*. It proposed an update to the coordinates of HSMs 26, 29, 36, 38, 39, 40, 41, 42 and 43, for which Argentina shared management responsibilities based on Measure 3 (2003). Argentina explained that the proposed amendments aimed to more precisely reflect the locations of the HSMs than was currently recorded in the list of HSMs. Argentina noted that a detailed review had made it possible to identify the locations to within a hundredth of a minute, with 20 m resolution on the ground, and to accordingly adjust the location of the HSMs. Argentina recommended that the CEP endorse the proposed updates to the location of these HSMs and forward them to the ATCM for adoption.

(131) The Committee thanked Argentina for the work it had done to update the coordinates of these historic sites and monuments, agreed to the suggested amendments to HSMs 26, 29, 36, 38, 39, 40, 41, 42, 43, and agreed to forward the modified details for the HSMs to the ATCM for adoption by means of a Measure.

CEP advice to the ATCM on proposed modifications to Historical Sites and Monuments

(132) The Committee agreed to forward ten proposals for modifications to the List of Historic Sites and Monuments to the ATCM for adoption by means of a Measure:

HSM #	Name
26	Ceremonial Installations of the San Martín base
29	Primero de Mayo Lighthouse
36	Dallmann Expedition Plaque
38	Swedish hut on Snow Hill
39	Hope Bay stone hut
40	Esperanza Base Ceremonial Facilities
41	Historic remains of *Antarctic*'s crew on Paulet Island
42	Laurie Island Observatories
43	Belgrano station cross
93	Wreck of *Endurance*

(133) With respect to HSM 93, the Committee agreed to advise the ATCM that it had agreed to the following additional updates to the fields of the HSM listing:

Field	Updated Text
(viii) Conservation status	Appears to be well preserved.
(xi) Management tools	A Conservation Management Plan is in development.

(134) The United Kingdom introduced WP 28 *Guidance for Conservation Management Planning for Historic Sites and Monuments in Antarctica*, prepared jointly with Australia, New Zealand, Norway and the United States. Recalling discussions at ATCM XLII relating to the responsible care of heritage in Antarctica, the co-authors proposed new guidance to be adopted to support Parties in developing conservation management plans as tools to protect Antarctic heritage. They noted that the new guidance would encourage Members to fulfil their responsibilities for heritage in Antarctica to a consistent standard that was in line with the principles of the Antarctic Treaty and Environmental Protocol, and comparable to the stewardship of heritage in other parts of the world.

(135) The Committee thanked the proponents for their paper and supported the proposal to update the Guidelines. The Committee recognised the importance of sharing information on conservation management plans related to HSMs and underlined their value for the conservation of Antarctic heritage. The Committee highlighted that, although they were not required for all HSMs, conservation management plans were a useful tool for protecting HSMs. One Member emphasised the need to consider the nature of HSMs when assessing whether the development of a conservation management plan was necessary.

(136) In response to a query, the United Kingdom clarified that it proposed a suggested bibliography and that the list was not intended to be fully comprehensive, and agreed to include additional links to strengthen the list.

(137) The Committee agreed to reaffirm the value of conservation management plans as an effective tool for the responsible stewardship of heritage in Antarctica; and to update the *Guidelines for the assessment and management of Heritage in Antarctica* as recommended by the proponents. The Committee encouraged Members to continue to share their conservation management plans and expertise with each other to improve the standard of heritage stewardship, and consider how this could be facilitated.

CEP advice to the ATCM on Guidance for Conservation Management Planning for Historic Sites and Monuments in Antarctica

(138) The Committee agreed to forward the revised *Guidelines for the Assessment and Management of Heritage in Antarctica* to the ATCM for adoption by means of a Resolution.

---

(139) Argentina presented IP 112 rev. 1 *Current Situation of the impact of climate change on the Sweden Refuge on Snow Hill Island (HSM No. 38)*, prepared jointly with Sweden. It provided a summary of the impacts of climate change on the Swedish refuge hut at Snow Hill, as observed by researchers from Argentina's National Antarctic Programme, and as part of a joint collaboration with Sweden. Argentina reported that the advanced state of erosion of the permafrost, which was caused by increased temperatures, the retreat of the adjacent glacier and increased fluvial erosion, posed an imminent risk to the refuge hut and highlighted the need to stabilise the terrain on which the refuge was located.

(140) The Committee thanked Argentina and Sweden for the paper and for their efforts to support to the conservation of this important historic monument.

(141) The Committee noted the following Information Paper submitted under this agenda item:

- IP 31 *Analysis of the accuracy of the location coordinates of some Historic Sites and Monuments* (Argentina).

9c) Site Guidelines

(142) The United Kingdom introduced WP 49 *Revised Visitor Site Guidelines for Site No. 22 Wordie House, Winter Island*, prepared jointly with Ukraine. The United Kingdom noted that Wordie House had been recognised as an HSM in Measure 4 (1995), and that the Site Guidelines for Wordie House had not been revised since their adoption through Resolution 4 (2009). It added that a number of editorial improvements and clarifications were made in the course of the review. In particular, a clearly defined visitor zone and recommended path to the top of the island's ice cap were added, and the site map for the Site Guidelines was updated and improved.

(143) The Committee thanked the United Kingdom and Ukraine for putting forward the revised Site Guidelines for Wordie House and highlighted the timeliness of the proposal. Following a minor amendment, the Committee agreed to approve the revised Site Guidelines and forward them to the ATCM for adoption. The Committee also requested that the Secretariat update the Site Guidelines on its website.

(144) IAATO thanked the proponents for the revised Site Guidelines for Wordie House. It emphasised that Visitor Site Guidelines were a critical tool for managing site visitation, and that IAATO valued the opportunity to participate in these discussions. IAATO reported that the revised Site Guidelines for Wordie House would be included in IAATO's 2022-23 Field Operations Manual. Noting that IP 97 *Revised Tourism Management Policy for Vernadsky Station, Galindez Island* covered a similar area to the Site Guidelines for Wordie House, IAATO offered to work with the proponents to clarify the interaction between the two ahead of the 2022-23 tourist season.

(145) The United Kingdom also thanked Ukraine for IP 97 and offered its support in providing any clarifications that would be helpful.

(146) With reference to WP 1 discussed under Agenda Item 9a, the Committee agreed that the closing of the Visitor Zone in ASMA 7 would entail that Site Guidelines for Torgersen Island, Arthur Harbour would no longer be relevant.

CEP advice to the ATCM on new and revised Site Guidelines

(147) The Committee agreed to forward the following revised Site Guidelines to the ATCM for adoption:

- Wordie House, Winter Island

(148) The Committee agreed to request *Torgersen Island, Arthur Harbour* be removed from the list of Site Guidelines maintained by the Antarctic Treaty Secretariat.

---

(149) Ukraine presented IP 97 *Revised Tourism Management Policy for Vernadsky Station, Galindez Island*, which presented a revised tourism management policy for Vernadsky Station. Ukraine noted the dynamic nature of this document, and that its tourism management policy for Vernadsky Station would be periodically reviewed.

(150) The Committee thanked Ukraine for its paper and welcomed the revised tourism management policy for Vernadsky Station.

(151) IAATO presented IP 43 *A Five-Year Overview and 2021–22 Season Report on IAATO Operator Use of Antarctic Peninsula Landing Sites and ATCM Visitor Site Guidelines*, which reported on data collected from IAATO Operator Post Visit Report Forms for the 2021-22 season. IAATO reported that, during the 2021-22 season, a total of 22 979 passengers made landings in the Antarctic Peninsula from 32 SOLAS vessels. It noted that IAATO operators saw fewer clients willing to travel during the 2021–22 season due to COVID-19 and therefore had lower occupancy. IAATO highlighted that most visited

sites were covered either by ATCM Site Guidelines for Visitors, IAATO operator landing site guidelines, or national programme management guidelines. It further observed that all visits were conducted in accordance with landing limits established in applicable guidelines, and that the IAATO ship scheduler had been used effectively to ensure that no limits had been exceeded.

(152) The Committee thanked IAATO for providing this useful information on its Antarctic activities.

9d) Marine Spatial Protection and Management

(153) No papers were submitted under this agenda item.

(154) The Chair made a note of the Committee's pending obligation to respond to the request from the ATCM in Resolution 5 (2017), where the CEP was asked to consider any appropriate actions within the ATCM's competence to contribute to the achievement of the specific objectives set forth in CCAMLR Conservation Measure 91-05.

9e) Other Annex V Matters

(155) Australia introduced WP 20 *Type localities in Antarctica*, which reported on recent research to develop an inventory of type localities for terrestrial and freshwater species on the Antarctic continent and offshore islands within the Antarctic Treaty area. The research also considered the extent to which those type localities occurred within ASPAs. Australia noted that this work could support implementation of the Environmental Protocol, including by providing information about areas that constituted the 'type locality or only known habitat of any species' and which, in accordance with Article 3.2(d) of Annex V, might warrant consideration for designation as ASPAs. Australia highlighted that its researchers had undertaken extensive efforts to review and collect the data to develop the inventory. It shared some of the key findings presented in the paper, including that: over 400 species have type localities on the Antarctic continent or offshore islands within the Antarctic Treaty area; over 100 of those species were located within or in close proximity to existing ASPAs; and that type localities occurred in 41 existing ASPAs.

(156) The Committee commended Australia for the development of a comprehensive body of work on type localities and recognised its value in enhancing the systematic protection of Antarctica.

(157) Some Members noted that, when considering ASPA designations, other aspects could be prioritised, including potential threats and risks, and that this newly developed tool should be considered along with many other existing tools.

(158) In responding to points raised by Members, Australia noted that the reported research represented the best available science relating to the provisions of Article 3.2 of Annex V regarding type localities, and was one of many important contributions to further develop the Antarctic protected area system. Australia referred to IP 47 *Research to inform CEP discussions about further development of the Antarctic protected areas system*, which reported on work being undertaken by Australian researchers to develop a suite of example scenarios for how a series of terrestrial protected areas might address the provisions of Article 3.2 of Annex V.

(159) ASOC thanked Australia for providing a useful scientific tool that could contribute to the expansion of protected areas in Antarctica. It noted that abundant data was available to systematically develop the protected area system in Antarctica and encouraged Members to use the newly developed tools when considering ASPA designations in the future.

(160) The Committee encouraged Members to draw on the research presented in WP 20, as well as other relevant tools, when: reviewing management plans for existing ASPAs; planning, assessing and conducting activities; and considering the designation of new ASPAs within a systematic environmental-geographic framework. The Committee also encouraged Members to continue to support efforts to improve Antarctic biodiversity knowledge, including research to determine the distribution, as well as status and trends, of species with type localities in the Antarctic Treaty area.

(161) The SGMP convenor, Dr Anoop Tiwari (India) introduced the second part of WP 8 *Subsidiary Group on Management Plans Report of activities during the intersessional period 2019-2022.* The SGMP's first task under ToRs 4 and 5 was to work with relevant Parties to ensure progress on review of management plans overdue for five-year review. The SGMP convenor reported that no requests were received from Parties that may need advice to initiate the five-year review of management plans and reminded Members that the SGMP was available to advise, facilitate or guide such review tasks when necessary.

(162) The SGMP's second task under ToRs 4 and 5 was to consider options for the efficient pre-meeting review of revised management plans submitted to the CEP for consideration and adoption.

(163) Dr Polly Penhale (United States), in her capacity as moderator of the SGMP's discussons on this task, addressed the Committee. Dr Penhale recalled that, at CEP XXIII, Members had suggested that the SGMP could consider options for efficient pre-meeting reviews of revised management plans submitted to the CEP for consideration and adoption. Members had requested that the SGMP discuss how to improve the management plan review process and report back to the Committee with suggestions on how to increase its efficiency. Dr Penhale reported that, as a result of these discussions, the SGMP had proposed a pre-meeting review of new and revised management plans submitted to the CEP for consideration and endorsement, aimed to encourage those Members and Observers who had interest and expertise in management plans in general, and with knowledge and familiarity of regional or site-specific environments, to comment on the submitted management plans prior to the CEP meeting in order to obtain the best possible recommendations. The SGMP had also highlighted that issues raised and suggested edits presented prior to the meeting would provide an opportunity for the proponent(s) of a management plan to consider comments and to provide responses to, or revisions of, the plans prior to the meeting. It had further noted that a summary of the pre-meeting discussions, with recommendations from the pre-meeting review, would be presented to all Members and that the formal conclusion of discussions would be taken during the CEP meeting. Dr Penhale emphasised that revising management plans was an important task of the CEP, which was increasing every year, and that the proposed process intended to save time and organised the workload in a more efficient way.

(164) The Committee thanked the SGMP convenor and the moderator of the SGMP's discussions about a pre-meeting review process for their presentations. Members supported the idea of a pre-meeting review of revised management plans as a way of guiding and streamlining the revision process, noting that early reviews could help save valuable time during the meeting. Some Members also emphasised that all CEP Members may become active members of the SGMP, and that broad participation in 2021 had proved to be effective.

(165) In responding to a concern raised, it was noted that the pre-meeting revision process would take place within the existing structure of the SGMP and would not require the establishment of a new group or mechanism.

(166) The Committee agreed to add a new SGMP Term of Reference to reflect the new regular task of pre-meeting review of Management Plans (see Appendix 4, ToR #4).

(167) The SGMP's third task under ToRs 4 and 5 was to review and update the SGMP work plan. In doing so, the SGMP had noted that the CCRWP included an action to 'review

and revise where necessary existing management tools to consider if they afford the best practical adaptation measure to areas at risk from climate change'. To deliver on this action, the SGMP and SGCCR Convenors discussed options to support a programme of work to develop guidance for addressing climate change in the process of identifying and managing protected areas, including identifying within which Subsidiary Group this work should reside. They concluded that this work should be undertaken by the SGMP as an additional task under ToR 5.

(168) The Committee thanked the SGMP for its advice and, following some minor amendments, agreed to adopt the SGMP work plan for 2022-23:

Terms of Reference	Suggested tasks
ToR 1 to 3	Review draft management plans referred by CEP for intersessional review and provide advice to proponents (including the four pending plans from previous intersessional period)
ToR 4 to 6	Work with relevant Parties to ensure progress on review of management plans overdue for five year review
	Pre-meeting review of all Management Plans with minor changes and submit a summary of recommendations to CEP as a separate Working Paper
	Review and update SGMP work plan
	To implement CCRWP action 2(e) "Review and revise where necessary existing management tools for protection and subsequent management of environments and habitats at risk from climate change", consider if and how they effectively take climate change issues into consideration.
Working Papers	Prepare report for CEP XXV against SGMP ToR 1 to 6.

(169) Brazil presented IP 66 rev. 1 *Report of the Joint Inspections' Program undertaken by Brazil, Ecuador, Peru, Poland, and the United States to the ASMA No. 1 - Admiralty Bay, King George Island,* prepared jointly with Ecuador, Peru, Poland, and the United States. It reported that officials from the proponent countries had made site visits to ASMA No. 1 to ensure that its designation as an ASMA provided continued protection of the special values based upon which it was initially designated. Brazil noted that the officials had concluded that the values for which the ASMA No. 1 was designated remained relevant, and that several measures were in place to ensure that the aims and objectives of the Management Plan were being met. The proponents recommended that: all personnel entering the ASMA No. 1 should be made aware of the provisions of the Management Plan and be required to follow the guidance; personnel should be trained to reduce the risk of introducing non-native species to the ASMA No. 1, including food-borne pathogens; personnel should be instructed to use vegetation-free walking routes whenever possible to minimise trampling; and coordination among members of the ASMA No. 1 Management Group should continue to ensure successful management of the area.

(170) The Committee thanked the proponents for their inspection of ASMA No. 1, and welcomed their report and recommendations.

(171) IAATO thanked Brazil, Ecuador, Peru, Poland and the United States for their paper and

for their continued engagement with IAATO about the management of this important area. IAATO noted that, during the 2021-22 season, tourist visits to active national Antarctic programme stations had not been undertaken. This IAATO guidance was currently under review in anticipation of the 2022-23 season. IAATO remarked that it looked forward to working with the ASMA No. 1 Management Group to ensure the continued successful management of this area.

(172) The Committee noted the following Information Paper had been submitted under this agenda item:

- IP 77 *A classification system of Antarctic inland aquatic ecosystems* (New Zealand).

Item 10: Conservation of Antarctic Flora and Fauna

10a) Quarantine and Non-native Species

(173) The Republic of Korea presented IP 9 *Report of a new non-native insect (moth fly) on King George Island, South Shetland Islands*, prepared jointly with Chile. It reported on the discovery of a new non-native insect, the moth fly *Psychoda albipennis*, at two research bases on King George Island during the 2019-20 and 2021-22 seasons. The moth fly had been identified through DNA barcoding. To avoid further spread of the moth fly in King George Island, the proponents urged all Parties operating their national Antarctic programmes on King George Island to undertake periodic monitoring inside and outside their facilities as well as their supply chains, and consider a coordinated response to this non-native species introduction.

(174) The Committee thanked the Republic of Korea and Chile for their paper, and their contribution to this priority issue in the CEP Five-year Work Plan.

(175) The United Kingdom presented IP 25 *International response under the Antarctic Treaty System to the establishment of a non-native fly on the South Shetland Islands*, prepared jointly with Uruguay. It summarised information concerning the potential development of an international non-native species management plan for the non-native fly *Trichocera maculipennis* in the South Shetland Islands and the wider maritime Antarctic region. The United Kingdom noted that, together with further guidelines on non-native species management from the CEP, such a plan could help deliver coordinated management of this increasingly widespread non-native species. It further noted that the academic paper attached to IP 25 detailed options for education, monitoring, awareness, reduction of fly dispersal, prevention of reintroduction, and eradication.

(176) The Committee thanked the United Kingdom and Uruguay for their paper. Several Members expressed support for an international management plan, as well as an exchange of experiences, with respect to *Trichocera maculipennis*.

(177) The Committee noted the following Information Papers had been submitted under this agenda item:

- IP 24 *Ship traffic connects Antarctica to worldwide locations, with implications for non-native marine species introduction risk* (United Kingdom).

- IP 30 *Detección de una especie no nativa de Díptero en el Refugio Elefante, ZAEP N°132, Isla 25 de Mayo / Rey Jorge* (Argentina, Uruguay).

- IP 84 *Definitive eradication of the presence of a Lepidoptera at Carlini Base* (Argentina, Germany).

(178) The Committee noted that the following Background Paper had been submitted under this agenda item:

- BP 18 *Seeds for Future - Global Wild Plant Seed Vault* (Italy).

10b) Specially Protected Species

(179) The United Kingdom introduced WP 34 *Report of the CEP Intersessional Contact Group established to develop a Specially Protected Species Action Plan for the emperor penguin*. It recalled that SCAR, in its review on the conservation status of the emperor penguin, had found that the emperor penguin was vulnerable to ongoing and projected climate change, and warranted protection as an Antarctic Specially Protected Species (SPS). SCAR had recommended that the Committee establish an ICG to review the draft Action Plan prepared by SCAR (ATCM XLIII - WP 37) and had suggested that the species might best be classified within the IUCN Red List as 'Vulnerable'. The United Kingdom reported that, after six rounds of discussion during the 2021-22 intersessional period, the ICG recommended that the CEP: consider the draft Specially Protected Species Action Plan for the emperor penguin developed by the ICG; forward the draft Action Plan and SCAR's assessment of the conservation status of the emperor penguin (ATCM XLIII - WP 37) to the ATCM for consideration; and recommend to the ATCM (i) the designation of the emperor penguin as a Specially Protected Species under Annex II to the Protocol through adoption of a draft Measure, and (ii) that it encourage Parties to undertake the timely implementation of the Specially Protected Species Action Plan.

(180) China introduced WP 24 *An Overview on the Legal Framework on Antarctic Specially Protected Species and Its Application*, which reviewed the legal framework on SPS and its application within the ATCM and the CEP, with a view to providing useful guidance on future designation of SPS. China outlined several observations on ATCM and CEP practices in relation to the legal framework on SPS. On the basis of its review, China recommended that the CEP: re-confirm the importance of designating SPS consistent with Annex II and the *Guidelines for CEP Consideration of Proposals for New and Revised Designations of Antarctic Specially Protected Species under Annex II of the Protocol*, particularly the conservation status of "Vulnerable or higher" as the threshold for the consideration of the potential designation, and the procedure for consideration of SPS proposals; align the future designation of SPS with previous ATCM and CEP practices, particularly on the application of criteria and approach on the basis of adequate scientific information; encourage SCAR to assess the risk of extinction of the species using the most up-to-date IUCN criteria consistent with its previous practice; and review and harmonise inconsistencies between the Guidelines and Annex II to the Protocol.

(181) China introduced WP 35 *Proposal for Development of a Targeted Research and Monitoring Plan for the Emperor Penguins*. The paper extracted the findings from the draft Action Plan as the outcome of six rounds of ICG, which built on CEP XXIII - WP 37 submitted by SCAR: the emperor penguins were currently listed as "Near Threatened" in the IUCN Red List; the population of the species had been increasing in the regional (Antarctic) scale; the northernmost emperor penguin colony on Snow Hill Island was stable; the known and emerging terrestrial and marine threats affecting emperor penguin were considered relatively small if not negligible; the threat assessment of climate change and sea ice reduction on the species was considerably uncertain; and the threat was predicted to take place only until after 2050. Following the scientific advice from SCAR in the paper ATCM XXVIII/CEP VIII - WP 34 and ATCM XXIX/CEP IX - WP 38, China recommended that the CEP establish an ICG to develop a targeted research and management plan for the emperor penguins as a "Near Threatened" species at the regional (Antarctic) scale, instead of designating it as a SPS, to ensure the consistency in the application of Annex II to the Protocol and the *Guidelines for CEP Consideration of Proposals for New and Revised Designations of Antarctic Specially Protected Species*.

(182) China also referred to IP 123 *The Case of Polar Bears Conservation informed by Climate Models and the Potential Similar Case of Emperor Penguins*, which put forward two articles respectively on polar bears and emperor penguins that China considered to be useful for the CEP's consideration of the status of the emperor penguin. One of the articles was about polar bears, noting they had been up-listed in 2006 from "Least Concern" to "Vulnerable" to extinction in the IUCN Red List, and was informed by a climate model, which predicted that the number of polar bears would decline by more than 30% over the next 45 years. It noted that the polar bear population had recovered in the 1980s and maintained stable. The article further provided the information that polar bear numbers are now the highest they have been over the past 60 years.

(183) The Committee thanked China for presenting WP 35, but noted that no other Member voiced its support for the recommendations in the paper. The Committee also thanked the United Kingdom for its work toward the protection of the emperor penguin. It particularly commended Dr Kevin Hughes for his work as ICG convener during the intersessional period. The Committee also thanked SCAR for the papers it presented to CEP XXIV, which had informed WP 34.

(184) The Committee emphasised the importance of drawing on best available science to support CEP management decisions such as listing specially protected species, and noted SCAR's advice on the need for the conservation of the emperor penguin. With one exception, Members expressed extensive support for the Action Plan outlined in WP 34 as a comprehensive document based on the best available science. Members noted that the Committee had sufficient scientific knowledge available to demonstrate the vulnerability of the emperor penguin to climate change, including as highlighted in the SCAR Lecture. Some Members and SCAR noted that the overall emperor penguin population trend was not increasing, as noted in WP 35. The aforementioned increase in number was due to the discovery of new colonies, but population projections continued to indicate a decline. With one exception, Members also emphasised that the need for further research should not undermine the importance of taking a precautionary approach to environmental protection as a fundamental component of the Environmental Protocol, which was a recognised tool that allowed necessary decisions or measures to be taken for the protection of the Antarctic environment, where needed. Members cautioned that failure to act in a timely manner would run contrary to the roles and responsibilities of the CEP and its commitment to the precautionary principle. Members emphasised that there was no prerequisite for a species to be listed in the IUCN Red List as Vulnerable or higher before it could be considered for SPS designation, and that the provisions of Annex II and current SPS Guidelines had been followed in basing the recommendations for designation on SCAR's assessment of conservation status. With one exception, Members voiced strong support for the recommendations put forward in WP 34 that the emperor penguin should be designated a SPS under Annex II of the Protocol, and that the Action Plan be implemented. Members highlighted that failure of the CEP and Parties to act in a timely manner on SPS designation would potentially render any actions taken to conserve the emperor penguin at a later stage too late to be effective. There was as a consequence no support for the recommendations of WP 35 on an alternative approach.

(185) With one exception, Members agreed that the current legal framework on SPS presented no impediments to advancing efforts to designate emperor penguins as SPS and that, although there was room to revisit some aspects of its guidance, the framework did not require further immediate consideration. There was therefore no support for the recommendations of WP 24.

(186) Many Members noted strong doubts about the scientific quality and accuracy of the information put forward in IP 123, and considered it had no relevance to the issues addressed in WP 34. It was noted that: the articles referred to in IP 123 had not been published in any credible scientific journals; the articles were published on a website well known for spreading disinformation to undermine confidence in climate science;

and they presented factual errors and misguided conclusions. Members underscored the importance of using peer-reviewed science as basis for management deliberations.

(187) ASOC thanked the authors of WPs 34 and 35 and expressed its strong support for the designation of the emperor penguin as a Specially Protected Species, which was a concrete step that could be taken by the ATCM to respond to climate change. ASOC considered that there was a precautionary basis for the designation, as well as a clear scientific case, and therefore believed that the designation should not be delayed.

(188) The Committee did not reach consensus on the recommendation in WP 34 proposing the listing of the emperor penguin as a Specially Protected Species despite receiving full support from all but one Member. Many Members and Observers expressed intent to use the draft Action Plan provided in WP 34 as guidance to support their actions on the management of this species, including conducting further monitoring of emperor penguin populations, and encouraged the Committee to do so. Members expressed an intent to return to the recommendations presented in WP 34 at CEP XXV, and urged all Members to engage in intersessional discussions to work towards consensus.

(189) The Committee noted the following Information Paper had been submitted under this agenda item:

- IP 10: *Recent status of emperor penguin population in Northern Victoria Land, Ross Sea* (Republic of Korea)

10c) Other Annex II Matters

(190) France introduced WP 25 *Important Marine Mammals Areas (IMMAs)*, prepared jointly with Chile, Germany, Monaco, South Africa and the United Kingdom. Recalling CEP XXIII - IP 24, which had discussed a 2018 scientific workshop convened to identify Important Marine Mammal Areas (IMMAs) in the Southern Ocean, the paper suggested that IMMAs could be a useful tool to assist Parties when planning and conducting a range of Antarctic activities. France reported that, during the workshop, experts from 11 countries had identified 15 IMMAs, which were submitted to an independent group of experts who validated and confirmed 13 of them. It noted that the paper considered four of those IMMAs, which were wholly or partially within the Antarctic Treaty area. It noted that the concept of IMMAs was modelled on the successful example of the BirdLife International process for determining IBAs. The IMMAs were identified according to specific criteria derived from IBAs and adapted to marine mammals integrating both activities on land and at sea. The proponents recommended that the Committee: welcome and acknowledge the content of the Final Report of the Fourth IMMA workshop for the three identified IMMAs that were within the Antarctic Treaty area and the section of the Scotia Arc IMMA that lay within the Antarctic Treaty area; consider the need to list tools of particular importance to the work of the Committee when planning and conducting activities in Antarctica in a single Resolution which could be amended as new scientific results became available; encourage Members to take account of the information in the report on IMMAs within the Antarctic Treaty area in the planning and conduct of their activities in Antarctica; encourage Members to consider the extent to which the scientific information behind these IMMAs could be useful to the development of new ASPAs with a marine component, or when reviewing existing management plans of ASPAs and ASMAs; and encourage Members to continue to undertake appropriate on-land and at-sea monitoring of marine mammal populations to inform future management actions that may be required.

(191) The Committee thanked the proponents for bringing this issue back to its attention and welcomed the information provided in the paper. It acknowledged the content of the Final Report of the Fourth IMMA workshop and agreed on the usefulness of taking into account IMMAs when planning and conducting activities in Antarctica. A Member stressed the importance of considering both the information from the IMMA e-Atlas and

the information from the research and monitoring projects of national Antarctic programmes. The Member noted the difference in geographical scale between the information in the e-Atlas, and the smaller scale of ASPAs and ASMAs. The Member also stated that the Committee's support for IMMAs should be limited to scientific information referring to the Antarctic Treaty area, since in other geographical areas it could contain references not shared by some Parties. The Committee encouraged Members to continue undertaking appropriate on-land and at-sea monitoring of marine mammal populations to inform future management activities, as suggested by one of the paper's recommendations.

(192) One Member expressed concern about the use of this tool and questioned the need to list all existing tools in a single and separate Resolution, stating that to do so would require a concrete proposal and assessment of whether the information included was acceptable.

(193) ASOC thanked the proponents and expressed support the recommendations in WP 25. In particular, ASOC considered the suggestion to collate this and other available tools into a single Resolution to be a practical way to centralise the growing number of science-based resources available for planning and conducting activities, and for environmental protection on the interface of land and sea.

(194) In responding to a question raised, France confirmed that population trends had been taken into account in the work put forward. It further clarified that the listed IMMAs were not proposed as potential ASMAs or ASPAs, noting that the information could be useful when considering the designation of ASMAs or ASPAs with marine components as IMMAs incorporate foraging areas for seals, and also areas where seals haul out on the ice or on the land to moult, breed, or rest.

(195) The Committee encouraged Members to consider this matter further and revisit discussions on IMMAs in a future meeting. With one exception, Members highlighted the importance of spatial tools and assessments to enhance both our understanding of the environment and management efforts. Some Members expressed their intent to begin using the information on IMMAs to inform planning moving forward.

(196) Germany introduced WP 14 *Do the Environmental Guidelines for operation of Remotely Piloted Air-craft Systems (RPAS) in Antarctica (v 1.1) need to be revised?* and referred to IP 39 *The usefulness of the Environmental Guidelines for operation of Remotely Piloted Aircraft Systems in Antarctica - Insights from a survey*. Germany reported on the results of its assessment to determine whether the *Environmental Guidelines for operation of RPAS in Antarctica (v 1.1)* adopted in Resolution 4 (2018) should be revised. Germany noted that it had reviewed and summarised the technical development of drone technology and evaluated the state of scientific knowledge on the impacts of RPAS use on Antarctic wildlife since the Guidelines were developed in 2017. In addition, it had conducted a survey among interested National Competent Authorities. As a result of its assessment, Germany recommended that the Committee: consider the need for a structural and substantive revision of the Guidelines; establish an informal ICG to discuss this issue further and set up Terms of Reference for a formal ICG with the aim of revising the guidelines commencing immediately after CEP XXV; and encourage Parties to carry out further studies and to collect information about the impacts of RPAS use on Antarctic wildlife.

(197) Germany also referred to IP 37 *Impact of RPAS (drone) use on emperor penguins*. Germany reported that its study had concluded that RPAS flights for monitoring purposes over emperor penguins could be reasonable, provided the drone only passed over the colony for short moments, and particularly if done above 70 metres. The study had also found that repeated activities, particularly with reoccurring changes of direction, should be avoided.

(198) The Committee thanked Germany for its papers and for conducting its assessments on RPAS use and guidelines in Antarctica. Several Members supported Germany's

recommendation to review the current guidelines on RPAS and expressed their willingness to participate in an ICG. The Committee noted that the use of RPAS in Antarctica was an increasingly frequent activity and that it required special attention. Some Members suggested that some of the guidelines, particularly related to operational and safety issues, were already covered by COMNAP's Antarctic Remotely Piloted (RPAS) Operator's Handbook, and questioned whether the CEP was the competent body to discuss operational and safety related risks of the use of RPAS in Antarctica. One Member suggested that it could be useful to work on the revision of the environmental part of the existing COMNAP guidelines. Some Members pointed out that it could be preferable to wait until new knowledge and research was available before working on updating the guidelines. Following further discussion, the Committee noted that there was no clear agreement on the immediate need to revise the RPAS guidelines.

(199) IAATO thanked Germany for its work. It noted that IAATO operators did not allow the use of recreational RPAS flights in wildlife rich coastal areas, and that its deep field operators did not allow the use of RPAS at wildlife sites, including at or near emperor penguin colonies. IAATO added that RPAS use was restricted near flight operations and not allowed within ASMA 5 at Amundsen-Scott South Pole Station. It further noted that IAATO members must adhere to Resolution 4 (2018), where applicable. Finally, IAATO remarked that it encouraged the sharing and collecting of information to inform decision-making on the use of RPAS, and valued continued engagement with Members, Observers and national competent authorities, including in support of future guideline revisions.

(200) COMNAP noted that it valued the reminder from Germany that it was important for RPAS operators to have robust, relevant guidelines, and to ensure such guidelines were available to others who made decisions about activities. COMNAP confirmed that many national Antarctic programmes contributed to the COMNAP Antarctic Remotely Piloted Aircraft Systems (RPAS) Operator's Handbook and that it continued to be reviewed and updated, and was available from COMNAP's website as version 6, 15 September 2021. COMNAP noted its appreciation for the IP 37 literature review which would be considered in its current review.

(201) In responding to Members' comments, Germany noted its intention to concentrate on the environmental aspects related to RPAS activities in Antarctica, in order to assist National Competent Authorities in permitting procedures and to find ways to prioritise actions.

(202) The Committee encouraged further intersessional discussion between interested Members and a report from such discussions at a future CEP meeting.

(203) China presented IP 122 *Group-size effect on vigilance and flight initiation distances of Adélie penguins in south-eastern Antarctica*, which reported on research conducted on Vigilance Initiation Distances and Flight Initiation Distances of Adélie penguins to potential disturbances from human activities in Cosmonaut Sea, the Cooperation Sea, and Prydz Bay. China suggested that: this research could be used to support the future development of possible guidelines for vessels operation; the Committee could encourage Members to conduct such research with their respective national programmes; and the Committee could encourage SCAR and IAATO to report their related data and results for future consideration.

(204) SCAR and IAATO indicated that they would report any relevant information to the CEP for future consideration.

(205) The Committee noted that the following Information Papers had been submitted under this agenda item:

- IP 36 *Population decline of Cape Petrel on Fildes Peninsula* (Germany).

- IP 38 *Update: Managing the Effects of anthropogenic noise in the Antarctic – Steps towards the development of an underwater noise protection concept for Antarctica* (Germany).

(206) The Committee noted that the following Background Paper had been submitted under this agenda item:

- BP 14 *State of Antarctic Penguins 2022 Report* (SCAR).

Item 11: Environmental Monitoring and Reporting

(207) SCAR introduced WP 10 *Antarctic Environments Portal,* noting that the Portal was an online independent source that supported the work of the CEP by providing impartial and up-to-date information based on the best available science. It further noted that SCAR had taken over management of the Portal and its website in 2020. SCAR provided an update on the operation of the Portal, including examples of Information Summaries that linked directly to issues of priority interest for the CEP. SCAR welcomed Members' support for the Portal. It thanked Spain and France for providing translations and acknowledged Members that had provided funding. SCAR recommended that the CEP continue to support the Portal and identify any additional Information Summaries it would like to see published.

(208) The Committee thanked SCAR for its extensive work on the Antarctic Environments Portal and highlighted that the Portal's Information Summaries provided a high-quality source of the best available science for policymakers to support decision making. The Committee noted that the Portal was a valuable tool for supporting Antarctic activities and decision making, and encouraged SCAR to continue its efforts in providing this highly relevant scientific data for Members' consideration. The Committee recognised the hard work undertaken by the Portal's previous editor, Neil Gilbert, and welcomed its new editor, Keith Reid. It acknowledged the role that national Antarctic programmes had played in the Portal's development, including through funding and the provision of translations. It also acknowledged their critical role in providing scientific support to the work of the CEP.

(209) Some Members highlighted the importance of considering geographical balance in relation to the Portal's authors and of engaging younger scientists and authors in this work. Members also underscored the need to ensure scientific neutrality in the summaries, as well as the importance of making information on the Portal available in all four official Treaty languages.

(210) The Committee thanked SCAR for its work and reiterated its continued support for the Portal, noting once more its value as a source of high-quality scientific information on subjects of relevance for the work of the Committee.

(211) Germany introduced WP 11 rev. 1 *Further steps towards a structured sample data collection of environmental contamination,* and referred to IP 7 rev. 1 *Update on current initiatives for a more structured sample and data collection of environmental contamination in the Antarctic,* prepared jointly with Australia, Italy, Sweden, United Kingdom and United States. Noting that global and regional activities were causing increased levels of chemical contamination in Antarctica, Germany drew the Committee's attention to the need for a more structured system of sampling and data collection for chemical contamination in the Antarctic. It highlighted the 2021 Expert Workshop 'Act now – Legacy and Emerging Contaminants in Polar Regions' and the report 'Emerging and legacy organic contaminants in the polar regions', and their calls for improved cooperation between experts, researchers, decision-makers and interested stakeholders with respect to screening, monitoring, assessment and data sharing.

(212) The Committee thanked the proponents for their paper and acknowledged the value of enhancing collective efforts towards the development of a structured sample database

of environmental contamination in Antarctica. The Committee recognised SCAR's valuable contribution with respect to sampling data and long-term monitoring of Antarctic contaminants and noted the valuable findings of the Expert Workshop on contaminants in the polar regions. The Committee expressed broad support for proponents' recommendations and requested SCAR to submit recommendations to CEP XXV on how a more systematic sampling and data collection of chemical contamination in the Antarctic could be delivered. The Committee also encouraged Members to intensify cooperation between all stakeholders to initiate a more structured sample and data collection of environmental contamination in the Antarctic.

(213) SCAR thanked the proponents for their papers, recalling its CEP XXIII - IP 137 *Persistent Organic Chemicals in Antarctica: A horizon scan of priority challenges* and drew Members' attention to the work of its ImPACT Action group on persistent organic pollutants. SCAR expressed support for the papers' recommendations and agreed to provide advice to CEP XXV on how a more systematic sampling and data collection of chemical contamination in the Antarctic could be delivered.

(214) IAATO thanked the proponents for their work and expressed its support for their recommendations. It remarked that it would continue working with interested parties on this matter.

(215) ASOC thanked the proponents for their work, and for addressing these gaps in current data collection and monitoring efforts on Antarctic contaminants.

(216) The Committee reiterated its thanks to Germany and the co-sponsors of these papers. It also thanked SCAR for its offer to provide advice on this matter and looked forward to progressing this work at CEP XXV.

(217) Spain introduced WP 22 *Towards adaptive and sustainable management of Antarctic tourism: Monitoring as a key tool for decision-making,* prepared jointly with Ecuador and the United States, which described the steady growth of tourism and non-governmental activities in the Antarctic since the 1960s and highlighted the disruption to this growth curve reflected in the 2020-2021 season due to COVID-19. It referred to ATCM Recommendations IV-27 (1966) and VI-7 (1970), which recognised that tourism activities could jeopardise the scientific research conducted, hinder fauna and flora conservation, and damage the Antarctic environment. With a view to achieving adaptive and sustainable tourism management in Antarctica and addressing information gaps in tourism monitoring programmes, the proponents recommended that the CEP: promote the establishment of monitoring programmes to assess the actual impacts arising from tourism activities; promote the development of these monitoring programmes and continue with its work to understand the cumulative impacts of tourism on the environment; and ensure that monitoring programs involve multiple stakeholders, including bodies such as SCAR, COMNAP and IAATO.

(218) The Committee thanked the proponents of WP 22 and acknowledged its contribution to improving the long-term monitoring of tourism impacts on the Antarctic environment. The Committee recalled its Five-year Work Plan and its request for advice from SCAR on the design of an environmental monitoring programme to assess the impacts of tourism. It also noted ongoing intersessional work being undertaken to identify and assess cumulative impacts and encouraged Members to participate in these discussions.

(219) Some Members commented on the inherent challenges of monitoring tourism impacts including the budgetary implications of remote monitoring, logistical difficulties of coordinating monitoring activities, issues with permit processing, and the interference of scientific activities by visitors. Members also noted the need to consider the importance of integrating the different sources of information regarding Antarctic tourism activities, including encouraging data collection of tourism activities through national monitoring programmes at the Antarctic stations as well as information collected at Antarctic gateways in order to contribute to developing tourism management tools based on this information.

(220) IAATO stated that long-term monitoring programmes were essential for understanding environmental impacts and changes, and noted its continued support of this research. It welcomed working with the Antarctic community towards the development of monitoring programmes and thanked the proponents for recommending a multiple stakeholder approach. IAATO reiterated that all human activity had the potential for impact and that effective management driven by informed decision-making, including from monitoring, was critically important. It encouraged Members and national competent authorities to continue their efforts towards a consistent and effective EIA process and sharing best-available information to ensure tourism had no more than a minor or transitory impact.

(221) SCAR thanked the authors and agreed on the need to provide further monitoring data to support decision-making on Antarctic tourism. It underlined that monitoring should involve multiple stakeholders and that an overarching strategy to coordinate and facilitate research was required. SCAR drew the meeting's attention to its recently formed Antarctic Tourism Action Group (ANTAG), which aimed to facilitate research collaboration within SCAR on topics related to tourism. It highlighted that SCAR experts were ready to contribute their evidence-based advice as required. It noted the importance of identifying the different elements of developing the scientific basis and planning of monitoring programmes, on one side, and the implementation of those programmes, on the other. In this regard, it suggested it would be useful to consider the different roles and contributions of stakeholders.

(222) The Committee expressed its support for the recommendations in WP 22. It highlighted the importance of developing programmes to assess impacts arising from tourism activities, and encouraged Members and Observers to work together to progress this work. The Committee also noted the upcoming Workshop on Tourism Monitoring in the Antarctic, being hosted by Germany on 28 May 2022, and encouraged Members to participate.

(223) Portugal introduced IP 1 *Microplastics in the Antarctic marine food web: evidence from penguins*, prepared jointly with the United Kingdom. This paper described recent research that reported the presence of microplastics in the marine food web of the wider Antarctic region, and noted that microplastics were found in 20% of examined penguin faecal samples. The co-authors encouraged future studies on the amount of microplastics in the Antarctic Treaty area and the potential effects of microplastic on penguins and other Antarctic organisms.

(224) The Committee thanked Portugal and the United Kingdom for their paper.

(225) ASOC thanked the proponents for the paper and noted its considerable concern around microplastics in the marine food web in the Southern Ocean. ASOC recommended that the CEP continue to monitor the situation and advise the ATCM on the appropriate response.

(226) SC-CAMLR drew the Committee's attention to the fact that several CCAMLR members regularly collected marine debris found on beaches and seabird colonies, and surveyed marine mammals entangled in fishery-related debris or soiled with hydrocarbons in the Convention area. SC-CAMLR communicated a willingness to provide a summary report on such work at a future CEP meeting.

(227) The Committee expressed its support for IP 1 and noted that it would welcome a summary report by SC-CAMLR at a future CEP meeting.

(228) Portugal introduced IP 2 *Effects of climate change on Antarctic marine food webs: new evidence from squid*, prepared jointly with the United Kingdom. This paper provided scientific evidence of the effects of climate change on the distribution and habitat of Southern Ocean squid. It highlighted the need for long-term monitoring programmes in

the Antarctic, and the value of organisations such as SCAR, COMNAP and national Antarctic programmes in developing such work.

(229) Portugal introduced IP 4 *Information on chemical pollution at Port Foster, Deception Island*, prepared jointly with Spain. The paper reported on emerging contaminants such as biocides, polycyclic aromatic hydrocarbons (PAH), persistent organic pollutants (POPs), pentachlorophenol (PCPs), and pharmaceuticals in phytoplankton samples collected from Port Foster, Deception Island. Portugal noted with concern that the most abundant elements were from pharmaceutical compounds. Noting its support for the findings in WP 11 and IP 54, the proponents recommended that the CEP: establish monitoring programmes to mitigate and remediate chemical pollutants from across the Antarctic Treaty area, to help inform future monitoring research and policy development; and consider implementing appropriate contamination control and remediation methods.

(230) The Committee thanked Portugal and Spain for their paper and affirmed the value of collaboration on pollution mitigation in Antarctica. It also thanked Argentina for sharing its research on the subject and welcomed Argentina's offer to present its results to an upcoming CEP meeting.

(231) Switzerland introduced IP 68 *Microplastic Pollution in the Southern Ocean*, which summarised recent research on microplastic pollution in the Southern Ocean and Antarctica. It explained that a collaborative project between Switzerland and Germany had investigated whether microplastics originated at research stations on the continent, from tourists on ships, or from other continents. The project had provided the first systematic data on microplastic pollution in the Southern Ocean, in particular the Weddell Sea, and in selected Antarctic and Southern Ocean species, as well as on microbial colonisation of microplastics under Southern Ocean conditions.

(232) The Committee thanked Switzerland for the paper and for its collaborative work with Germany.

(233) ASOC presented IP 91 *Antarctic tourism policies after the "pandemic pause"*. ASOC highlighted the pause in Antarctic tourism caused by the pandemic is easing, and that recovery is likely. ASOC suggested Members should be proactive in identifying emerging tourism trends and shaping tourism management for the next decade. Noting that the paper suggested five approaches to identifying emerging tourism trends and management over the next decade, ASOC highlighted the three of most relevance to the CEP: expanding area protection under Annex V; developing dedicated programmes for monitoring of tourism impacts; and ensuring consistent assessment of tourism activities. ASOC noted that the paper was of relevance to the upcoming workshop on "Tourism monitoring in Antarctica: development of a concept for the monitoring of the effects of tourism on the Antarctic environment or dependent or associated ecosystems in Antarctica", which had been commissioned by the German Environment Agency, and that it looked forward to participating in the workshop.

(234) The Committee thanked ASOC for presenting the paper and noted a call for intersessional discussion between Members on the subject.

(235) The Committee noted that the following Information Paper had been submitted under this agenda item:

- IP 76 *Wastewater management practices at Antarctic stations: Preliminary survey results* (COMNAP).

(236) The Committee noted that the following Background Papers had been submitted under this agenda item:

- BP 11 *A seismic swarm at the Bransfield Rift, Antarctica* (Uruguay).

- BP 13 *First evidence of airborne microplastic pollution in Antarctic air and snow* (New Zealand, Spain).

Item 12: Inspection Reports

(237) No papers were submitted under this agenda item.

Item 13: General Matters

(238) Norway introduced WP 21 *Communication of CEP science needs to researchers and national science funding agencies*, prepared jointly with the United Kingdom. Norway highlighted the CEP's practice of drawing on the best available science to inform its advice to the ATCM. It also recalled that the Chair of CEP XX had consolidated existing CEP science needs into a single list. After examining this list, the proponents had found that CEP science needs were not being framed in a manner that could be easily translated into scientific efforts. Norway expressed its concern that science funding agencies were not sufficiently informed about prioritised science needs for the support of the management of the Antarctic environment. For this reason, the proponents recommended that the Committee initiate a process to consider how the list of CEP science needs for Antarctic management, in the CEP Five-year Work Plan, could be further developed to clarify research needs in a way that could be more easily understood and actioned by researchers and funding agencies. They further recommended that the Committee advise the ATCM that Parties should ensure that CEP science needs were regularly communicated to national science funding agencies, with the aim of supporting timely delivery of policy-relevant science to inform CEP advice to the ATCM.

(239) The Committee thanked Norway and the United Kingdom for raising this important matter for consideration. It noted that that this issue was relevant to all Members, especially those Members whose funding agencies and national Antarctic programmes were not closely linked. Many Members highlighted the importance of an effective Antarctic science-policy interface and several Members shared insights into the experiences of their respective countries. The Committee discussed a number of opportunities for communicating CEP science needs to the research community in the future.

(240) Concerns were raised about the ability of some Members' national funding agencies to translate CEP science needs into funded research based on the particularities of national funding systems. In relation to this challenge, several Members suggested that the recommendations outlined in WP 21 could be implemented in such a way as to facilitate the development of international collaborative programmes that would be responsive to policy needs. It was also noted that effective communication of CEP science needs could impact individual scientists' proposed research agendas, to the benefit of CEP activities. One Member raised a concern about the appropriateness of asking scientists to undertake policy-relevant research rather than neutral, impartial, and objective science. Some Members noted the utility to add these actions into the CEP Five-year Work Plan.

(241) SCAR thanked Norway and the United Kingdom for their paper, noting that it addressed important challenges that cut across many of the issues under consideration by the CEP. It agreed that strengthening dialogue between the CEP and national science funding agencies would be valuable and noted that the creation of a list of science needs provided a good foundation for this. SCAR expressed its interest in contributing to efforts to clarify research needs that were both accessible to and actionable by researchers and national science funding agencies.

(242) WMO responded to concerns raised about the appropriateness of asking scientists to undertake policy-relevant research rather than neutral, impartial, and objective science

by clarifying that independent research and policy-relevant research were not mutually exclusive.

(243) The Committee agreed to initiate a process to consider how the list of CEP science needs for Antarctic management in the CEP Five-Year Work Plan can be further developed to clarify research needs in a way that can be more easily understood and actioned by researchers and funding agencies; and advise the ATCM that Parties should ensure that CEP science needs are regularly communicated to national science funding agencies with the aim of supporting timely delivery of science to inform CEP advice to the ATCM.

(244) Portugal introduced IP 3 *UN Ocean Conference 2022 in Lisbon, Portugal*, prepared jointly with Sweden and WMO. It noted that in 2022, Portugal and Kenya would be hosting the second UN Ocean Conference, which had been delayed by COVID-19 constraints. The proponents suggested that the Antarctic Treaty System had the capacity and expertise to be one of the key contributors to the success of the event.

(245) The Committee thanked Portugal for the invitation to participate in the UN Ocean Conference in Lisbon.

(246) WMO introduced IP 74 *Education and Outreach Activities of the World Climate Research Programme*, which discussed the Education and Outreach activities of its co-sponsored World Climate Research Programme (WCRP). WMO highlighted two new WCRP initiatives: the WCRP Academy Lighthouse Activity and the Climate and Cryosphere Fellowships and Grants. It noted that these initiatives aimed to ensure that the next generation of climate science leaders would be ready to take on important roles in guiding the climate research agenda and that all scientists would be equipped to engage with society in the context of climate change.

(247) WMO presented IP 106 *WMO Unified Data Policy and the Global Basic Observing Network (GBON)*. This paper explained that the Unified Data Policy integrated all WMO-relevant Earth system discipline and domain areas under a single umbrella policy statement. WMO expected the Global Basic Observing Network to strengthen global observational data availability. It emphasised a commitment to free and unrestricted data exchange and noted that sustained access to observations taken from stations operated under the ATS was an integral component of meeting the goals of the global Numerical Weather Prediction systems.

(248) The Committee thanked WMO for its paper and noted its completed and ongoing work.

(249) SCAR introduced IP 107 rev. 1 *The Southern Ocean contribution to the United Nations Decade of Ocean Science for Sustainable Development*, prepared jointly with Belgium, IAATO, the Netherlands, and WMO. SCAR drew the Committee's attention to the work of the Southern Ocean Task Force, which comprised organisations from across the scientific research community, industry sectors, and national and international management bodies. The Task Force was formed as part of the UN Decade of Ocean Science, which aimed to gather ocean stakeholders worldwide behind a common framework for research to support a sustainable future for the world's oceans. SCAR reported that the Southern Ocean community had engaged in a stakeholder-oriented process to develop the Southern Ocean Action Plan, which was published in April 2022 to identify research challenges, strengthen the links between science, industry and policy, and encourage internationally collaborative activities to address gaps in knowledge and data coverage.

(250) ASOC thanked the proponents for the paper, and noted that the Pew Charitable Trust and World Wide Fund for Nature supported the development of the Southern Ocean Action Plan, which drew from the expertise of a wide range of Antarctic scientists and other stakeholders. ASOC noted it was encouraged by the framework which provided a useful roadmap for developing the science needed to protect one of the world's last great wilderness areas.

(251) The Committee thanked the proponents for IP 107 rev.1, and recognised all contributions to the UN Decade of the Ocean.

(252) France presented IP 108 *The Ice Memory Programme*, prepared jointly with Italy. This paper provided an update on the status of the Ice Memory (IM) Programme and proposed additional collaboration from interested Members to further advance the programme. France explained that the IM Programme intended to collect an ice core archive from the deep layers of key endangered glaciers before they lost their ability to preserve environmental history in optimal conditions. It proposed to store these ice cores in repository caves to be constructed on the Antarctic Plateau close to Concordia Station, where the cores would be preserved by naturally cold temperatures on a long-term basis for future scientists and for humanity. The co-authors explained that an IM Foundation had been created in order to ensure the IM Programme would be a global initiative. The co-authors invited all Members to join the IM Foundation and to exchange information to further the work of the IM Programme.

(253) The Committee welcomed the update on the IM Programme provided by France and Italy. Several Members expressed a desire for further updates relating to: the progress and content of the EIA of the activity; how the proponents would address biosecurity issues; and the impact of greenhouse gas emissions from transporting the ice cores. The Committee noted the proponents' willingness to share further information on the programme and to collaborate with Members on these issues in the intersessional period.

(254) The Secretariat introduced SP 7 *Waste Management Plans and Contingency Plans: Analysis of the information provided by the Parties in the EIES*. The document provided an analysis of the status and evolution of the data corresponding to the information exchange requirements for waste management plans and contingency plans contained in the Annual Report and Permanent Information that Parties had submitted to EIES during the period 2012-2021. It recalled that the ATCM had expressed the need for the EIES to be continuously updated and improved and highlighted its usefulness for decision-making. The document reported that, with respect to the provisions of Annex III and Annex IV to the Environmental Protocol, data submitted on waste management and contingency plans appeared to be incomplete and were not consistent among the Parties. The Secretariat stated that it stood ready to serve the needs of the Parties, should they consider it appropriate to advance on these matters.

(255) The Committee thanked the Secretariat for its work and for its efforts to gather and present this information. It highlighted the importance of having easily accessible information on waste management plans and contingency plans, and took note of the paper's findings that information exchange on these topics was incomplete and not consistent among Members. The Committee recalled that Article 9 (3) of Annex III to the Environmental Protocol clearly outlined Members' responsibilities to circulate and review waste management plans. It also noted the importance of updating waste management plans and contingency plans on vessels to minimise environmental impacts to the Antarctic environment. The Committee encouraged Members to share relevant information through the EIES tool.

(256) Noting that the Secretariat's useful analysis had highlighted issues of inconsistencies in reporting, some Members suggested that the Secretariat perform an annual review of information on the EIES. Several Members commented on the usefulness of virtual training sessions run by the Secretariat and suggested similar training sessions be run in the future. The Secretariat expressed its willingness to assist Members as required.

(257) While echoing the need for improved information exchange, it was noted that, just because a Member may not have shared information on waste management and contingency plans via the EIES, did not necessarily mean that these plans had not been prepared.

(258) In response to concerns by Members raised regarding the duplication of information exchange required by COMNAP and the Secretariat, COMNAP and the Secretariat expressed their willingness to work together to streamline the information exchange process.

(259) IAATO expressed its strong support for the exchange of information and encouraged strong relationships between tourism operators and their national competent authorities.

(260) The Committee noted that the following Information Paper had been submitted under this agenda item:

- IP 83 *On the Permit to carry out activities in the area of the Antarctic Treaty to the State Institution "Republican Center for Polar Research" during the period 2021-2026* (Belarus).

Item 14: Election of Officers

(261) The Committee elected Dr Heike Herata from Germany as the Vice-Chair for a two-year term and congratulated her on her appointment to the role.

(262) The Committee warmly thanked Dr Kevin Hughes for the effective, friendly and systematic work he completed during his four-year term. The Committee recognised the substantial time and wisdom he brought to the role and congratulated him on his contributions.

Item 15: Preparation for the Next Meeting

(263) The Committee adopted the Preliminary Agenda for CEP XXV (Appendix 5).

Item 16: Adoption of the Report

(264) The Committee adopted its Report.

Item 17: Closing of the Meeting

(265) The Chair closed the Meeting on Friday 27th May.

CEP Five-year Work Plan

Issue / Environmental Pressure: Introduction of non-native species	
Priority: 1	
Actions:	
1. Continue developing practical guidelines & resources for all Antarctic operators.	
2. Implement related actions identified in the Climate Change Response Work Programme.	
3. Consider the spatially explicit, activity-differentiated risk assessments to mitigate the risks posed by terrestrial non-native species.	
4. Develop a surveillance strategy for areas at high risk of non-native species establishment.	
5. Give additional attention to the risks posed by intra-Antarctic transfer of propagules.	
Intersessional period 2022/23	• Initiate work to develop a non-native species response strategy, including appropriate responses to diseases of wildlife • To help the Committee in assessing the effectiveness of the Manual, request a report from COMNAP on the implementation of quarantine and biosecurity measures by its members
CEP XXV 2023	• Discuss the intersessional work concerning the development of a response strategy for inclusion in the Non-native Species Manual, and the implementation of quarantine and biosecurity measures by COMNAP members. Review IMO report on biofouling guidelines • SCAR to present information on existing mechanism to assist with the identification of non-native species
Intersessional period 2023/24	• Ask SCAR to compile a list of available biodiversity information sources and databases to help Parties establish which native species are present at Antarctic sites and thereby assist with identifying the scale and scope of current and future introductions • Develop generally applicable monitoring guidelines. More detailed or site-specific monitoring may be required for particular locations • Request a report from Parties and Observers on the application of biosecurity guidelines by their members
CEP XXVI 2024	• Discuss the intersessional work concerning the development of monitoring guidelines for inclusion in the NNS Manual. • Consider the reports from Parties and Observers on the application of biosecurity guidelines by their members

Intersessional period 2024/25	• Initiate work to assess the risk of marine non-native species introductions
CEP XXVII 2025	• Discuss the intersessional work concerning the risks of marine non-native species
Intersessional period 2025/26	• Develop specific guidelines to reduce non-native species release with wastewater discharge • Review the progress and contents of the CEP Non-native Species Manual
CEP XXVIII 2026	• CEP to consider if intersessional work is required to review/update the Non-native Species Manual
Intersessional period 2026/27	• As appropriate, intersessional work to review the Non-native Species Manual
CEP XXIX 2027	• CEP to consider report of ICG, if established, and consider adoption of revised Non-native Species Manual by the ATCM through a resolution

Science knowledge and information needs:

- Identify terrestrial and marine regions and habitats at risk of introduction

- Identify native species at risk of relocation and vectors and pathways for intra-continental transfer

- Synthesise knowledge of Antarctic biodiversity, biogeography and bioregionalisation and undertake baseline studies to establish which native species are present

- Identify pathways for the introduction of marine species (including risks associated with wastewater discharge)

- Assess risks and pathways for introduction of microorganisms that might impact on existing microbial communities

- Monitor for non-native species in the terrestrial and marine environments (including microbial activity near sewage treatment plant discharges)

- Identify techniques to rapidly respond to non-native species introductions

- Identify pathways for introduction of non-native species without any direct human intervention

Issue / Environmental Pressure: Tourism and NGO activities	
Priority: 1	
Actions:	
1. Provide advice to ATCM as requested.	
2. Advance recommendations from ship-borne tourism ATME.	
Intersessional period 2022/23	• Work on framework for pre-assessment relating to new, novel or particularly concerning activities

	• Continued work on site sensitivity methodology
CEP XXV 2023	• Consideration of advice from SCAR on potential design of an environmental monitoring programme to assess the impacts of tourism • Consider outcomes of discussions relating to pre-assessment relating to new, novel or particularly concerning activities • Discuss the trial site sensitivity methodology • Consider report from SCAR and others on wilderness values and their practical application • Report from SCAR on carrying capacity
Intersessional period 2023/24	
CEP XXVI 2024	
Intersessional period 2024/25	
CEP XXVII 2025	
Intersessional period 2025/26	
CEP XXVIII 2026	
Intersessional period 2026/27	
CEP XXIX 2027	

Science knowledge and information needs:

- Consistent and dedicated monitoring of tourism impacts
- Monitor visitor sites covered by Site Guidelines

Issue / Environmental Pressure: Climate Change Implications for the Environment	
Priority: 1	
Actions:	

1. Consider implications of climate change for management of Antarctic environment.
2. Implement the Climate Change Response Work Programme.

Intersessional period 2022/23	• Subsidiary group conducts work in accordance with agreed work plan
CEP XXV 2023	• Standing agenda item

	• Consider subsidiary group report, including CCRWP updates • Plan for five-yearly joint SC-CAMLR/CEP workshop during 2022/23 intersessional period
Intersessional period 2023/24	
CEP XXVI 2024	• Finalise plans for joint SC-CAMLR/CEP workshop during 2022/23 intersessional period
Intersessional period 2024/25	• Regular five-yearly joint SC-CAMLR CEP workshop
CEP XXVII 2025	
Intersessional period 2025/26	
CEP XXVIII 2026	
Intersessional period 2026/27	
CEP XXIX 2027	

Science knowledge and information needs:

• Improve understanding of current and future change to the terrestrial (including aquatic) biotic and abiotic environment due to climate change

• Long-term monitoring of change to the terrestrial (including aquatic) biotic and abiotic environment due to climate change

• Continue to develop biogeographic tools to provide a sound basis for informing Antarctic area protection and management at regional and continental scales in light of climate change, including identifying the need to set aside reference areas for future research and identifying areas resilient to climate change

• Identify and prioritise Antarctic biogeographic regions most vulnerable to climate change

• Understand and predict near-shore marine changes and impacts of the change.

• Long-term monitoring of change to the near-shore marine biotic and abiotic environment due to climate change

• Assessment on impact of ocean acidification to marine biota and ecosystems

• Understand population status, trends, vulnerability and distribution of key Antarctic species

• Understand habitat status, trends, vulnerability and distribution

• Southern Ocean observations and modelling to understand climate change

• Identify areas that may be resilient to climate change

• Monitor emperor penguin colonies, including using remote sensing and complementary techniques, to identify trends in populations and potential climate change *refugia*

Issue / Environmental Pressure: Processing new and revised protected / managed area management plans	
Priority: 1	

Actions:

1. Refine the process for reviewing new and revised management plans.
2. Update existing guidelines.
3. Develop guidelines to ASMA preparation.

Intersessional period 2022/23	• SGMP conducts work as per agreed work plan
CEP XXV 2023	• Consider SGMP report
Intersessional period 2023/24	• SGMP conducts work as per agreed work plan
CEP XXVI 2024	• Consider SGMP report
Intersessional period 2024/25	• SGMP conducts work as per agreed work plan
CEP XXVII 2025	• Consider SGMP report
Intersessional period 2025/26	• SGMP conducts work as per agreed work plan
CEP XXVIII 2026	• Consider SGMP report
Intersessional period 2026/27	• SGMP conducts work as per agreed work plan
CEP XXIX 2027	• Consider SGMP report

Science knowledge and information needs:

- Monitoring to assess the status of values at ASPA 107 Emperor Island
- Use remote sensing techniques to monitor changes in vegetation within ASPAs
- Long-term monitoring of biological values in ASPAs

Issue / Environmental Pressure: Implementing and improving the EIA provisions of Annex I

Priority: 1

Actions:

1. **Refine the process for considering CEEs and advising the ATCM accordingly.**
2. **Develop guidelines for assessing cumulative impacts.**
3. **Review EIA guidelines and consider wider policy and other issues.**
4. **Consider application of strategic environmental assessment in Antarctica.**

Intersessional period 2022/23	• Discuss changes to the EIA database with a view to giving proposals to the Secretariat. Discuss the mechanisms to provide answers to the comments that are transmitted through the intersessional contact groups or other means on the global environmental impact assessments • Consider potential changes required to EIA database to improve its utility • Establish ICG to review draft CEEs as required • Members and Observers work to progress and coordinate information that will assist development of guidance on identifying and assessing cumulative impacts • Members to work on further guidance with regards to commenting processes related to CEEs. • Informal intersessional discussions to take forward work to improve effectiveness of the Antarctic EIA system.
CEP XXV 2023	• Consideration of ICG reports on draft CEE, as required • Consider outcomes of intersessional discussions to take forward work to improve effectiveness of the Antarctic EIA system.
Intersessional period 2023/24	• Establish ICG to review draft CEEs as required • Consider Members' work related to commenting processes related to CEEs. • Members and Observers work to progress and coordinate information that will assist development of guidance on identifying and assessing cumulative impacts
CEP XXVI 2024	• Ask SCAR to provide guidance on how to do an environmental baseline condition survey, and consider their advice in due course • Consideration of ICG reports on draft CEE, as required
Intersessional period 2024/25	• Establish ICG to review draft CEEs as required

	• Members and Observers work to progress and coordinate information that will assist development of guidance on identifying and assessing cumulative impacts
CEP XXVII 2025	• Encourage Parties to provide feedback on the utility of the revised set of *Guidelines for Environmental Impact Assessment in Antarctica* in the preparation of EIAs • Consideration of the options for preparing guidance on identifying and assessing cumulative impacts • Consideration of ICG reports on draft CEE, as required
Intersessional period 2025/26	• Establish ICG to review draft CEEs as required
CEP XXVIII 2026	• Consideration of ICG reports on draft CEE, as required
Intersessional period 2026/27	• Establish ICG to review draft CEEs as required
CEP XXIX 2027	• Consideration of ICG reports on draft CEE, as required

Issue / Environmental Pressure: Operation of the CEP and Strategic Planning	
Priority: 2	
Actions: 1. Keep the five-year work plan up to date based on changing circumstances and ATCM requirements. 2. Identify opportunities for improving the effectiveness of the CEP. 3. Consider long-term objectives for Antarctica (50-100 years' time). 4. Consider opportunities for enhancing the working relationship between the CEP and the ATCM.	
Intersessional period 2022/23	• Intersessional discussions to prepare for a workshop in Helsinki prior to CEP XXV • Discuss strategic priorities and 5YWP in an informal workshop in Helsinki prior to CEP XXV
CEP XXV 2023	• Dedicated discussions on strategic priorities and 5YWP on basis of intersessional discussions and outcomes of informal workshop held in Helsinki prior to CEP XXV
Intersessional period 2023/24	
CEP XXVI 2024	
Intersessional period 2024/25	

CEP XXVII 2025	
Intersessional period 2025/26	
CEP XXVIII 2026	
Intersessional period 2026/27	
CEP XXIX 2027	

Issue / Environmental Pressure: Repair or Remediation of Environmental Damage

Priority: 2

Actions:

1. Respond to further request from the ATCM related to repair and remediation, as appropriate.

2. Monitor progress on the establishment of Antarctic-wide inventory of sites of past activity.

3. Consider guidelines for repair and remediation.

4. Members develop practical guidelines and supporting resources for inclusion in the Clean-up Manual.

5. Continue developing bioremediation and repair practices for inclusion in the Clean-up Manual.

Intersessional period 2022/23	• Continuous review of the Manual. Parties to work on the development of new techniques or guidelines.
CEP XXV 2023	• Insertion of new tools and guidelines as they become available and agreed by the Committee.
Intersessional period 2023/24	• Continuous review of the Manual. Parties to work on the development of new techniques or guidelines.
CEP XXVI 2024	• Continuous review of the Manual and insertion of new tools and guidelines as they become available.
Intersessional period 2024/25	• Continuous review of the Manual. Parties to work on the development of new techniques or guidelines.
CEP XXVII 2025	• Continuous review of the Manual and insertion of new tools and guidelines as they become available.
Intersessional period 2025/26	• Continuous review of the Manual. Parties to work on the development of new techniques or guidelines.
CEP XXVIII 2026	• Continuous review of the Manual and insertion of new tools and guidelines as they become available.

Intersessional period 2026/27	• Continuous review of the Manual. Parties to work on the development of new techniques or guidelines.
CEP XXIX 2027	• Continuous review of the Manual and insertion of new tools and guidelines as they become available.

Science knowledge and information needs:

• Research to inform the establishment of appropriate environmental quality targets for the repair or remediation of environmental damage in Antarctica

• Techniques to prevent mobilisation of contaminants such as melt water diversion and containment barriers

• Techniques for *in situ* and *ex situ* remediation of sites contaminated by fuel spills or other hazardous substances

---

Issue / Environmental Pressure: Monitoring and state of the environment reporting

Priority: 2

Actions:

1. Identify key environmental indicators and tools.

2. Establish a process for reporting to the ATCM.

3. SCAR to support information to COMNAP and CEP.

Intersessional period 2022/23	• SCAR to consider systematic sampling and data collection of chemical contamination in the Antarctic
CEP XXV 2023	• Consider monitoring report by UK on ASPA 107 • Consider SCAR's advice on systematic sampling and data collection of chemical contamination in the Antarctic
Intersessional period 2023/24	
CEP XXVI 2024	
Intersessional period 2024/25	
CEP XXVII 2025	
Intersessional period 2025/26	
CEP XXVIII 2026	
Intersessional period 2026/27	

CEP XXIX 2027	

Science knowledge and information needs:

- Long-term monitoring of change to the terrestrial (including aquatic) biotic and abiotic environment due to climate change
- Long-term monitoring of change to the near-shore marine biotic and abiotic environment due to climate change
- Monitor bird populations to inform future management actions
- Use remote sensing techniques to monitor changes in vegetation within ASPAs and more widely
- Monitor emperor penguin colonies, using remote sensing and complementary techniques, to identify potential climate change *refugia*
- Long-term monitoring of biological values in ASPAs
- Long-term monitoring to verify or detect environmental impacts associated with human activities
- Long-term monitoring and sustained observations of environmental change
- Consistent and dedicated monitoring of tourism impacts
- Systematic and regular monitoring of visitor sites covered by Site Guidelines
- Long-term monitoring of biological indicators at sites visited by tourists

---

Issue / Environmental Pressure: Marine spatial protection and management

Priority: 2

Actions:

1. Cooperation between the CEP and SC-CAMLR on common interest issues.
2. Cooperate with CCAMLR on Southern Ocean bioregionalisation and other common interests and agreed principles.
3. Identify and apply processes for spatial marine protection.
4. Consider connectivity between land and ocean, and complementary actions that could be taken by Parties with respect to MPAs.

Intersessional period 2022/23	
CEP XXV 2023	• Continue to consider advice relating to Resolution 5 (2017)
Intersessional period 2023/24	
CEP XXVI 2024	
Intersessional period 2024/25	

CEP XXVII 2025	
Intersessional period 2025/26	
CEP XXVIII 2026	
Intersessional period 2026/27	
CEP XXIX 2027	

Issue / Environmental Pressure: Site specific guidelines for tourist-visited sites

Priority: 2

Actions:

1. Periodically review the list of sites subject to Site Guidelines and consider whether development of guidelines is needed for additional sites.
2. Regular review of all existing Site Guidelines to ensure that they are accurate and up to date, including precautionary updates where appropriate.
3. Provide advice to ATCM as required.
4. Review the format of the Site Guidelines.

Intersessional period 2022/23	• Consider developing guidelines for short overnight stays to ensure consistent application of best practices and minimise impacts to the Antarctic environment. • Germany to lead informal discussions concerning a new layout template for Visitor Site Guidelines
CEP XXV 2023	• Committee to consider outcome of discussions on a new layout template for Visitor Site Guidelines • Standing agenda item; Parties to report on their reviews of Site Guidelines
Intersessional period 2023/24	• Development of a repository of pictures to aid in the regular review of Site Guidelines
CEP XXVI 2024	• Standing agenda item; Parties to report on their reviews of Site Guidelines
Intersessional period 2024/25	
CEP XXVII 2025	
Intersessional period 2025/26	

CEP XXVIII 2026	
Intersessional period 2026/27	
CEP XXIX 2027	

Science knowledge and information needs:

- Long-term monitoring to assess the status and recovery of vegetation at Barrientos Island
- Systematic and regular monitoring of visitor sites covered by Site Guidelines

Issue / Environmental Pressure: Overview of the protected areas system	
Priority: 2	
Actions:	
1. Apply the Environmental Domains Analysis (EDA) and Antarctic Conservation Biogeographic Regions (ACBR) to enhance the protected areas system. 2. Maintain and develop Protected Area database. 3. Assess the extent to which Antarctic IBAs are or should be represented within the series of ASPAs.	
Intersessional period 2022/23	• Undertake work to advance actions agreed by the Committee from discussions on the protected areas workshop • SCAR to provide advice on selection criteria that might be applied to identified IBAs or other bird areas when considering ASPA designation
CEP XXV 2023	• Committee to consider advice from SCAR on selection criteria that might be applied to identified IBAs or other bird areas when considering ASPA designation • Review progress on the work to advance actions agreed by the Committee from discussions on the protected areas workshop
Intersessional period 2023/24	• Undertake work to advance actions agreed by the Committee from discussions on the protected areas workshop
CEP XXVI 2024	• Review progress on the work to advance actions agreed by the Committee from discussions on the protected areas workshop
Intersessional period 2024/25	
CEP XXVII 2025	
Intersessional period 2025/26	
CEP XXVIII 2026	

Intersessional period 2026/27	
CEP XXIX 2027	

Science knowledge and information needs:

- Continue to develop biogeographic tools to provide a sound basis for informing Antarctic area protection and management at regional and continental scales in light of climate change, including identifying the need to set aside reference areas for future research and identifying areas resilient to climate change
- Use remote sensing techniques to monitor changes in vegetation within ASPAs and more widely, to inform the further development of the Antarctic protected areas system

---

Issue / Environmental Pressure: Designation and management of Historic Sites and Monuments

Priority: 2

Actions:

1. Maintain the list and consider new proposals as they arise.
2. Consider strategic issues as necessary, including issues relating to designation of HSM versus clean-up provisions of the Protocol.
3. Review the presentation of the HSM list with the aim to improve information availability.

Intersessional period 2022/23	• Develop further guidance with regard to the listing of HSMs with no known location • Consider how environmental impact assessments can form a part of Historic Site and Monument assessment
CEP XXV 2023	• Consider guidance concerning the listing of HSMs with no known location • Review proposals relating to EIAs and the HSM listing process
Intersessional period 2023/24	
CEP XXVI 2024	
Intersessional period 2024/25	
CEP XXVII 2025	
Intersessional period 2025/26	
CEP XXVIII 2026	
Intersessional period	

2026/27	
CEP XXIX 2027	

Issue / Environmental Pressure: Biodiversity knowledge
Priority: 2
Actions:

1. Maintain awareness of threats to existing biodiversity.
2. CEP to consider further scientific advice on wildlife disturbance.

Intersessional period 2022/23	• Informal intersessional discussions relating to assessing the protection of Antarctic seals. • Continue informal discussions on the recommendations in CEP XXIV - WP 34
CEP XXV 2023	• Report on informal intersessional discussions relating to assessing the protection of Antarctic seals
Intersessional period 2023/24	
CEP XXVI 2024	
Intersessional period 2024/25	
CEP XXVII 2025	
Intersessional period 2025/26	
CEP XXVIII 2026	
Intersessional period 2026/27	
CEP XXIX 2027	

Science knowledge and information needs:

- Research on the environmental impacts of remotely piloted aircraft systems (RPAS), particularly on wildlife responses including:
    - a range of species including flying seabirds and seals;
    - both behavioural and physiological responses;
    - demographic effects, including breeding numbers and breeding success;
    - ambient environmental conditions, for example, wind and noise;
    - the effects of RPAS of different sizes and specifications;

- o   the contribution of RPAS noise to wildlife disturbance;
- o   comparisons with control sites and human disturbance; and
- o   habituation effects.
- Collection and submission of further spatially explicit biodiversity data
- Research on the impacts of underwater noise on Antarctic marine mammals
- Synthesis of available knowledge on the biogeography, bioregionalisation and endemism within Antarctica
- Site-specific, timing-specific and species-specific studies to understand the impacts arising from interactions between human activities and wildlife and support evidence-based guidelines to avoid disturbance
- Inventory of Mt Erebus ice caves and microbial communities
- Regular population counts and research to understand the status and trends in the southern giant petrel population

Issue / Environmental Pressure: Outreach and education	
Priority: 3	
Actions:	
1. Review current examples and identify opportunities for greater education and outreach.	
2. Encourage Members to exchange information regarding their experiences in this area.	
3. Establish a strategy and guidelines for exchanging information between Members on Education and Outreach for long-term perspective.	
Intersessional period 2022/23	
CEP XXV 2023	
Intersessional period 2023/24	
CEP XXVI 2024	
Intersessional period 2024/25	
CEP XXVII 2025	
Intersessional period 2025/26	
CEP XXVIII 2026	
Intersessional period 2026/27	

CEP XXIX 2027	

Issue / Environmental Pressure: Protection of outstanding geological values	
Priority: 3	
Actions: 1. Consider further mechanisms for protection of outstanding geological values.	
Intersessional period 2022/23	
CEP XXV 2023	
Intersessional period 2023/24	
CEP XXVI 2024	
Intersessional period 2024/25	
CEP XXVII 2025	
Intersessional period 2025/26	
CEP XXVIII 2026	
Intersessional period 2026/27	
CEP XXIX 2027	

Text for an SGMP webpage on the Antarctic Treaty Secretariat website

Subsidiary Group on Management Plans (SGMP)

Background

Since its first meeting in 1998, the CEP has discussed the need for effective and efficient procedures for reviewing new and revised Management Plans for Antarctic Specially Protected Areas (ASPAs) and Antarctic Specially Managed Areas (ASMAs). In 2008, ATCM XXXI agreed to establish the Subsidiary Group on Management Plans (SGMP) in accordance with Rule 10 of the CEP Rules of Procedure. The SGMP provides practical advice on draft management plans referred by the CEP for intersessional review, in clarity, consistency and effectiveness etc., and on improving management plans and the process for their intersessional review.

SGMP Terms of Reference

The original four Terms of Reference for the SGMP were defined in Appendix 3 of the CEP XI (2008) report. Following a review of the effectiveness of the SGMP at CEP XIII (2010), a fifth Term of Reference was added. In 2022, an additional Term of Reference was introduced to reflect the new regular task of pre-meeting review of Management Plans. The current Terms of Reference are presented in Appendix 4 to the CEP XXIV report:

1) Examine any draft new or revised Management Plan recommended by the Committee for intersessional review to consider, in consultation with relevant experts if appropriate:

  • whether it is consistent with the provisions of Annex V to the Protocol, particularly Articles 3, 4 and 5, and with relevant CEP guidelines;

  • its content, clarity, consistency and likely effectiveness;

  • whether it clearly states the primary reason for designation; and

  • whether it clearly states how the proposed Area complements the Antarctic protected areas system as a whole.

2) Advise proponents of suggested amendments to the draft Management Plan to address issues in relation to 1) above.

3) Submit a Working Paper to the CEP with recommendations for the adoption or otherwise of each new or revised draft Management Plan, identifying where the Plan reflects comments received by Members, and where they have not been, the reasons for not doing so. The Working Paper is to include all revised Management Plans and the information required by the ATCM's Legal and Institutional Working Group.

4) Operate a pre-meeting subforum on the review of all revised Management Plans with minor changes, irrespective of whether or not they have been submitted to the SGMP, and provide a summary of the recommendations arising from the pre-meeting review for consideration by the CEP during the discussion of revised management plans.

5) Provide advice to the CEP as necessary for the purpose of improving Management Plans and the process for their intersessional review.

6) Develop and suggest procedures that would assist in achieving a long-term goal aiming at ensuring that all ASPA and ASMA management plans contain adequate content, and are clear, consistent and likely to be effective.

SGMP Operating Mechanisms

Under Rule 22 of the CEP Rules of Procedure, English, French, Russian and Spanish shall be the official languages of subsidiary bodies. There is an agreement to conduct the work of the SGMP in English and to translate key documents into the official languages. The Subsidiary Group undertakes its intersessional work via the CEP Forum and produces an annual report to the CEP.

Relevant links

- CEP Handbook: Subsidiary Group on Management Plans
- CEP Forum (password required)
- CEP Workspace (password required)
- Area Protection and Management / Monuments
- Tools for Delegates

Text for an SGCCR webpage on the Antarctic Treaty Secretariat website

Subsidiary Group on Climate Change Response (SGCCR)

Background

The Climate Change Response Work Programme (CCRWP) was adopted through ATCM Resolution 4 (2015), which recommended that Governments:

1. encourage the CEP to begin implementing the CCRWP as a matter of priority, and provide annual progress reports to the Antarctic Treaty Consultative Meeting on its implementation;

2. request the CEP to keep the CCRWP under regular review, with the input of the Scientific Committee on Antarctic Research (SCAR) and the Council of Managers of National Antarctic Programs (COMNAP) on scientific and practical matters respectively; and

3. give consideration, within their own national scientific funding systems and national Antarctic research programmes, as to how they can address the science needs and actions identified in the CEP's CCRWP.

'Climate Change Implications for the Environment' is a Priority 1 issue on the CEP Five-Year Work Plan, with 'Implementing the CCRWP' a key action.

SGCCR Terms of Reference

Following discussions within CEP regarding updating, implementation and follow-up of the CCRWP, a decision was made at ATCM XL (Decision 1 (2017)) to establish a new Subsidiary Group on Climate Changes Response (SGCCR).

The Terms of Reference for the SGCCR are to facilitate the efficient and timely implementation of the CCRWP by:

1. Facilitating the coordination and communication of the CCRWP between Members, Observers and Experts, highlighting actions identified for the coming year(s) and requesting relevant updates on planned activities;

2. Drafting proposed annual updates of the CCRWP, including management, research or monitoring actions;

3. Drafting annual progress reports on the implementation of the CCRWP for the CEP to draw on in their updates to the ATCM.

SGCCR operating mechanisms

In addition to the Terms of Reference, the Committee tasked the SGCCR to develop operating mechanisms to support good participation and efficient handling of work (CEP XX Final Report, para 74). The SGCCR maintains flexibility regarding membership and welcomes new members. The Subsidiary Group undertakes its intersessional work via the CEP Forum and produces an annual report to the CEP.

Relevant links
- Climate Change Response Work Programme

- CEP Handbook: Subsidiary Group on Climate Change Response
- CEP Science Needs
- CEP Forum (password required)
- Antarctic Treaty Meeting of Experts on implications of climate change for Antarctic management and governance: Co-chairs' report

Revised SGMP Terms of Reference

The original four Terms of Reference for the SGMP were defined in Appendix 3 of the CEP XI (2008) report. Following a review of the effectiveness of the SGMP at CEP XIII (2010), a fifth Term of Reference was added. In 2022, an additional Term of Reference was introduced to reflect the new regular task of pre-meeting review of Management Plans. The current Terms of Reference are presented in Appendix 4 to the CEP XXIV report:

1. Examine any draft new or revised Management Plan recommended by the Committee for intersessional review to consider, in consultation with relevant experts if appropriate:

    -   whether it is consistent with the provisions of Annex V to the Protocol, particularly, Articles 3, 4 and 5[1], and with relevant CEP guidelines[2];
    -   its content, clarity, consistency and likely effectiveness[3];
    -   whether it clearly states the primary reason for designation[4]; and
    -   whether it clearly states how the proposed Area complements the Antarctic protected areas system as a whole[5].

2. Advise proponents of suggested amendments to the draft Management Plan to address issues in relation to 1) above.

3. Submit a Working Paper to the CEP with recommendations for the adoption or otherwise of each new or revised draft Management Plan, identifying where the Plan reflects comments received by Members, and where they have not been, the reasons for not doing so. The Working Paper is to include all revised Management Plans and the information required by the ATCM's Legal and Institutional Working Group.

4. Operate a pre-meeting subforum on the review of all revised Management Plans with minor changes, irrespective of whether or not they have been submitted to the SGMP, and provide a summary of the recommendations arising from the pre-meeting review for consideration by the CEP during the discussion of revised management plans.

5. Provide advice to the CEP as necessary for the purpose of improving Management Plans and the process for their intersessional review.

6. Develop and suggest procedures that would assist in achieving a long-term goal aiming at ensuring that all ASPA and ASMA management plans contain adequate content, and are clear, consistent and likely to be effective[6].

---

[1] Modified from "Terms of Reference for an Intersessional Contact Group to Consider draft Management Plans" ToR #2 (CEP VII Report, Annex 4).

[2] Currently including – for ASPAs – Resolution 2 (1998) Guide for the Preparation of Management Plans for Antarctic Specially Protected Areas, Resolution 1 (2000) Guidelines for Implementation of the Framework for Protected Areas set forth in Article 3, Annex V of the Environmental Protocol and Resolution 2 (2021) Revised Guide to the presentation of Working Papers containing proposals for Antarctic Specially Protected Areas, Antarctic Specially Managed Areas or Historic Sites and Monuments

[3] From "Guidelines for CEP Consideration of New and Revised Draft ASPA and ASMA Management Plans" paragraph 8 (CEP VI Report, Annex 4), and "Terms of Reference for an Intersessional Contact Group to Consider draft Management Plans" ToR #2 (CEP VII Report, Annex 4).

[4] Agreement at CEP VIII (Report paragraph 187).

[5] Agreement at CEP VIII (Report paragraph 187).

[6] Term of Reference added at CEP XIII (Report paragraph 162)

Preliminary Agenda for CEP XXV (2023)

1. Opening of the Meeting

2. Adoption of the Agenda

3. Strategic Discussions on the Future Work of the CEP

4. Operation of the CEP

5. Cooperation with other Organisations

6. Repair and Remediation of Environment Damage

7. Climate Change Implications for the Environment:

     a. Strategic Approach

     b. Implementation and Review of the Climate Change Response Work Programme

8. Environmental Impact Assessment (EIA):

     a. Draft Comprehensive Environmental Evaluations

     b. Other EIA Matters

9. Area Protection and Management Plans:

     a. Management Plans

     b. Historic Sites and Monuments

     c. Site Guidelines

     d. Marine Spatial Protection and Management

     e. Other Annex V Matters

10. Conservation of Antarctic Flora and Fauna:

     a. Quarantine and Non-native Species

     b. Specially Protected Species

     c. Other Annex II Matters

11. Environmental Monitoring and Reporting

12. Inspection Reports

13. General Matters

14. Election of Officers

15. Preparation for the Next Meeting

16. Adoption of the Report

17. Closing of the Meeting

3. Appendices

Ad Hoc Guidelines for ATCM XLIV – CEP XXIV Hybrid Meeting

The Antarctic Treaty Consultative Parties (ATCPs) agree that ATCM XLIV - CEP XXIV take the form of hybrid meetings. These meetings will be conducted in accordance with the ATCM Rules of Procedure (RoPs), the CEP RoPs, and the *ad hoc* guidelines listed below.

Context:

1. These *ad hoc* guidelines shall apply for the hybrid meetings of ATCM XLIV - CEP XXIV (2022). The hybrid format will allow in-person participation, virtual participation (with voice and asking for the floor) and virtual audience (without voice nor asking for the floor). The following guidelines only apply to delegates participating virtually with the understanding that the delegation, in particular in Guideline 11, comprises delegates participating both virtually and in-person.

2. Hybrid meetings of ATCM XLIV - CEP XXIV (2022) shall take place following the ATCM/CEP RoPs and these *ad hoc* guidelines. Guidelines are complementary to the RoPs and do not replace or have precedence over them.

3. If unforeseen circumstances arise during the course of the hybrid meetings, in which the ATCM or CEP RoPs cannot be applied directly and for which none of the following guidelines apply, the ATCPs or CEP Members respectively shall decide how to apply the RoPs in the circumstances and/or modify these guidelines at the request of the Chair or an ATCP/CEP Member pursuant to a point of order.

Engagement:

4. Only registered delegates shall be admitted to meetings. Separate registration for CEP, Working Groups and Plenary will be requested for secure meeting management.

5. Delegates attending virtually shall provide official and alternative electronic contact information on registration, including telephone numbers which may be used by the Secretariat to contact them in case of connectivity difficulties. The Host Country Secretariat will provide delegates with emergency contact information, including telephone, to allow them to contact relevant Host Country Secretariat staff in case of losing connectivity or interpretation.

6. For each meeting for which a Party has virtually registered, the Head of Delegation (HoD) or CEP Representative, as appropriate, shall identify one or more Alternate Representative (AR) and authorise them to make relevant decisions should the HoD or CEP Representative lose connectivity or interpretation services.

7. A preliminary test of the selected platform functionality and connectivity will be conducted well before the start of the virtual meeting with all delegates willing to participate.

8. All delegates attending virtually should join the meeting at least 10 minutes before the scheduled start. The meeting will be open for access 30 minutes before the scheduled start.

9. The Chair shall conduct a roll call at the start of each session of the meeting to establish that the HoD, CEP Representative, or AR of each delegation attending virtually is connected and receiving interpretation. If both HoD/CEP Representative and AR of a Consultative Party/CEP Member are absent, the Chair shall confirm, via alternative communication channels, whether they wish to be present at the session. In case they confirm that they wish to be present and are trying to connect, the Chair shall suspend the meeting for a time that is reasonable to solve the connectivity difficulty. In case they are also not reachable via the alternative communication channels provided beforehand, the Chair will proceed with the meeting.

10. The Chair will periodically check with HoDs, CEP Representative or AR attending virtually, as appropriate, that they are able to engage with proceedings.

11. Should both HoD/CEP Representative and AR of a Consultative Party/CEP Member attending virtually lose connectivity or interpretation, it is the responsibility of the delegation to notify the Host Country Secretariat. Any Consultative Party/CEP Member may request the Chair to suspend the meeting until connectivity/interpretation to the HoD/CEP Representative-or AR is restored. This request may be made by alternative communication methods.-

12. Should both HoD/CEP Representative and AR from a delegation attending virtually lose connectivity or interpretation, the Chair shall–suspend the meeting until one of them reconnects or interpretation is resumed, unless the delegation that had lost connectivity or interpretation advises otherwise.

13. If members of the delegation that are not a HoD/CEP Representative/AR lose connectivity, it is the responsibility of the delegation to contact the Secretariat and restore connectivity. The meeting will not be suspended in the case of loss of connectivity/interpretation of a delegate who is not a HoD/CEP Representative/AR.

Decision-making:

14. When decisions are about to be made in Plenary, the Chair will confirm with all HoDs attending virtually that they understand and approve the decision.

15. At the end of each Plenary session, the Chair will report the decisions that in his record have been made by the ATCPs and note the issues that have been discussed but where no decision and/or consensus was reached.

16. All decisions will be confirmed at report adoption.

Reporting:

17. The draft report of the session will be placed on the Meeting documents platform within 12 hours of the close of the session and be made available for comments for twelve hours

from that time. Subsequently, the Secretariat and the responsible Chair will review all comments on the draft report.

18. A consolidated draft report will be available prior to consideration and adoption under the agenda item "Adoption of the Report" for both the ATCM and CEP respectively. Consideration and amendments shall be conducted in a way that each proposed amendment to report text can be viewed by all delegations. The ATCM report shall be adopted at the end of the meeting in accordance with Rule 25 of the Rules of Procedure of the ATCM. The CEP report shall be adopted at the end of the CEP meeting and thereafter translated and presented to the ATCM in accordance with Rule 22 of the CEP RoPs. Technical and factual corrections will be accepted 24 hours after the close of the meeting.

Preliminary Agenda for ATCM XLV, Working Groups and Allocation of Items

Plenary

1) Opening of the Meeting
2) Election of Officers and Creation of Working Groups
3) Adoption of the Agenda, Allocation of Items to Working Groups and Consideration of the Multi-year Strategic Work Plan
4) Operation of the Antarctic Treaty System: Reports by Parties, Observers and Experts
5) Report of the Committee for Environmental Protection
6) Operation of the Antarctic Treaty System:
   a. Request from Belarus to become a Consultative Party
   b. Request from Canada to become a Consultative Party
   c. Implementation of IMO Polar Code
   d. Climate Change

Working Group 1: *(Policy, Legal, Institutional)*

6) Operation of the Antarctic Treaty System:
   e. General matters
7) Operation of the Antarctic Treaty System: Matters related to the Secretariat
8) Liability
9) Biological Prospecting in Antarctica
10) Exchange of Information
11) Education Issues
12) Multi-year Strategic Work Plan
   a. Policy, Legal and Institutional priorities

Working Group 2: *(Science, Operations, Tourism)*

12) Multi-year Strategic work Plan
   b. Science, Operations and Tourism priorities
13) Safety and Operations in Antarctica
14) Inspections under the Antarctic Treaty and Environment Protocol
15) Science issues, future science challenges, scientific cooperation and facilitation
16) Implications of Climate Change for Management of the Antarctic Treaty Area
17) Tourism and Non-governmental Activities in the Antarctic Treaty Area, including Competent Authorities Issues

Plenary

18) Preparation of the 46th Meeting
19) Any other Business
20) Adoption of the Final Report
21) Close of the Meeting

XLIV ANTARCTIC TREATY CONSULTATIVE MEETING

BERLIN, 23 May – 2 June 2022

HOST COUNTRY COMMUNIQUÉ

From 22 May to 2 June, 2022, Germany was the host state to the XLIV Antarctic Treaty Consultative Meeting (ATCM) as well as the XXIV meeting of the Committee for Environmental Protection (CEP), bringing together the 54 States Party to the Antarctic Treaty, as well as Observers and Experts. The meetings took place in Berlin and were held, for the first time, in hybrid format. Ms. Tania von Uslar-Gleichen, Director of International Law at the Federal Foreign Office, served as Chair of ATCM XLIV. The CEP was chaired by Ms. Birgit Njåstad (Norway).

A total of 448 delegates were registered for the ATCM XLIV, 104 participated virtually.

Ms Jennifer Lee Morgan, State Secretary and Special Envoy for International Climate Action at the Federal Foreign Office, and Dr Bettina Hoffmann, Parliamentary State Secretary at the Federal Ministry for the Environment, Nature Conservation, Nuclear Safety and Consumer Protection, officially opened the conference, both condemning in the strongest possible terms Russia's unjustifiable, unprovoked and illegal war of one consultative state against another. They called on Russia to put an end to the war against Ukraine, noting that this breach of international law was also contrary to the spirit of the Antarctic Treaty. Ukraine presented an Information Paper on the consequences of the military aggression against its country for its Antarctic Program. The overwhelming majority of the Parties expressed their solidarity with Ukraine and aligned themselves with the condemnation of the Russian aggression.

Many Parties stressed that the ATCM's work for peace, research and environmental protection should not be compromised by the military aggression of one Party against another. The Antarctic Treaty has long been seen as an example of successful international cooperation for the benefit of humanity, and to fight against the global crises of climate change, biodiversity loss and pollution. The fact that the Meeting was able to adopt Measures, Resolutions and Decisions in consensus shows the strength and resilience of the Antarctic Treaty System.

In accordance with its theme "From Science via Policy to Protection", the ATCM stressed the importance of research in Antarctica in order to take the right political decisions on how to protect it. In this vein, the meeting considered the decadal synopsis report "Antarctic Climate Change and the Environment" by the Scientific Committee on Antarctic Research as the best available science and acknowledged the advice that urgent action is required to prevent irreversible loss of Antarctic values and consequences for the planet. All parties agreed that the ATCM has an important role in addressing the threat of global climate change, and decided to focus even more on the subject at the next ATCM.

Over the years, 75 areas across the white continent have been designated as Antarctic Specially Protected Areas at the Consultative Meetings. At ATCM XLIV, the management of seventeen of these areas has undergone a review and revision. Four new protected areas will be added in the future, as the ATCM endorsed the next steps for their special protection.

In addition the Meeting focused on a specific species: the emperor penguin. The world's largest penguin is increasingly at risk, in particular because of global warming. An overwhelming majority of Parties held the opinion that there is sufficient scientific evidence for the species to be put under the special protection of the Protocol on Environmental Protection. While a formal decision on Special Protection Status was blocked by one party, most Parties indicated that they would nonetheless implement the draft action plan that had been developed intersessionally on a national basis.

The Meeting also discussed the issue of the growing tourism to Antarctica, with the forecast that the total number of visitors to Antarctica would exceed 100.000 in the 2022-2023 season. The sharp rise in interest around the world, especially in Antarctic cruises, is increasing the pressure on those Antarctic regions in particular that are already hit hard by climate change. The Parties agreed that a precautionary approach should aim at the development of a strategic and coordinated approach towards the sustainable management of tourism to Antarctica.

The CEP emphasized the importance of its Climate Change Response Work Programme (CCRWP) and showed its results. Outstanding among these is the collaboration of organizations working in Antarctica to address global issues to protect the Antarctic environment and the associated and dependent ecosystems. Engaged discussions were held on improving the system of environmental impact assessments for all activities in Antarctica. The Committee agreed on several aspects that will be addressed intersessionally to enhance the effectiveness of the environmental assessment system even more. The CEP also gave special attention to the dangers of chemical contamination and the introduction of plastics into the Antarctic ecosystem.

The ATCM highlighted the importance of ensuring that everyone working in Antarctica is safe, welcome, respected and free from discrimination. Participants affirmed their commitment to enhancing diversity and promoting an inclusive culture for everyone contributing to the work of the Antarctic Treaty system.

In accordance with Parties' commitment to protect the Antarctic environment, ATCM XLIV was organized in accordance with the Federal Government's "Guidelines for the Sustainable Organization of Events" to minimize the impact on the environment, such as paper consumption, minimization of waste and carbon offset.

Parties discussed a request from Canada for Consultative Status. Though widespread support was declared, two parties were not ready to decide on Canada's application at this meeting. The request will therefore be discussed again at ATCM 45, which will take place in Helsinki from 29 May to 8 June 2023.

PART II

Measures, Decisions and Resolutions

1. Measures

Measure 1 (2022)

Antarctic Specially Managed Area No 7 (Southwest Anvers Island and Palmer Basin): Revised Management Plan

The Representatives,

Recalling Articles 4, 5 and 6 of Annex V to the Protocol on Environmental Protection to the Antarctic Treaty, providing for the designation of Antarctic Specially Managed Areas ("ASMA") and the approval of Management Plans for those Areas;

Recalling
- Measure 1 (2008), which designated Southwest Anvers Island and Palmer Basin as Antarctic Specially Managed Area No 7 and annexed a Management Plan for the Area;
- Measures 2 (2009), 14 (2010) and 11 (2019) which adopted a revised Management Plan for ASMA 7;

Noting that the Committee for Environmental Protection ("CEP") has endorsed a revised Management Plan for ASMA 7;

Noting Measure 14 (2022) concerning Antarctic Specially Protected Area ("ASPA") No 139 (Biscoe Point, Anvers Island), Measure 5 (2022) concerning ASPA 113 (Litchfield Island, Arthur Harbor, Anvers Island, Palmer Archipelago) and Measure 19 (2021) concerning ASPA 176 (Rosenthal Islands, Anvers Island, Palmer Archipelago), which are all located within ASMA 7;

Desiring to replace the existing Management Plan for ASMA 7 with the revised Management Plan;

Recommend to their Governments the following Measure for approval in accordance with paragraph 1 of Article 6 of Annex V to the Protocol on Environmental Protection to the Antarctic Treaty:

That:

1.   the revised Management Plan for Antarctic Specially Managed Area No 7 (Southwest Anvers Island and Palmer Basin), which is annexed to this Measure, be approved; and

2.   the Management Plan for Antarctic Specially Managed Area No 7 annexed to Measure 11 (2019) be revoked.

Measure 2 (2022)

Antarctic Specially Protected Area No 109 (Moe Island, South Orkney Islands): Revised Management Plan

The Representatives,

Recalling Articles 3, 5 and 6 of Annex V to the Protocol on Environmental Protection to the Antarctic Treaty providing for the designation of Antarctic Specially Protected Areas ("ASPA") and approval of Management Plans for those Areas;

Recalling
- Recommendation IV-13 (1966), which designated Moe Island, South Orkney Islands as Specially Protected Area ("SPA") No 13 and annexed a map of the Area;
- Recommendation XVI-6 (1991), which annexed a revised description of SPA 13 and a Management Plan for the Area;
- Measure 1 (1995), which annexed a revised description and a revised Management Plan for SPA 13;
- Decision 1 (2002), which renamed and renumbered SPA 13 as ASPA 109;
- Measures 1 (2007), 1 (2012) and 1 (2017), which adopted a revised Management Plan for ASPA 109;

Recalling
- Recommendation IV-13 (1966) was designated as no longer current by Decision 1 (2011);
- Resolution 9 (1995) was designated as no longer current by Resolution 1 (2008);
- Recommendation XVI-6 (1991) did not become effective and was withdrawn by Decision 3 (2017); and
- Measure 1 (1995) did not become effective and was withdrawn by Measure 3 (2012);

Noting that the Committee for Environmental Protection has endorsed a revised Management Plan for ASPA 109;

Desiring to replace the existing Management Plan for ASPA 109 with the revised Management Plan;

Recommend to their Governments the following Measure for approval in accordance with paragraph 1 of Article 6 of Annex V to the Protocol on Environmental Protection to the Antarctic Treaty:

That:

1.   the revised Management Plan for Antarctic Specially Protected Area No 109 (Moe Island, South Orkney Islands), which is annexed to this Measure, be approved; and

2.   the Management Plan for Antarctic Specially Protected Area No 109 annexed to Measure 1 (2017) be revoked.

Measure 3 (2022)

Antarctic Specially Protected Area No 110 (Lynch Island, South Orkney Islands): Revised Management Plan

The Representatives,

Recalling Articles 3, 5 and 6 of Annex V to the Protocol on Environmental Protection to the Antarctic Treaty providing for the designation of Antarctic Specially Protected Areas ("ASPA") and approval of Management Plans for those Areas;

Recalling
- Recommendation IV-14 (1966), which designated Lynch Island, South Orkney Islands as Specially Protected Area ("SPA") No 14 and annexed a map of the Area;
- Recommendation XVI-6 (1991), which annexed a Management Plan for the Area;
- Measure 1 (2000), which annexed a revised Management Plan for SPA 14;
- Decision 1 (2002), which renamed and renumbered SPA 14 as ASPA 110;
- Measures 2 (2012) and 2 (2017), which adopted a revised Management Plan for ASPA 110;

Recalling that Recommendation XVI-6 (1991) and Measure 1 (2000) did not become effective and were withdrawn by Decision 3 (2017);

Noting that the Committee for Environmental Protection has endorsed a revised Management Plan for ASPA 110;

Desiring to replace the existing Management Plan for ASPA 110 with the revised Management Plan;

Recommend to their Governments the following Measure for approval in accordance with paragraph 1 of Article 6 of Annex V to the Protocol on Environmental Protection to the Antarctic Treaty:

That:

1.   the revised Management Plan for Antarctic Specially Protected Area No 110 (Lynch Island, South Orkney Islands), which is annexed to this Measure, be approved; and

2.   the Management Plan for Antarctic Specially Protected Area No 110 annexed to Measure 2 (2017) be revoked.

Measure 4 (2022)

Antarctic Specially Protected Area No 111 (Southern Powell Island and adjacent islands, South Orkney Islands): Revised Management Plan

The Representatives,

Recalling Articles 3, 5 and 6 of Annex V to the Protocol on Environmental Protection to the Antarctic Treaty providing for the designation of Antarctic Specially Protected Areas ("ASPA") and approval of Management Plans for those Areas;

Recalling
- Recommendation IV-15 (1966), which designated Southern Powell Island and adjacent islands, South Orkney Islands as Specially Protected Area ("SPA") No 15 and annexed a map of the Area;
- Recommendation XVI-6 (1991), which annexed a Management Plan for SPA 15;
- Measure 1 (1995), which annexed a modified description and a revised Management Plan for SPA 15;
- Decision 1 (2002), which renamed and renumbered SPA 15 as ASPA 111;
- Measures 3 (2012) and 3 (2017), which adopted a revised Management Plan for ASPA 111;

Recalling that Recommendation XVI-6 (1991) did not become effective and was withdrawn by Decision 3 (2017) and Measure 1 (1995) did not become effective and was withdrawn by Measure 3 (2012);

Noting that the Committee for Environmental Protection has endorsed a revised Management Plan for ASPA 111;

Desiring to replace the existing Management Plan for ASPA 111 with the revised Management Plan;

Recommend to their Governments the following Measure for approval in accordance with paragraph 1 of Article 6 of Annex V to the Protocol on Environmental Protection to the Antarctic Treaty:

That:

1.   the revised Management Plan for Antarctic Specially Protected Area No 111 (Southern Powell Island and adjacent islands, South Orkney Islands), which is annexed to this Measure, be approved; and

2.   the Management Plan for Antarctic Specially Protected Area No 111 annexed to Measure 3 (2017) be revoked.

Measure 5 (2022)

Antarctic Specially Protected Area No 113 (Litchfield Island, Arthur Harbor, Anvers Island, Palmer Archipelago): Revised Management Plan

The Representatives,

Recalling Articles 3, 5 and 6 of Annex V to the Protocol on Environmental Protection to the Antarctic Treaty providing for the designation of Antarctic Specially Protected Areas ("ASPA") and approval of Management Plans for those Areas;

Recalling
- Recommendation VIII-1 (1975), which designated Litchfield Island, Arthur Harbor, Palmer Archipelago as Specially Protected Area ("SPA") No 17 and annexed a map for the Area;
- Decision 1 (2002), which renamed and renumbered SPA 17 as ASPA 113;
- Measure 2 (2004), which adopted a Management Plan for ASPA 113;
- Measure 1 (2008), which designated Southwest Anvers Island and Palmer Basin as Antarctic Specially Managed Area No 7, within which ASPA 113 is located;
- Measures 4 (2009) and 1 (2014), which adopted a revised Management Plan for ASPA 113;

Recalling that Recommendation VIII-1 (1975) was designated as no longer effective by Measure 4 (2009);

Noting that the Committee for Environmental Protection has endorsed a revised Management Plan for ASPA 113;

Desiring to replace the existing Management Plan for ASPA 113 with the revised Management Plan;

Recommend to their Governments the following Measure for approval in accordance with paragraph 1 of Article 6 of Annex V to the Protocol on Environmental Protection to the Antarctic Treaty:

That:

1. the revised Management Plan for Antarctic Specially Protected Area No 113 (Litchfield Island, Arthur Harbor, Anvers Island, Palmer Archipelago), which is annexed to this Measure, be approved; and

2. the Management Plan for Antarctic Specially Protected Area No 113 annexed to Measure 1 (2014) be revoked.

Measure 6 (2022)

Antarctic Specially Protected Area No 115 (Lagotellerie Island, Marguerite Bay, Graham Land): Revised Management Plan

The Representatives,

Recalling Articles 3, 5 and 6 of Annex V to the Protocol on Environmental Protection to the Antarctic Treaty providing for the designation of Antarctic Specially Protected Areas ("ASPA") and approval of Management Plans for those Areas;

Recalling
- Recommendation XIII-11 (1985), which designated Lagotellerie Island, Marguerite Bay, Graham Land as Specially Protected Area ("SPA") No 19 and annexed a map of the Area;
- Recommendation XVI-6 (1991), which annexed a Management Plan for the Area;
- Measure 1 (2000), which annexed a revised Management Plan for SPA 19;
- Decision 1 (2002), which renamed and renumbered SPA 19 as ASPA 115;
- Measures 5 (2012) and 4 (2017), which adopted a revised Management Plan for ASPA 115;

Recalling that Recommendation XVI-6 (1991) and Measure 1 (2000) did not become effective and were withdrawn by Decision 3 (2017);

Noting that the Committee for Environmental Protection has endorsed a revised Management Plan for ASPA 115;

Desiring to replace the existing Management Plan for ASPA 115 with the revised Management Plan;

Recommend to their Governments the following Measure for approval in accordance with paragraph 1 of Article 6 of Annex V to the Protocol on Environmental Protection to the Antarctic Treaty:

That:

1.	the revised Management Plan for Antarctic Specially Protected Area No 115 (Lagotellerie Island, Marguerite Bay, Graham Land), which is annexed to this Measure, be approved; and

2.	the Management Plan for Antarctic Specially Protected Area No 115 annexed to Measure 4 (2017) be revoked.

Measure 7 (2022)

Antarctic Specially Protected Area No 119 (Davis Valley and Forlidas Pond, Dufek Massif, Pensacola Mountains): Revised Management Plan

The Representatives,

Recalling Articles 3, 5 and 6 of Annex V to the Protocol on Environmental Protection to the Antarctic Treaty providing for the designation of Antarctic Specially Protected Areas ("ASPA") and approval of Management Plans for those Areas;

Recalling
- Recommendation XVI-9 (1991), which designated Forlidas Pond and Davis Valley Ponds as Specially Protected Area ("SPA") No 23 and annexed a Management Plan for the Area;
- Decision 1 (2002), which renamed and renumbered SPA 23 as ASPA 119;
- Measures 2 (2005), 6 (2010) and 7 (2015), which adopted a revised Management Plan for ASPA 119;

Recalling that Recommendation XVI-9 (1991) has not become effective and was withdrawn by Measure 6 (2010);

Noting that the Committee for Environmental Protection has endorsed a revised Management Plan for ASPA 119;

Desiring to replace the existing Management Plan for ASPA 119 with the revised Management Plan;

Recommend to their Governments the following Measure for approval in accordance with paragraph 1 of Article 6 of Annex V to the Protocol on Environmental Protection to the Antarctic Treaty:

That:

1. the revised Management Plan for Antarctic Specially Protected Area No 119 (Davis Valley and Forlidas Pond, Dufek Massif, Pensacola Mountains), which is annexed to this Measure, be approved; and

2. the Management Plan for Antarctic Specially Protected Area No 119 annexed to Measure 7 (2015) be revoked.

Measure 8 (2022)

Antarctic Specially Protected Area No 122 (Arrival Heights, Hut Point Peninsula, Ross Island): Revised Management Plan

The Representatives,

Recalling Articles 3, 5 and 6 of Annex V to the Protocol on Environmental Protection to the Antarctic Treaty providing for the designation of Antarctic Specially Protected Areas ("ASPA") and approval of Management Plans for those Areas;

Recalling
- Recommendation VIII-4 (1975), which designated Arrival Heights, Hut Point Peninsula, Ross Island as Site of Special Scientific Interest ("SSSI") No 2 and annexed a Management Plan for the Site;
- Recommendations X-6 (1979), XII-5 (1983), XIII-7 (1985), XIV-4 (1987), Resolution 3 (1996) and Measure 2 (2000), which extended the expiry date of SSSI 2;
- Decision 1 (2002), which renamed and renumbered SSSI 2 as ASPA 122;
- Measures 2 (2004), 3 (2011) and 3 (2016), which adopted a revised Management Plan for ASPA 122;

Recalling that Measure 2 (2000) was withdrawn by Measure 5 (2009);

Recalling that Recommendations VIII-4 (1975), X-6 (1979), XII-5 (1983), XIII-7 (1985), XIV-4 (1987) and Resolution 3 (1996) were designated as no longer current by Decision 1 (2011);

Noting that the Committee for Environmental Protection has endorsed a revised Management Plan for ASPA 122;

Desiring to replace the existing Management Plan for ASPA 122 with the revised Management Plan;

Recommend to their Governments the following Measure for approval in accordance with paragraph 1 of Article 6 of Annex V to the Protocol on Environmental Protection to the Antarctic Treaty:

That:

1.   the revised Management Plan for Antarctic Specially Protected Area No 122 (Arrival Heights, Hut Point Peninsula, Ross Island), which is annexed to this Measure, be approved; and

2.   the Management Plan for Antarctic Specially Protected Area No 122 annexed to Measure 3 (2016) be revoked.

Measure 9 (2022)

Antarctic Specially Protected Area No 124 (Cape Crozier, Ross Island): Revised Management Plan

The Representatives,

Recalling Articles 3, 5 and 6 of Annex V to the Protocol on Environmental Protection to the Antarctic Treaty providing for the designation of Antarctic Specially Protected Areas ("ASPA") and approval of Management Plans for those Areas;

Recalling
- Recommendation IV-6 (1966), which designated Cape Crozier, Ross Island as Specially Protected Area ("SPA") No 6 and annexed a map for the Area;
- Recommendation VIII-2 (1975), which terminated Recommendation IV-6 (1966);
- Recommendation VIII-4 (1975), which designated Cape Crozier, Ross Island as Site of Special Scientific Interest ("SSSI") No 4 and annexed a Management Plan for the Site;
- Recommendations X-6 (1979), XII-5 (1983), XIII-7 (1985) and XVI-7 (1991) and Measure 3 (2001), which extended the expiry date for SSSI 4;
- Decision 1 (2002), which renamed and renumbered SSSI 4 as ASPA 124;
- Measures 1 (2002), 7 (2008) and 3 (2014), which adopted a revised Management Plan for ASPA 124;

Recalling that Recommendations VIII-2 (1975), X-6 (1979), XII-5 (1983), XIII-7 (1985) and XVI-7 (1991) were designated as no longer current by Decision 1 (2011);

Recalling that Measure 3 (2001) has not become effective and was withdrawn by Measure 4 (2011);

Noting that the Committee for Environmental Protection has endorsed a revised Management Plan for ASPA 124;

Desiring to replace the existing Management Plan for ASPA 124 with the revised Management Plan;

Recommend to their Governments the following Measure for approval in accordance with paragraph 1 of Article 6 of Annex V to the Protocol on Environmental Protection to the Antarctic Treaty:

That:

1.   the revised Management Plan for Antarctic Specially Protected Area No 124 (Cape Crozier, Ross Island), which is annexed to this Measure, be approved; and

2.   the Management Plan for Antarctic Specially Protected Area No 124 annexed to Measure 3 (2014) be revoked.

Measure 10 (2022)

Antarctic Specially Protected Area No 126 (Byers Peninsula, Livingston Island, South Shetland Islands): Revised Management Plan

The Representatives,

Recalling Articles 3, 5 and 6 of Annex V to the Protocol on Environmental Protection to the Antarctic Treaty providing for the designation of Antarctic Specially Protected Areas ("ASPA") and approval of Management Plans for those Areas;

Recalling
- Recommendation IV-10 (1966), which designated Byers Peninsula, Livingston Island, South Shetland Islands as Specially Protected Area ("SPA") No 10;
- Recommendation VIII-2 (1975), which terminated SPA 10, and Recommendation VIII-4 (1975), which redesignated the Area as Site of Special Scientific Interest ("SSSI") No 6 and annexed the first Management Plan for the Site;
- Recommendations X-6 (1979), XII-5 (1983), XIII-7 (1985) and Measure 3 (2001), which extended the expiry date of SSSI 6;
- Recommendation XVI-5 (1991), which adopted a revised Management Plan for SSSI 6;
- Decision 1 (2002), which renamed and renumbered SSSI 6 as ASPA 126;
- Measures 1 (2002), 4 (2011) and 4 (2016), which adopted a revised Management Plan for ASPA 126;

Recalling that Recommendation XVI-5 (1991) and Measure 3 (2001) had not become effective and were withdrawn by Measure 4 (2011);

Recalling that Recommendations VIII-2 (1975), X-6 (1979), XII-5 (1983), XIII-7 (1985) and XVI-5 (1991) were designated as no longer current by Decision 1 (2011);

Noting that the Committee for Environmental Protection has endorsed a revised Management Plan for ASPA 126;

Desiring to replace the existing Management Plan for ASPA 126 with the revised Management Plan;

Recommend to their Governments the following Measure for approval in accordance with paragraph 1 of Article 6 of Annex V to the Protocol on Environmental Protection to the Antarctic Treaty:

That:

1.   the revised Management Plan for Antarctic Specially Protected Area No 126 (Byers Peninsula, Livingston Island, South Shetland Islands), which is annexed to this Measure, be approved; and

2.   the Management Plan for Antarctic Specially Protected Area No 126 annexed to Measure 4 (2016) be revoked.

Measure 11 (2022)

Antarctic Specially Protected Area No 127 (Haswell Island): Revised Management Plan

The Representatives,

Recalling Articles 3, 5 and 6 of Annex V to the Protocol on Environmental Protection to the Antarctic Treaty providing for the designation of Antarctic Specially Protected Areas ("ASPA") and approval of Management Plans for those Areas;

Recalling
- Recommendation VIII-4 (1975), which designated Haswell Island as Site of Special Scientific Interest ("SSSI") No 7 and annexed a Management Plan for the Site;
- Recommendations X-6 (1979), XII-5 (1983), XIII-7 (1985), XVI-7 (1987) and Measure 3 (2001), which extended the expiry date of SSSI 7;
- Decision 1 (2002), which renamed and renumbered SSSI 7 as ASPA 127;
- Measure 4 (2005), which extended the expiry date of the Management Plan for ASPA 127;
- Measures 1 (2006), 5 (2011) and 5 (2016), which adopted a revised Management Plan for ASPA 127;

Recalling that Recommendations VIII-4 (1975), X-6 (1979), XII-5 (1983), XIII-7 (1985) and XVI-7 (1987) were designated as no longer current by Decision 1 (2011);

Noting that the Committee for Environmental Protection has endorsed a revised Management Plan for ASPA 127;

Desiring to replace the existing Management Plan for ASPA 127 with the revised Management Plan;

Recommend to their Governments the following Measure for approval in accordance with paragraph 1 of Article 6 of Annex V to the Protocol on Environmental Protection to the Antarctic Treaty:

That:

1. the revised Management Plan for Antarctic Specially Protected Area No 127 (Haswell Island), which is annexed to this Measure, be approved; and

2. the Management Plan for Antarctic Specially Protected Area No 127 annexed to Measure 5 (2016) be revoked.

Measure 12 (2022)

Antarctic Specially Protected Area No 129 (Rothera Point, Adelaide Island): Revised Management Plan

The Representatives,

Recalling Articles 3, 5 and 6 of Annex V to the Protocol on Environmental Protection to the Antarctic Treaty providing for the designation of Antarctic Specially Protected Areas ("ASPA") and approval of Management Plans for those Areas;

Recalling
- Recommendation XIII-8 (1985), which designated Rothera Point, Adelaide Island as Site of Special Scientific Interest ("SSSI") No 9 and annexed a Management Plan for the Site;
- Resolution 7 (1995), which extended the expiry date of SSSI 9;
- Measure 1 (1996), which annexed a revised description and a revised Management Plan for SSSI 9;
- Decision 1 (2002), which renamed and renumbered SSSI 9 as ASPA 129;
- Measure 1 (2007), which adopted a revised Management Plan for ASPA 129 and revised its boundaries;
- Measures 6 (2012) and 5 (2017), which adopted a revised Management Plan for ASPA 129;

Recalling that Resolution 7 (1995) was designated as no longer current by Decision 1 (2011) and that Measure 1 (1996) did not become effective and was withdrawn by Measure 10 (2008);

Noting that the Committee for Environmental Protection has endorsed a revised Management Plan for ASPA 129;

Desiring to replace the existing Management Plan for ASPA 129 with the revised Management Plan;

Recommend to their Governments the following Measure for approval in accordance with paragraph 1 of Article 6 of Annex V to the Protocol on Environmental Protection to the Antarctic Treaty:

That:

1. the revised Management Plan for Antarctic Specially Protected Area No 129 (Rothera Point, Adelaide Island), which is annexed to this Measure, be approved; and

2. the Management Plan for Antarctic Specially Protected Area No 129 annexed to Measure 5 (2017) be revoked.

Measure 13 (2022)

Antarctic Specially Protected Area No 133 (Harmony Point, Nelson Island, South Shetland Islands): Revised Management Plan

The Representatives,

Recalling Articles 3, 5 and 6 of Annex V to the Protocol on Environmental Protection to the Antarctic Treaty providing for the designation of Antarctic Specially Protected Areas ("ASPA") and approval of Management Plans for those Areas;

Recalling
- Recommendation XIII-8 (1985), which designated Harmony Point, Nelson Island, South Shetland Islands as Site of Special Scientific Interest ("SSSI") No 14;
- Resolution 7 (1995), which extended the expiry date for SSSI 14;
- Measure 3 (1997), which adopted a revised Management Plan for SSSI 14;
- Decision 1 (2002), which renamed and renumbered SSSI 14 as ASPA 133;
- Measures 2 (2005) and 7 (2012), which annexed a revised Management Plan for ASPA 133;

Recalling that Resolution 7 (1995) was designated as no longer current by Decision 1 (2011);

Recalling that Measure 3 (1997) did not become effective and was withdrawn by Measure 6 (2011);

Noting that the Committee for Environmental Protection has endorsed a revised Management Plan for ASPA 133;

Desiring to replace the existing Management Plan for ASPA 133 with the revised Management Plan;

Recommend to their Governments the following Measure for approval in accordance with paragraph 1 of Article 6 of Annex V to the Protocol on Environmental Protection to the Antarctic Treaty:

That:

1. the revised Management Plan for Antarctic Specially Protected Area No 133 (Harmony Point, Nelson Island, South Shetland Islands), which is annexed to this Measure, be approved; and

2. the Management Plan for Antarctic Specially Protected Area No 133 annexed to Measure 7 (2012) be revoked.

Measure 14 (2022)

Antarctic Specially Protected Area No 139 (Biscoe Point, Anvers Island, Palmer Archipelago): Revised Management Plan

The Representatives,

Recalling Articles 3, 5 and 6 of Annex V to the Protocol on Environmental Protection to the Antarctic Treaty providing for the designation of Antarctic Specially Protected Areas ("ASPA") and approval of Management Plans for those Areas;

Recalling
- Recommendation XIII-8 (1985), which designated Biscoe Point, Anvers Island, Palmer Archipelago as Site of Special Scientific Interest ("SSSI") No 20 and annexed a Management Plan for the Site;
- Resolution 3 (1996) and Measure 2 (2000), which extended the expiry date of SSSI 20;
- Decision 1 (2002), which renamed and renumbered SSSI 20 as ASPA 139;
- Measures 2 (2004), 7 (2010) and 6 (2014), which adopted a revised Management Plan for ASPA 139;

Recalling that Resolution 3 (1996) was designated as no longer current by Decision 1 (2011);

Recalling that Measure 2 (2000) did not become effective and was withdrawn by Measure 5 (2009);

Noting that the Committee for Environmental Protection has endorsed a revised Management Plan for ASPA 139;

Desiring to replace the existing Management Plan for ASPA 139 with the revised Management Plan;

Recommend to their Governments the following Measure for approval in accordance with paragraph 1 of Article 6 of Annex V to the Protocol on Environmental Protection to the Antarctic Treaty:

That:

1.   the revised Management Plan for Antarctic Specially Protected Area No 139 (Biscoe Point, Anvers Island, Palmer Archipelago), which is annexed to this Measure, be approved; and

2.   the Management Plan for Antarctic Specially Protected Area No 139 annexed to Measure 6 (2014) be revoked.

Measure 15 (2022)

Antarctic Specially Protected Area No 140 (Parts of Deception Island, South Shetland Islands): Revised Management Plan

The Representatives,

Recalling Articles 3, 5 and 6 of Annex V to the Protocol on Environmental Protection to the Antarctic Treaty providing for the designation of Antarctic Specially Protected Areas ("ASPA") and approval of Management Plans for those Areas;

Recalling
- Recommendation XIII-8 (1985), which designated Shores of Port Foster, Deception Island, South Shetland Islands as Site of Special Scientific Interest ("SSSI") No 21 and annexed a Management Plan for the Site;
- Resolution 7 (1995) and Measure 2 (2000), which extended the expiry date for SSSI 21;
- Decision 1 (2002), which renamed and renumbered SSSI 21 as ASPA 140;
- Measures 3 (2005), 8 (2012) and 6 (2017), which adopted a revised Management Plan for ASPA 140;

Recalling that Resolution 7 (1995) was designated as no longer current by Decision 1 (2011) and that Measure 2 (2000) did not become effective and was withdrawn by Measure 5 (2009);

Noting that the Committee for Environmental Protection has endorsed a revised Management Plan for ASPA 140;

Desiring to replace the existing Management Plan for ASPA 140 with the revised Management Plan;

Recommend to their Governments the following Measure for approval in accordance with paragraph 1 of Article 6 of Annex V to the Protocol on Environmental Protection to the Antarctic Treaty:

That:

1.   the revised Management Plan for Antarctic Specially Protected Area No 140 (Parts of Deception Island, South Shetland Islands), which is annexed to this Measure, be approved; and

2.   the Management Plan for Antarctic Specially Protected Area No 140 annexed to Measure 6 (2017) be revoked.

Measure 16 (2022)

Antarctic Specially Protected Area No 149 (Cape Shirreff and San Telmo Island, Livingston Island, South Shetland Islands): Revised Management Plan

The Representatives,

Recalling Articles 3, 5 and 6 of Annex V to the Protocol on Environmental Protection to the Antarctic Treaty providing for the designation of Antarctic Specially Protected Areas ("ASPA") and approval of Management Plans for those Areas;

Recalling
- Recommendation IV-11 (1966), which designated Cape Shirreff, Livingston Island, South Shetland Islands as Specially Protected Area ("SPA") No 11;
- Recommendation XV-7 (1989), which terminated SPA 11 and redesignated the Area as Site of Special Scientific Interest ("SSSI") No 32 and annexed a Management Plan for the Site;
- Resolution 3 (1996) and Measure 2 (2000), which extended the expiry date of SSSI 32;
- Decision 1 (2002), which renamed and renumbered SSSI 32 as ASPA 149;
- Measures 2 (2005), 7 (2011) and 7 (2016), which adopted a revised Management Plan for ASPA 149;

Recalling that Recommendation XV-7 (1989) and Measure 2 (2000) did not become effective, and that Measure 2 (2000) was withdrawn by Measure 5 (2009);

Recalling that Recommendation XV-7 (1989) and Resolution 3 (1996) were designated as no longer current by Decision 1 (2011);

Noting that the Committee for Environmental Protection has endorsed a revised Management Plan for ASPA 149;

Desiring to replace the existing Management Plan for ASPA 149 with the revised Management Plan;

Recommend to their Governments the following Measure for approval in accordance with paragraph 1 of Article 6 of Annex V to the Protocol on Environmental Protection to the Antarctic Treaty:

That:

1.	the revised Management Plan for Antarctic Specially Protected Area No 149 (Cape Shirreff and San Telmo Island, Livingston Island, South Shetland Islands), which is annexed to this Measure, be approved; and

2.	the Management Plan for Antarctic Specially Protected Area No 149 annexed to Measure 7 (2016) be revoked.

Measure 17 (2022)

Antarctic Specially Protected Area No 164 (Scullin and Murray Monoliths, Mac.Robertson Land): Revised Management Plan

The Representatives,

Recalling Articles 3, 5 and 6 of Annex V to the Protocol on Environmental Protection to the Antarctic Treaty providing for the designation of Antarctic Specially Protected Areas ("ASPA") and approval of Management Plans for those Areas;

Recalling
- Measure 2 (2005), which designated Scullin and Murray Monoliths, Mac.Robertson Land, East Antarctica as ASPA 164 and annexed a Management Plan for the Area;
- Measures 13 (2010) and 16 (2015), which adopted a revised Management Plan for ASPA 164;

Noting that the Committee for Environmental Protection has endorsed a revised Management Plan for ASPA 164;

Desiring to replace the existing Management Plan for ASPA 164 with the revised Management Plan;

Recommend to their Governments the following Measure for approval in accordance with paragraph 1 of Article 6 of Annex V to the Protocol on Environmental Protection to the Antarctic Treaty:

That:

1. the revised Management Plan for Antarctic Specially Protected Area No 164 (Scullin and Murray Monoliths, Mac.Robertson Land), which is annexed to this Measure, be approved; and

2. the Management Plan for Antarctic Specially Protected Area No 164 annexed to Measure 16 (2015) be revoked.

Measure 18 (2022)

Revised List of Antarctic Historic Sites and Monuments: Updating information for Historic Sites and Monuments No 26, 29, 36, 38, 39, 40, 41, 42, 43 and 93

The Representatives,

Recalling the requirements of Article 8 of Annex V to the Protocol on Environmental Protection to the Antarctic Treaty to maintain a list of current Historic Sites and Monuments ("HSM") and that such sites "shall not be damaged, removed or destroyed";

Recalling
- Resolution 3 (2009), which adopted the Guidelines for the designation and protection of Historic Sites and Monuments;
- Resolution 2 (2018), which adopted the Guidelines for the assessment and management of Heritage in Antarctica;
- Recommendation VII-9, which designated HSM 26, 29, 36, 38, 39, 40, 41, 42 and 43, and Measure 5 (1997) which amended HSM 41;
- Measure 12 (2019), which added the wreck of the *Endurance* to the list of HSM;
- Decision 1 (2019), which added new information fields to the List of HSM;
- Decision 1 (2021), which sets out the information contained in fields that continue to be a formal part of the List of HSM and that changes to these fields would require adoption through a Measure; and
- Measure 23 (2021), which adopted the reformatted List of HSM;

Recommend to their Governments the following Measure for approval in accordance with paragraph 2 of Article 8 of Annex V to the Protocol on Environmental Protection to the Antarctic Treaty:

That:

1.   the information in the List of Historic Sites and Monuments ("HSM") for HSM 93, Wreck of *Endurance*, be amended as in the table below:

No	Name	Description	Location	Physical features of the environment and cultural and local context
93	Wreck of *Endurance*	Wreck of the vessel *Endurance*, including all artefacts contained within or formerly contained within the ship, which may be lying on the seabed in or near the wreck within a 500m radius. This includes all fixtures and fittings associated with the ship, including ship's wheel, bell, etc. The designation also includes all items of personal possessions left on the ship by the ship's company at the time of its sinking.	68°44'21" S, 52°19'47" W	The wreck is located on the floor of the Weddell Sea at a depth of 3,008m.

2.   the information in the List of HSM for HSM 26, 29, 36, 38, 39, 40, 41, 42 and 43, be amended as in the table below:

No	Name	Location
26	Ceremonial facilities of the San Martín Base	68°07'47"S, 67°06'05"W
29	Lighthouse 'Primero de Mayo"	64°17'58"S, 62°58'08"W
36	Dallmann Expedition Plaque	62°14'26"S, 58°40'45"W
38	Snow hill Swedish hut	64°21'50"S, 56°59'32"W
39	Hope Bay stone hut	63°23'44"S, 56°59'51"W
40	Ceremonial facilities of the Esperanza Base	63°23'49"S, 56°59'57"W
41	Historical remains of *Antarctic's* crew in Paulet island	63°34'29"S, 55°47'06"W
42	Laurie island observatories	60°44'18"S, 44°44'19"W
43	Belgrano station's cross	77°52'34"S, 34°37'43"W

3.   the Secretariat of the Antarctic Treaty be requested to update the list annexed to Measure 23 (2021) and make it available on its website.

2. Decisions

Decision 1 (2022)

Secretariat Report, Programme and Budget

The Representatives,

Recalling Measure 1 (2003) on the establishment of the Secretariat of the Antarctic Treaty ("the Secretariat");

Bearing in mind the Financial Regulations for the Secretariat of the Antarctic Treaty annexed to Decision 4 (2003) and amended by Decision 6 (2005);

Decide:

1.   to approve the audited Financial Report for 2020/21 annexed to this Decision (Annex 1);

2.   to take note of the Secretariat Report 2021/22, which includes the Provisional Financial Report for 2021/22, annexed to this Decision (Annex 2);

3.   to take note of the Five Year Forward Budget Profile 2023/24-2027/28 and approve the Secretariat Programme 2022/23, including the Budget for 2022/23 and the Forecast Budget 2023/24, annexed to this Decision (Annex 3); and

4.   to request that the Executive Secretary of the Secretariat open at the Antarctic Treaty Consultative Meeting ("ATCM") forum a topic to report to the Consultative Parties on financial issues.

Opinion of the Auditor

Secretary
of the Secretariat of the Antarctic Treaty,
Maipu 757, 4° piso
CUIT (Tax No.) 30-70892567-1

Re: ATCM XLIV - CEP XXIV Antarctic Treaty Consultative Meeting, 2022 – Berlin, Germany.

1.   Report on Financial Statements

We have audited the attached Financial Statements of the Antarctic Treaty Secretariat, which
include the following: Statement of Income and Expenditure, Statement of Financial Position,
Statement of Equity, Cash Flow Statement and Explanatory Notes for the financial period
commencing 1 April 2020 and ending 31 March 2021.

2.   Management Responsibility for Financial Statements

The Antarctic Treaty Secretariat, constituted under Argentine Act No. 25 888 of 14 May 2004,
is responsible for the preparation and reasonable presentation of the attached financial
statements according to accounting methods based on cash movements in accordance with
International Accounting Standards and the specific Standards for Antarctic Treaty Consultative
Meetings. Such responsibility includes: designing, implementing and maintaining internal
controls for the preparation and presentation of the Financial Statements such that they are free
of misstatements, due to error or fraud, selecting and implementing appropriate accounting
policies, and preparing accounting estimates which are reasonable under the circumstances.

3.   Auditor's Responsibility

Our responsibility is to express our opinion on these Financial Statements based on our audit.

The audit was conducted in accordance with International Auditing Standards and the Annex to
Decision 3 (2012) of the XXXI Antarctic Treaty Consultative Meeting, which describes the
tasks to be carried out by the external auditor.

These standards require compliance with ethical requirements, and planning and execution of
the audit so as to provide reasonable assurance that the Financial Statements are free of material
errors.

An audit includes the execution of procedures in order to obtain evidence of the amounts and
the exposure reflected in the Financial Statements. The procedures selected depend on the
auditor's judgement, including an assessment of the risks of material errors in the Financial
Statements.

In conducting such a risk assessment, the auditor considers the internal control relevant to the
preparation and reasonable presentation of the Financial Statements by the organisation, in order
to design suitable procedures that are appropriate to the circumstances.

An audit also includes an assessment of appropriateness of the accounting principles used, an
opinion on whether the accounting estimates made by management are reasonable, as well as an
assessment of the general presentation of the Financial Statements.

We believe that the audited evidence we have obtained is sufficient and appropriate to provide a basis for our opinion as auditors.

4.   Opinion

In our opinion, the attached Financial Statements of the Antarctic Treaty Secretariat corresponding to the financial period ending 31 March 2021 have been prepared, in all material aspects, in accordance with International Accounting Standards, the specific standards for Antarctic Treaty Consultative Meetings, and methods of accounting based on cash flow.

5.   Other Matters

The information contained in Note 1 to the attached financial statements, indicates that they have been prepared by the Antarctic Treaty Secretariat following the guidelines established in the Financial Regulations, Annexed to Decision 4 (2003), which differ in certain aspects of valuation and presentation from the professional accounting standards in force in the Autonomous City of Buenos Aires, Argentina.

In addition, the information mentioned in the preceding paragraph reflects the currency conversion differences generated over a year in a context of strong devaluation of the legal tender of the Argentine Republic.

6.   Additional information required by law

Pursuant to the analysis described in point 3, I report that the above-mentioned Financial Statements are based on accounting records that are not transcribed into books in accordance with current Argentine standards.

We also report that, according to the accounting entries as of 31 March 2021, the liabilities accrued in favour of the Argentine Single Social Security System in Argentine pesos and pursuant to settlements made by the Secretariat amounting to ARS 1 037 612.96 (USD 10 642.18), there was no debt due and payable in Argentine pesos as of that date.

It is worth noting that labour relations are governed by Antarctic Treaty Secretariat Staff Regulations.

Autonomous city of Buenos Aires, 31 March 2022

SINDICATURA GENERAL DE LA NACIÓN

BOZZANO Ariel Digitally signed by
Maximiliano BOZZANO Ariel Maximiliano Date: 2022.04.21 11:38:31

Ariel Maximiliano Bozzano
Contador Público (U.B.A.)
C.P.C.E.C.A.B.A. – T°379 – F°044

Annex I - Final Report for 2020/21

1. **Income and Expenditure Statement for all funds for the period 1 April 2020 to 31 March 2021 and comparison with the previous period.**

	31/3/2020	Budget 31/3/2021	31/3/2021
INCOME			
Contributions (Note 10)	1 378 097	1 378 097	1 378 097
General Fund (Note 1.11)	0	0	0
Other income (Note 2)	6 492	2 700	734
Total income	1 384 589	1 380 797	1 378 831
EXPENDITURE			
Salaries and wages	704 087	682 247	678 136
Translation and interpretation services	324 089	72 000	22 840
Travel and accommodation	99 173	39 500	10 230
Information technology	50 517	54 450	46 011
Printing, editing and copying	15 693	4 500	1 801
General services	56 309	54 488	35 295
Communications	14 763	17 900	13 827
Office expenses	11 466	17 500	12 711
Administration	6 570	7 200	6 750
Representation expenses	2 895	4 000	169
Financing (Note 9)	45 775	73 700	54 571
Total expenditure	1 331 338	1 027 485	882 340
ALLOCATION OF FUNDS			
Staff termination fund	25 359	25 813	25 813
Staff replacement fund	-	-	-
Working Capital fund	-	-	-
Translation contingency fund	-	-	-
Total allocation of funds	25 359	25 813	25 813
Total expenditure and allocations	1 356 696	1 053 298	908 153
(Loss) / Profit for the period	27 893	327 499	470 678

This statement must be read in conjunction with the accompanying Notes 1 to 10

199

Annex I - Final Report for 2020/21

2. Statement of Financial Position as of 31 March 2021 and comparison with the previous period

ASSETS

	31/3/2020	31/3/2021
Current assets		
Cash and cash equivalents (Note 3)	1 203 852	1 541 947
Contributions due (Note 10)	60 852	128 674
Other receivables (Note 4)	56 383	31 971
Other current assets (Note 5)	73 526	86 424
Total current assets	1 394 612	1 789 016
Non-current assets		
Fixed assets (Notes 1.3 and 6)	86 457	88 999
Total non-current assets	86 457	88 999
Total Assets	1 481 070	1 878 015

LIABILITIES

	31/3/2020	31/3/2021
Current liabilities		
Accounts payable (Note 7)	40 050	36 748
Contributions received in advance (Note 10)	493 543	387 197
Special voluntary fund for specific purposes (Note 1.9)	3 465	9 461
Remuneration and contributions payable (Note 8)	31 530	33 096
Total current liabilities	568 588	466 502
Non-current liabilities		
Staff termination fund (Note 1.4)	44 316	70 129
Staff replacement fund (Note 1.5)	50 000	50 000
Translation contingency fund (Note 1.6)	30 000	30 000
Involuntary separation from service fund (Note 1.7)	80 291	80 291
Fixed assets replacement fund (Note 1.8)	20 161	22 702
Total non-current liabilities	224 768	253 122
Total Liabilities	793 356	719 624
NET ASSETS	687 713	1 158 391

This statement must be read in conjunction with the accompanying Notes 1 to 10

Annex I - Final Report for 2020/21

3. **Statement of Changes in Net Assets as of 31 March 2021 and comparison with the previous period.**

Represented by	Net assets 31/3/2020	Income	Expenditure and Appropriations	Others income	Net assets 31/3/2021
General fund	457 761	1 378 097	-908 153	734	928 439
- to cover translation contingency fund					0
- to set up an involuntary separation from service fund					0
Working Capital fund (Note 1.9)	229 952				229 952
Net assets	687 713				1 158 391

This statement must be read in conjunction with the accompanying Notes 1 to 10

Annex I - Final Report for 2020/21

4   **Cash flow statement for the period 1 April 2020 to 31 March 2021 and comparison with the previous period.**

Variations in cash and cash equivalents		31/3/2021		31/3/2020	
Cash and cash equivalents at year-start		1 203 852		1 305 710	
Cash and cash equivalents at year-end		1 541 947		1 203 852	
Net increase in cash and cash equivalents			338 094		-101 858
Causes of the variations in cash and cash equivalents					
Operating activities					
Contributions received	816 731			1 004 398	
Payment of remunerations and salaries	-676 725			-703 648	
Payment of translation services	-15 880			-304 539	
Payment of travel, accommodation, etc.	0			-158 198	
Payment of printing, editing and copying services	-1 801			-15 693	
Payment of general services	-38 692			-51 974	
Other payments to suppliers	-67 207			-45 089	
Net cash flow from operating activities		16 426			-274 743
Investment activities					
Purchase of fixed assets	-16 172			-36 589	
Net cash flow from investment activities		-16 172			-36 589
Financing activities					
Contributions received in advance	387 197			493 543	
Payment of severance and replacement expenses	0			-185 160	
Preparation for ATCM XLI	0			0	
Collection pt. 5.6 Staff Regulations	167 620			190 707	
Payment pt. 5.6 Staff Regulations	-165 545			-214 302	
Net advance rent	13 532			20 866	
Net movement AFIP	-38 593			14 341	
Sundry income / (expenditure)	4 272			-65 211	
Net cash flow from financing activities		368 483			254 784
Foreign currency activities					
Net loss	-30 643			-45 310	
Net cash flow from foreign currency activities		-30 643			-45 310
Net increase in cash and cash equivalents			338 094		-101 858

This statement must be read in conjunction with the accompanying Notes 1 to 10

Notes to the Financial Statements as of 31 March 2020 and 2021

1 BASIS FOR PREPARATION OF FINANCIAL STATEMENTS

These financial statements are expressed in US dollars, pursuant to the guidelines established in the Financial Regulations, Annex to Decision 4 (2003). These statements were prepared in accordance with the International Financial Reporting Standards (IFRS) of the International Accounting Standards Board (IASB). The accounting method used is accrual-based.

1.1 Historical Cost

The financial statements have been prepared under the historical cost convention, unless indicated otherwise.

1.2 Office

The office of the Secretariat is provided by the Ministry of Foreign Affairs, Foreign Trade and Worship of the Argentine Republic. Its use is free of rent and common expenses.

1.3 Fixed assets

All items are valued at historical cost, less accumulated depreciation. Depreciation is calculated on a straight-line basis at annual rates appropriate to extinguish their values at the end of their estimated useful life. The aggregate residual value of fixed assets does not exceed their economic utilisation value.

1.4 Staff termination fund

In accordance with Staff Regulation 10.4, the fund shall be sufficiently funded to compensate executive staff members at a rate of one month basic pay for each year of service.

1.5 Staff replacement fund

The fund is used to cover the travel costs of the Secretariat's executive staff to and from the headquarters of the Secretariat.

1.6 Translation contingency fund

In accordance with Decision 4 (2009), the Fund was set up to cover translation expenses, which may be incurred by by the unforeseen increase in the volume of documents submitted to the ATCM for translation.

1.7 Involuntary separation from service fund

Comply with Article 10.5 of the Antarctic Treaty Secretariat's Staff Regulations for general services staff.

1.8 Fixed assets replacement fund

In accordance with the IAS, assets whose useful life exceeds one financial year must be disclosed as an asset in the Statement of Financial Position. Up to March 2010, the balancing entry was an adjustment to the General Fund. As of April 2010 the balancing entry of these assets will be shown in liabilities under this item.

1.9 Working Capital fund

According to Financial Regulation Article 6.2 (a), this must not exceed one-sixth (1/6) of the budget for the current financial year. In the current financial year, this fund was unallocated.

1.10 Special voluntary fund for specific purposes

Pt (82) of the XXXV ATCM Final Report, to receive voluntary contributions by the parties. The Voluntary Fund is money to meet the payment of rent and common expenses for the financial year.

1.11 General fund

This Fund was set up to account for the Secretariat's income and expenditure.

Notes to the Financial Statements as of 31 March 2020 and 2021

		31/3/2020	31/3/2021
2 Other Income			
	Interest earned	6 014	0
	Discounts obtained	478	734
	Total	6 492	734
3 Cash and cash equivalents			
	Cash in dollars	1 530	1 530
	Cash in Argentine pesos	60	150
	BNA special account in dollars	1 108 286	1 521 302
	BNA account in Argentine pesos	93 976	18 964
	Investments	-	-
	Total	1 203 852	1 541 947
4 Other receivables			
	Staff regulations pt. 5.6	56 383	31 971
5 Other current assets			
	Advance payments	38 514	31 738
	VAT receivable	28 448	50 456
	Other expenses to be recovered	6 563	4 230
	Total	73 526	86 424
6 Fixed assets			
	Books and subscriptions	16 704	16 704
	Office equipment	41 611	40 227
	Furniture	50 971	52 436
	Computer hardware and software	139 284	143 719
	Total original cost	248 569	253 086
	Accumulated depreciation	-162 112	-164 087
	Total	86 457	88 999
7 Accounts payable			
	Commercial suppliers	2 921	3 219
	Accrued expenditure	36 977	33 359
	Others	152	170
	Total	40 050	36 748
8 Remuneration and contributions payable			
	Remuneration	8 090	9 500
	Contributions	23 441	23 596
	Total	31 530	33 096
9 Financing			
	Exchange gains/(losses) due to payment	22 179	22 723
	Exchange gains/(losses) disbursement A	10 296	15 264
	Exchange gains/(losses) VAT refund	13 299	16 584
	Total	45 774	54 571

Notes to the Financial Statements as of 31 March 2020 and 2021

10 Contributions due, committed, cancelled and received in advance.

Contributions Parties	Due 31/3/2020	Com- mitted	Cancelled $	Due 31/3/2021	Advanced 31/3/2021
Argentina		60 347	60 347		-
Australia	25	60 347	60 372		-
Belgium		40 021	40 021		-
Brazil	60 728	40 021	0	100 749	-
Bulgaria		33 923	33 923		-
Chile		46 119	46 119		-
China	25	46 119	46 144		-
Czech Republic		40 021	40 021		40 009
Ecuador		33 923	33 923		-
Finland		40 021	40 021		40 021
France		60 347	60 347		-
Germany	12	52 217	52 229		-
India		46 119	46 119		-
Italy		52 217	52 217		-
Japan		60 347	60 347		-
Netherlands		46 119	46 119		-
New Zealand		60 347	60 347		60 322
Norway		60 347	60 347		60 327
Peru	16	33 923	6 013	27 926	-
Poland		40 021	40 021		40 021
Republic of Korea		40 021	40 021		40 021
Russian Federation		46 119	46 119		46 119
South Africa		46 119	46 119		-
Spain		46 119	46 119		-
Sweden	10	46 119	46 129		10
Ukraine	12	40 021	40 033		-
United Kingdom		60 347	60 347		60 347
United States		60 347	60 347		-
Uruguay	25	40 021	40 046		-
Total	60 852	1 378 097	1 310 275	128 674	387 197

Albert Lluberas Bonaba
Executive Secretary

Roberto A. Fennell
Financial Manager

Provisional Financial Report FY 2021/22

APPROPRIATION LINES	Audited Statement 2020/21		Budget 2021/22		Prov Statement 2021/22	
INCOME						
Contributions pledged	$	1 378 097	$	1 378 097	$	1 378 097
Voluntary contributions	$	-	$	-	$	-
Other income	$	734	$	1 000	$	975
Total Income	**$**	**1 378 831**	**$**	**1 379 097**	**$**	**1 379 072**
EXPENSES						
SALARIES						
Executive	$	297 522	$	303 468	$	303 468
General staff	$	380 443	$	390 542	$	388 841
ATCM support staff	$	-	$	9 900	$	8 900
Trainee	$	-	$	600	$	-
Overtime	$	170	$	2 000	$	6 254
Total Salaries	$	678 136	$	706 510	$	707 463
TRANSLATION AND INTERPRETATION						
Translation and Interpretation	$	22 840	$	220 000	$	215 954
TRAVEL						
Travel, lodging, allowance, misc.	$	10 230	$	30 000	$	18 625
INFORMATION TECHNOLOGY						
Hardware	$	7 209	$	10 750	$	9 800
Software	$	2 844	$	3 000	$	3 451
Development	$	28 573	$	29 800	$	22 752
Hardware & software maintenance	$	2 720	$	2 800	$	3 870
Support	$	4 666	$	7 500	$	6 000
Total Information Technology	$	46 011	$	53 850	$	45 873
PRINTING, EDITING & COPYING						
Final Report	$	1 330	$	14 000	$	11 401
Other publications	$	471	$	2 500	$	1 117
Total Printing Editing & Copying	$	1 801	$	16 500	$	12 518
GENERAL SERVICES						
Legal advice & counselling	$	446	$	7 000	$	571
Payroll services	$	9 061	$	8 400	$	8 194
External audit	$	11 619	$	11 908	$	11 618
Rapporteur services	$	-	$	-	$	-
Cleaning, maintenance & security	$	5 237	$	8 000	$	2 725
Training	$	1 612	$	5 000	$	2 530
Banking	$	5 013	$	7 000	$	7 322
Rental of equipment	$	2 308	$	1 500	$	892
Total General Services	$	35 295	$	48 808	$	33 852
COMMUNICATION						
Telephone	$	1 609	$	3 200	$	3 068
Internet	$	2 981	$	4 000	$	4 046
Web hosting	$	9 086	$	11 500	$	9 180
Postage	$	150	$	1 200	$	204
Total Communication	$	13 827	$	19 900	$	16 498

	Audited Statement 2020/21		Budget 2021/22		Prov Statement 2021/22
OFFICE					
Stationery & consumables	$	304	$	3 000	$	3 111
Books & subscriptions	$	15	$	1 000	$	303
Insurance	$	2 683	$	4 000	$	2 976
Furniture	$	1 464	$	1 500	$	1 476
Office equipment	$	2 096	$	3 500	$	1 100
Office improvement	$	6 149	$	5 500	$	5 430
Total Office	$	12 711	$	18 500	$	14 396
ADMINISTRATIVE					
Office supplies	$	1 353	$	2 500	$	741
Local transport	$	2 809	$	1 500	$	1 232
Miscellaneous	$	249	$	2 000	$	1 197
Utilities	$	2 340	$	3 000	$	1 910
Total Administrative	$	6 750	$	9 000	$	5 080
REPRESENTATION					
Representation	$	169	$	4 000	$	770
FINANCING					
Expenditures exchange (gain)/loss	$	22 723	$	22 000	$	11 662
Host Country Payments exchange (gain)/loss	$	15 264	$	15 000	$	8 540
VAT Refunds net (gain)/loss	$	16 584	$	18 000	$	7 771
Total Financing (gain)/loss	$	54 571	$	55 000	$	27 973
SUBTOTAL EXPENSES	**$**	**882 340**	**$**	**1 182 068**	**$**	**1 099 002**
FUND APPROPRIATIONS					
Working Capital Fund	$	-	$	-	$	-
Staff Replacement Fund	$	-	$	-	$	-
Staff Termination Fund	$	25 813	$	26 768	$	26 768
Involuntary Separation from Service	$	-	$	-	$	-
Translation Contingency Fund	$	-	$	-	$	-
Total Fund Appropriation	$	25 813	$	26 768	$	26 768
TOTAL EXPENSES & APPROPRIATIONS	**$**	**908 153**	**$**	**1 208 836**	**$**	**1 125 770**
Surplus / (Deficit) for the period	**$**	**470 678**	**$**	**170 261**	**$**	**253 302**

	Audited Statement 2020/21		Net Movements 2021/22		Prov Statement 2021/22	

FUND ACTIVITY

GENERAL FUND

Audited start balance	$	928 439				
Surplus/(Deficit) for the current period			$	253 302		
Provisional end balance					$	1 181 741

WORKING CAPITAL FUND

Audited start balance	$	229 952				
Provisional end balance			$	-	$	229 952

*) STAFF REPLACEMENT FUND

Audited start balance	$	50 000				
Provisional end balance			$	-	$	50 000

*) STAFF TERMINATION FUND

Audited start balance	$	70 129				
Appropriation in the current period			$	26 768		
Provisional end balance					$	96 897

**) INVOLUNTARY SEPARATION FROM SERVICE

Audited start balance	$	80 291				
Provisional end balance					$	80 291

***) TRANSLATION CONTINGENCY FUND

Audited start balance	$	30 000				
Provisional end balance					$	30 000

FINANCIAL REGULATION 6.3

General Fund	$	928 439	$	253 302	$	1 181 741
****) Unpaid Contributions	$	(128 839)			$	(141 962)
Cash Surplus	$	799 600			$	1 039 779

*) Decision 1 (2006)

**) Decision 3 (2019)

***) Decision 4 (2009)

****) Unpaid contributions as of 31 March 2021 and 31 March 2022

Secretariat Programme 2022 / 2023

Introduction

This work programme outlines the activities proposed for the Secretariat in the Financial Year 2022/23 (from 1 April 2022 to 31 March 2023).

The programme focuses on the Secretariat's regular activities, such as the preparation of the ATCM XLV, the publication of Reports, tasks assigned to the Secretariat under Measure 1 (2003), and the various specific tasks requested by the latest ATCMs. The programme and the accompanying budget figures for 2022/23 are based on the approved Forecast Budget for the Financial Year 2022/2023 (D3 (2021)).

Support for intersessional activities

During recent years, both the ATCM and the CEP have produced a substantial amount of intersessional work, mainly through Intersessional Contact Groups (ICGs) and informal discussion forums. The Secretariat will continue to provide support to these discussions, issue regular reminders of discussions in progress, and regularly provide detailed updates on the status of these discussions on the forum. The Secretariat will maintain close contact with ATCM Working Group Chairs to provide assistance for the preparation of the next meeting.

Concerning the CEP, the Secretariat will continue to work with the CEP Chair and the conveners of the Subsidiary Group on Climate Change Response (SGCCR) and the Subsidiary Group on Management Plans (SGMP). The Secretariat will also continue to take part in monthly video calls coordinated by the CEP Chair to facilitate the intersessional work of the CEP and prepare for the next meeting.

Planned support for ATCM XLV (2023) and ATCM XLVI (2024)

The Government of Finland and the Secretariat of the Antarctic Treaty will jointly organise ATCM XLV and CEP XXV, which will take place in Helsinki from 29 May to 8 June 2023. The responsibilities of the Host Country Secretariat and the Antarctic Treaty Secretariat are described in the Organisational Manual, updated annually by the Antarctic Treaty Secretariat. The main tasks of the Secretariat at the meeting are document management, supervision of technical services, organisation of translation and interpretation services, and support for the compilation and publication of the Final Report. The host country is responsible for the organisation of the venue, the provision of technical services, the rapporteur services and the accompanying programme.

The Secretariat will organise the translation and interpretation services. These comprise the translation of documents before, during and after the meeting, and interpretation during sessions. The Secretariat will also organise the note-taking services during the meeting and is responsible for the compilation and editing of the reports of the ATCM and CEP Meeting. The Secretariat will also establish a section of its website to make documents and other relevant materials available for delegates and to provide online registration to the meeting.

The Secretariat will start preliminary contact with the Government of India in relation to the organisation of ATCM XLVI (2024), including issues such as office and meeting room layouts and capacity, IT and audio-visual support and planning of events.

Coordination and contact

Aside from maintaining constant contact via email, telephone and other means with the Parties and international institutions of the Antarctic Treaty System, attendance at meetings is an important tool to maintain coordination and communication. However, at the time of preparing this programme, both the COMNAP and CCAMLR 2022 meetings are not yet confirmed. The Executive Secretary (ES) plans to participate virtually or physically at both of them.

Based on the valuable experiences of the past year, the Secretariat will be ready to perform virtual training and discussion sessions with delegates, at Parties' request, to support the use of the EIES, explain new features and exchange views on how to continue enhancing it. The Secretariat also stands ready to assist Parties at any time in relation to the services provided through the website, the management of information, documents, contacts and intersessional activities, among others.

Website and Information Systems

Redesign and improvement of the Contacts Database

The interface of the contacts database will be redesigned to achieve a full visual integration with the current design of the Secretariat website. This redesign will also include improvements in the functionality offered to users, as well as the possible integration with other services provided by the Secretariat that require restricted access to registered users. The development will also aim to maintain the highest standards of availability and security of the information contained in the database by adding enhanced security features.

Development of the Secretariat website

The Secretariat will continue improving the website by incorporating a new section to provide easy access to material useful to delegates and other registered users. The section, which will work similarly to the current CEP Handbook, will be called "ATCM Tools for Delegates".

Under the guidance of the CEP Chair, the Secretariat will work on continued improvements to the Historic Site and Monuments (HSM) section of the Secretariat website.

The Secretariat will assess likely ways to re-define the categories and topics currently used to classify ATCM measures in the Antarctic Treaty database with the aim of facilitating the search and filtering of measures.

The new online mechanism for the submission of documents to the meetings will be further adjusted, based on experience gained during the first year of use and feedback from users.

Mapping tools

The Secretariat will continue to explore the possibility of using the existing web-based geographical information platform for representing a variety of georeferenced content already existing in its databases or that could result from new information exchange requirements. As a complement to the improvements to be made to the list of historic sites and monuments, the Secretariat will apply adjustments to the new map that provides information on the location, description, and photographic material of each of the HSMs in Antarctica.

Information Exchange and the Electronic Information Exchange System (EIES)

The Secretariat will continue to assist Parties in posting their information exchange materials, as well as to process information uploaded using the File Upload functionality. In this regard, alternatives will continue to be assessed for the production of tutorials and/or training programs for EIES operators.

Additional Summarized Reports from the EIES will be added to complement and expand information provided by Parties in their reports.

Publications

ATCM Final Report and CEP Report

For ATCM XLIV in Berlin, the Secretariat has prepared for the timely translation in the four Treaty languages of the CEP Chair's non-paper on the CEP advice to the ATCM.

The Secretariat will translate, publish and distribute the ATCM XLIV Final Report and its Annexes in the four Treaty languages pursuant to the Procedures for the Submission, Translation and Distribution of Documents for the ATCM and the CEP Meeting, and other requirements established by the ATCM (ATCM XXXII Final Report, paragraph 72). The Final Report will be available on the Secretariat's website and hard copies will be distributed by courier and diplomatic channels. Hard copies will also be available for purchase through online retailers. The Secretariat will adjust its internal procedures to continue to improve the editorial quality of the report, including pre-meeting and post-meeting document formatting.

Other Publications

The Secretariat will publish an updated edition of the *Rules of Procedure of the Antarctic Treaty Consultative Meeting and the Committee for Environmental Protection* in the four Treaty languages. This book will be available on the Secretariat website and hard copies will also be available from online retailers worldwide. The Secretariat is ready to produce a new edition of the *Compilation of Key Documents of the Antarctic Treaty System* in the four Treaty languages, if needed.

Documentation and Public Information

Documents of the ATCM

The Secretariat will continue its efforts to complete its archive of the Final Reports and other records of the ATCM and other meetings of the Antarctic Treaty System in the four Treaty languages. We would like to reiterate our invitation to the Parties to search for their files to achieve a complete archive at the Secretariat. Please contact the Secretariat for a detailed list of missing documents.

The Secretariat will create a web platform to improve access to additional documents arising from ATCM XLIV, including reports from Observers and Experts and other documents, in line with the provisions established by the ATCM (ATCM XXXII Final Report, paragraph 72).

Glossaries and Editorial Guidelines

The Secretariat will continue to maintain the glossary of terms and expressions of the ATCM to generate a nomenclature in the four Treaty languages. The Secretariat will update its editorial guidelines, aimed at standardising the work of rapporteurs, translators, proofreaders and Secretariat staff. The Secretariat will update its web-based technical glossary for internal use, with the aim of improving consistency in the translation of ATCM documents.

Image Bank

The Secretariat will continue to incorporate to the image bank photographic material currently available in its archive. We would like to reiterate our invitation to provide the Secretariat with original photographic material to be published in the image bank under a Creative Commons license. We would especially appreciate receiving photographs corresponding to Antarctic Treaty Meetings before the establishment of the Secretariat, as well as those related to field work carried out by Parties in Antarctica in pursuit of compliance with the regulations established by the ATCM and the CEP, such as inspection activities.

Likewise, the Secretariat enabled a section of the image bank aimed at the collection and public dissemination of videos in digital format. With a criterion similar to that applied for the bank of still images, we would appreciate receiving videos related to the Consultative Meetings, such as the presentation videos displayed each year by the host country of the following meeting during the closing plenary session.

Personnel

On 1 April 2022 the Secretariat staff consisted of the following personnel:

Position	Since	Rank	Step	Term
Executive staff				
Executive Secretary	1-09-2017	E1	5	31-08-2025
Assistant Executive Secretary	15-07-2019	E3	3	31-07-2023
General staff				
Information Officer	1-11-2004	G1	6	
Support Officer (part time)	1-02-2020	G2	3	
Finance Officer (part time)	1-12-2008	G2	6	
Editor	1-02-2006	G2	6	
IT Specialist	1-02-2019	G3	4	
Communications Specialist (part time)	1-10-2010	G4	6	
Office Manager	15-11-2012	G4	6	
Cleaning Assistant (part time)	1-07-2015	G7	6	

No changes are foreseen in the staff positions of the Secretariat.

On 31 July 2023 the first term of the contract of the AES, Diego Wydler, will end. Mr. Wydler has demonstrated a high commitment and efficiency in his tasks during the last years. In addition, the ES considers that Mr. Wydler will prove an invaluable asset for the assistance of the next Executive Secretary, whose first term will start in 2025. Therefore, it is the intention of the ES to continue with Mr. Wydler's assistance and renew his contract for an additional four-year period.

To this end, considering that Staff Regulation 6.3 (e) reads: " (e) for executive staff the period of appointment [...] may be renewed in consultation with the ATCM", the ES will take a decision after further consultation during the ATCM XLIV.

Organizational review process

As explained in the Secretariat Report 2020/21, the Secretariat will continue the review process of the descriptions of roles and responsibilities of its staff, with the aim of keeping the Secretariat a small but dynamic, effective, robust and modern organisation, and plans to apply further actions during the current period.

A full confidential report which includes the description of still pending and possible future actions will be distributed to the Heads of Delegation during ATCM XLIV.

Financial Matters

The Budget for the Financial Year 2022/23 and the Forecast Budget for the Financial Year 2023/24 are included in Appendix 1.

Draft Budget for the Financial Year 2022/23

Allocation to the appropriation lines follows closely the proposed forecast from last year. Only smaller adjustments to the foreseen expenses in the Financial Year 2022/23 have been introduced.

The cost of living continued to rise sharply in Argentina in the year 2021. The inflation rate (Índice de Precios al Consumidor) for 2021 published by INDEC (Instituto Nacional de

Estadística y Censos de la República Argentina) was 50.9% and was only minimally compensated by a rise of the US Dollar against the Argentine Peso of 20.73%.

While this significant loss in 2021 was partially balanced by minor gains in previous years, the trend of the first quarter of 2022 is still one of inflation largely outpacing the US Dollar rise. Global inflation has also peaked in this period.[1]

For this reason, the Executive Secretary proposes to increase the salaries by 1.5% calculated to cover half the additional loss of Q1 2022 (approximately 3%).

The salary scale, which has not been updated since 2016, is provided in Appendix 3.

Despite the impact of local and global inflation on most of the costs, because expenditures are still largely based on contracts signed in 2021, and savings were applied in some lines, a balanced budget was attained.

Quarterly reports of budget implementation will be provided to the Parties in accordance with Decision 3 (2021).

Funds

Working Capital Fund

According to Financial Regulation 6.2 (a), the Working Capital Fund must be maintained at 1/6 of the Secretariat's budget (currently 229 952 US$).

Staff Termination Fund

The Staff Termination Fund will be credited with 29 592 US$ in accordance with Staff Regulation 10.4 (see Appendix 1).

Forecast Budget for the Financial Year 2023/24

It is expected that most of the regular activities of the Secretariat will continue in the Financial Year 2022/23 including meetings in person in 2023 in Helsinki and therefore, unless the programme undergoes major changes, no major change in appropriation lines is foreseen.

However, rise adjustments in US$ for local costs in Argentina are expected to affect operational costs while global inflation would bring rising costs to Travel and Translation & Interpretation.

Therefore, the Forecast Budget for this period is expected to show a deficit of approximately US$ 18 000 which would be covered by accumulated surplus in the General Fund.

The contributions for the Financial Year 2023/24 will not rise. Appendix 2 shows the contribution scale for the Financial Year 2023/24.

Five-Year Forward Budget profile 2023/24 - 2027/28

Under reasonable assumptions the budget profile allows a zero-nominal increase in contributions until 2027/28 as explained in the Five-Year Budget Profile document presented separately by the Secretariat.

---

[1] Inflation 2021, international inflation figures from 2021 (global-rates.com)

Budget FY 2022/23 and Forecast FY 2023/24

APPROPRIATION LINES	Prov Statement 2021/22		Forecast 2022/23		Budget 2022/23		Forecast 2023/24	
INCOME								
Contributions pledged	$	1 378 097	$	1 378 097	$	1 378 097	$	1 378 097
Voluntary contributions	$	-	$	-	$	-	$	-
Other income	$	975	$	3 500	$	3 500	$	3 500
Total Income	$	1 379 072	$	1 381 597	$	1 381 597	$	1 381 597

EXPENSES
SALARIES

Executive	$	303 468	$	309 199	$	313 825	$	319 574
General staff	$	388 841	$	394 800	$	405 842	$	410 187
ATCM support staff	$	8 900	$	15 467	$	15 220	$	16 000
Trainee	$	-	$	1 200	$	1 200	$	1 200
Overtime	$	6 254	$	13 000	$	12 000	$	12 000
Total Salaries	$	707 463	$	733 666	$	748 087	$	758 961

TRANSLATION AND INTERPRETATION

Translation and Interpretation	$	215 954	$	310 200	$	310 000	$	312 000

TRAVEL

Travel, lodging, allowance, misc.	$	18 625	$	109 000	$	108 500	$	111 300

INFORMATION TECHNOLOGY

Hardware	$	9 800	$	11 000	$	11 000	$	11 000
Software	$	3 451	$	3 000	$	3 500	$	3 500
Development	$	22 752	$	27 500	$	26 000	$	27 500
Hardware & software maintenance	$	3 870	$	2 500	$	3 500	$	3 500
Support	$	6 000	$	7 500	$	8 000	$	8 000
Total Information Technology	$	45 873	$	51 500	$	52 000	$	53 500

PRINTING, EDITING & COPYING

Final Report	$	11 401	$	15 000	$	12 000	$	12 500
Other publications	$	1 117	$	2 500	$	2 500	$	3 000
Total Printing Editing & Copying	$	12 518	$	17 500	$	14 500	$	15 500

GENERAL SERVICES

Legal advice & counselling	$	571	$	7 000	$	3 500	$	4 000
Payroll services	$	8 194	$	8 400	$	8 400	$	8 400
External audit	$	11 618	$	11 908	$	11 618	$	11 618
Rapporteur services	$	-	$	-	$	-	$	-
Cleaning, maintenance & security	$	2 725	$	8 000	$	8 000	$	8 000
Training	$	2 530	$	7 000	$	7 000	$	7 000
Banking	$	7 322	$	6 500	$	7 900	$	8 000
Rental of equipment	$	892	$	1 000	$	1 000	$	1 000
Total General Services	$	33 852	$	49 808	$	47 418	$	48 018

COMMUNICATION

Telephone	$	3 068	$	2 500	$	2 500	$	2 500
Internet	$	4 046	$	4 000	$	4 500	$	4 500
Web hosting	$	9 180	$	10 500	$	10 000	$	10 000
Postage	$	204	$	1 000	$	1 000	$	1 000
Total Communication	$	16 498	$	18 000	$	18 000	$	18 000

	Prov Statement 2021/22		Forecast 2022/23		Budget 2022/23		Forecast 2023/24	
OFFICE								
Stationery & consumables	$	3 111	$	2 500	$	2 500	$	2 500
Books & subscriptions	$	303	$	1 000	$	1 000	$	1 000
Insurance	$	2 976	$	4 000	$	3 500	$	3 500
Furniture	$	1 476	$	1 500	$	1 500	$	1 500
Office equipment	$	1 100	$	3 000	$	3 000	$	3 500
Office improvement	$	5 430	$	3 500	$	4 500	$	4 000
Total Office	$	**14 396**	$	**15 500**	$	**16 000**	$	**16 000**
ADMINISTRATIVE								
Office supplies	$	741	$	2 500	$	2 500	$	3 000
Local transport	$	1 232	$	700	$	1 000	$	700
Miscellaneous	$	1 197	$	2 500	$	2 200	$	2 700
Utilities	$	1 910	$	3 500	$	2 500	$	3 000
Total Administrative	$	**5 080**	$	**9 200**	$	**8 200**	$	**9 400**
REPRESENTATION								
Representation	$	770	$	4 000	$	4 000	$	4 000
FINANCING								
Expenditures exchange (gain)/loss	$	11 662	$	16 500	$	11 500	$	11 500
Host Country Payments exchange (gain)/	$	8 540	$	11 000	$	5 800	$	4 800
VAT Refunds net (gain)/loss	$	7 771	$	8 000	$	8 000	$	7 700
Total Financing (gain)/loss	$	**27 973**	$	**35 500**	$	**25 300**	$	**24 000**
SUBTOTAL EXPENSES	$	**1 099 002**	$	**1 353 874**	$	**1 352 005**	$	**1 370 679**
FUND APPROPRIATIONS								
Working Capital Fund	$	-	$	-	$	-	$	-
Staff Replacement Fund	$	-	$	-	$	-	$	-
Staff Termination Fund	$	26 768	$	27 723	$	29 592	$	29 108
Involuntary Separation from Service	$	-	$	-	$	-	$	-
Translation Contingency Fund	$	-	$	-	$	-	$	-
Total Fund Appropriation	$	**26 768**	$	**27 723**	$	**29 592**	$	**29 108**
TOTAL EXPENSES & APPROPRIATIONS	$	**1 125 770**	$	**1 381 597**	$	**1 381 597**	$	**1 399 787**
Surplus / (Deficit) for the period	$	**253 302**	$	**-**	$	**-**	$	**(18 190)**

FUND BALANCE

Working Capital Fund	$	229 952	$	229 952	$	229 952	$	229 952
Staff Replacement Fund	$	50 000	$	50 000	$	50 000	$	50 000
Staff Termination Fund	$	96 897	$	124 620	$	126 489	$	153 728
Involuntary Separation from Service	$	80 291	$	80 291	$	80 291	$	80 291
Translation Contingency Fund	$	30 000	$	30 000	$	30 000	$	30 000

Contribution Scale FY 2023/24

Party	Cat.	Mult.	Variable	Fixed	Total
Argentina	A	3.6	$ 36 587	$ 23 760	$ 60 347
Australia	A	3.6	$ 36 587	$ 23 760	$ 60 347
Belgium	D	1.6	$ 16 261	$ 23 760	$ 40 021
Brazil	D	1.6	$ 16 261	$ 23 760	$ 40 021
Bulgaria	E	1	$ 10 163	$ 23 760	$ 33 923
Chile	C	2.2	$ 22 359	$ 23 760	$ 46 119
China	C	2.2	$ 22 359	$ 23 760	$ 46 119
Czech Republic	D	1.6	$ 16 261	$ 23 760	$ 40 021
Ecuador	E	1	$ 10 163	$ 23 760	$ 33 923
Finland	D	1.6	$ 16 261	$ 23 760	$ 40 021
France	A	3.6	$ 36 587	$ 23 760	$ 60 347
Germany	B	2.8	$ 28 456	$ 23 760	$ 52 217
India	C	2.2	$ 22 359	$ 23 760	$ 46 119
Italy	B	2.8	$ 28 456	$ 23 760	$ 52 217
Japan	A	3.6	$ 36 587	$ 23 760	$ 60 347
Republic of Korea	D	1.6	$ 16 261	$ 23 760	$ 40 021
Netherlands	C	2.2	$ 22 359	$ 23 760	$ 46 119
New Zealand	A	3.6	$ 36 587	$ 23 760	$ 60 347
Norway	A	3.6	$ 36 587	$ 23 760	$ 60 347
Peru	E	1	$ 10 163	$ 23 760	$ 33 923
Poland	D	1.6	$ 16 261	$ 23 760	$ 40 021
Russian Federation	C	2.2	$ 22 359	$ 23 760	$ 46 119
South Africa	C	2.2	$ 22 359	$ 23 760	$ 46 119
Spain	C	2.2	$ 22 359	$ 23 760	$ 46 119
Sweden	C	2.2	$ 22 359	$ 23 760	$ 46 119
Ukraine	D	1.6	$ 16 261	$ 23 760	$ 40 021
United Kingdom	A	3.6	$ 36 587	$ 23 760	$ 60 347
United States	A	3.6	$ 36 587	$ 23 760	$ 60 347
Uruguay	D	1.6	$ 16 261	$ 23 760	$ 40 021

Total Pledged   **$ 1 378 097**

Salary Scale FY 2022/23

Schedule A
SALARY SCALE FOR THE EXECUTIVE STAFF
(United States Dollar)

2022/23 Level		STEPS I	II	III	IV	V	VI	VII	VIII	IX	X	XI	XII	XIII	XIV	XV
E1	A	$ 137 332	$ 139 886	$ 142 442	$ 144 998	$ 147 554	$ 150 108	$ 152 663	$ 155 220							
E1	B	$ 171 664	$ 174 858	$ 178 052	$ 181 248	$ 184 442	$ 187 636	$ 190 829	$ 194 025							
E2	A	$ 115 641	$ 117 816	$ 119 991	$ 122 164	$ 124 339	$ 126 512	$ 128 685	$ 130 860	$ 133 035	$ 135 209	$ 137 382	$ 137 629	$ 139 775		
E2	B	$ 144 551	$ 147 269	$ 149 989	$ 152 706	$ 155 423	$ 158 139	$ 160 856	$ 163 575	$ 166 295	$ 169 011	$ 171 728	$ 172 036	$ 174 718		
E3	A	$ 96 432	$ 98 529	$ 100 627	$ 102 725	$ 104 824	$ 106 921	$ 109 019	$ 111 118	$ 113 215	$ 115 312	$ 117 410	$ 118 669	$ 119 926	$ 121 996	$ 124 064
E3	B	$ 120 539	$ 123 161	$ 125 784	$ 128 407	$ 131 030	$ 133 651	$ 136 274	$ 138 898	$ 141 518	$ 144 140	$ 146 763	$ 148 335	$ 149 908	$ 152 496	$ 155 080
E4	A	$ 79 961	$ 81 903	$ 83 848	$ 85 786	$ 87 732	$ 89 672	$ 91 611	$ 93 557	$ 95 500	$ 97 440	$ 99 384	$ 99 925	$ 101 841	$ 103 756	$ 105 672
E4	B	$ 99 951	$ 102 379	$ 104 811	$ 107 233	$ 109 665	$ 112 091	$ 114 514	$ 116 945	$ 119 375	$ 121 799	$ 124 229	$ 124 906	$ 127 300	$ 129 695	$ 132 089
E5	A	$ 66 295	$ 68 034	$ 69 770	$ 71 509	$ 73 244	$ 74 981	$ 76 720	$ 78 452	$ 80 192	$ 81 930	$ 83 663				
E5	B	$ 82 869	$ 85 043	$ 87 213	$ 89 386	$ 91 556	$ 93 727	$ 95 899	$ 98 066	$ 100 240	$ 102 412	$ 104 580	$ 105 282			
E6	A	$ 52 482	$ 54 151	$ 55 819	$ 57 491	$ 59 158	$ 60 827	$ 62 499	$ 64 167	$ 65 835	$ 66 850	$ 67 506				
E6	B	$ 65 601	$ 67 689	$ 69 773	$ 71 863	$ 73 948	$ 76 034	$ 78 124	$ 80 209	$ 82 294	$ 83 563	$ 84 382				

Note: Row B is the base salary (shown in Row A) with an additional 25% for salary on-costs (retirement fund and insurance premiums, installation and repatriation grants, education allowances etc.) and is the total salary entitlement for executive staff in accordance with regulation 5.1.

Schedule B
SALARY SCALE FOR THE GENERAL STAFF
(United States Dollar)

Level	STEPS I	II	III	IV	V	VI	VII	VIII	IX	X	XI	XII	XIII	XIV	XV
G1	$ 66 746	$ 69 859	$ 72 975	$ 76 088	$ 79 333	$ 82 717									
G2	$ 55 622	$ 58 216	$ 60 812	$ 63 406	$ 66 112	$ 68 932									
G3	$ 46 350	$ 48 512	$ 50 676	$ 52 838	$ 55 093	$ 57 445									
G4	$ 38 626	$ 40 428	$ 42 230	$ 44 033	$ 45 910	$ 47 870									
G5	$ 31 909	$ 33 399	$ 34 887	$ 36 378	$ 37 931	$ 39 552									
G6	$ 26 156	$ 27 375	$ 28 595	$ 29 816	$ 31 089	$ 32 416									
G7	$ 14 139	$ 14 750	$ 15 362	$ 15 974	$ 16 611	$ 17 277									

Decision 2 (2022)

Liability arising from environmental emergencies

The Representatives,

Recalling the undertaking in Article 16 of the Protocol on Environmental Protection to the Antarctic Treaty ("the Protocol") to elaborate rules and procedures relating to liability for damage arising from activities taking place in the Antarctic Treaty area and covered by the Protocol;

Recalling Measure 1 (2005) and the adoption of Annex VI to the Protocol, as a step towards the establishment of a liability regime in accordance with Article 16 of the Protocol;

Noting that Annex VI has yet to become effective;

Recalling Decisions 1 (2005), 4 (2010) and 5 (2015) regarding the annual evaluation of progress towards Annex VI becoming effective and the establishment of a time-frame for the resumption of negotiations on liability in accordance with Article 16 of the Protocol;

Acknowledging the advice provided by the Committee for Environmental Protection in 2013 on environmental issues related to the practicality of specific instances of repair or remediation of environmental damage in the circumstances of Antarctica;

Decide:

1.   to continue to evaluate annually the progress made towards Annex VI becoming effective in accordance with Article IX of the Antarctic Treaty, and what action may be necessary and appropriate to encourage Parties to approve Annex VI in a timely manner;

2.   to continue to share with one another information and experience, to support progress towards Annex VI becoming effective;

3.   to take a decision in 2025 on the establishment of a time-frame for the resumption of negotiations on liability in accordance with Article 16 of the Protocol, or sooner if Parties so decide in light of progress made in approving Measure 1 (2005); and

4.   that Decision 5 (2015) is no longer current.

Decision 3 (2022)

Multi-year Strategic Work Plan for the Antarctic Treaty Consultative Meeting

The Representatives,

Reaffirming the values, objectives and principles contained in the Antarctic Treaty and its Protocol on Environmental Protection;

Recalling Decision 3 (2012) on the Multi-year Strategic Work Plan ("the Plan") and its principles;

Bearing in mind that the Plan is complementary to the agenda of the Antarctic Treaty Consultative Meeting ("ATCM") and that the Parties and other ATCM participants are encouraged to contribute as usual to other matters on the ATCM agenda;

Decide:

1.   to adopt the Plan annexed to this Decision; and

2.   that the Plan annexed to Decision 5 (2021) is no longer current.

ATCM Multi-year Strategic Work Plan

	Priority	ATCM XLIV (2022)	Intersessional	ATCM XLV (2023)	Intersessional	ATCM XLVI (2024)	Intersessional	ATCM XLVII (2025)
1.	Consider coordinated outreach to non-party states whose nationals or assets are active in Antarctica and states that are Antarctic Treaty Parties but not yet to the Protocol	ATCM to identify and reach out to non-party states whose nationals are active in Antarctica	Coordination to be considered within Competent Authority online forum	ATCM to identify and reach out to non-party states whose nationals are active in Antarctica				
2.	Contribute to nationally and internationally coordinated education and outreach activities from an Antarctic Treaty perspective	WG 1 to consider the report of the ICG on Education and Outreach	ICG on Education and Outreach	WG1 to consider the report of the ICG on Education and Outreach				
3.	Share and discuss strategic science priorities in order to identify and pursue opportunities for collaboration as well as capacity building in science, particularly in relation to climate change	SCAR will report on the outcomes of the ACCE update, which represents a comprehensive decadal update

The ATCM to consider if its results would indicate the need for some additional priorities and opportunities for cooperation

The ATCM will invite SCAR lecture on the outcome of the report | | Parties, Observers and Experts encouraged to report on activities relating to promoting the implications of climate change in Antarctica | | | | |

Priority	ATCM XLIV (2022)	Intersessional	ATCM XLV (2023)	Intersessional	ATCM XLVI (2024)	Intersessional	ATCM XLVII (2025)
4. To bring Annex VI into force and to continue to gather information on repair and remediation of environmental damage and other relevant issues to inform future negotiations on liability	ATCM to evaluate progress made towards Annex VI becoming effective in accordance with Article IX of the Antarctic Treaty, and what action may be necessary and appropriate to encourage Annex VI in a timely manner		ATCM to evaluate progress made towards Annex VI becoming effective in accordance with Article IX of the Antarctic Treaty, and what action may be necessary and appropriate to encourage Parties to approve Annex VI in a timely manner				
	ATCM to consider the implications of liability limits in other relevant international instruments for the potential future amendment of the limits in Article 9 of Annex VI		ATCM to consider the implications of liability limits in other relevant international instruments for the potential future amendment of the limits in Article 9 of Annex VI				

	Priority	ATCM XLIV (2022)	Intersessional	ATCM XLV (2023)	Intersessional	ATCM XLVI (2024)	Intersessional	ATCM XLVII (2025)
		ATCM to take a decision in 2022 on the establishment of a timeframe for the resumption of negotiations on liability in accordance with Article 16 of the Protocol on Environmental Protection, or sooner if the Parties so decide in light of progress made in approving Measure 1 (2005) – see Decision 5 (2015)		ATCM to take a decision in 2025 on the establishment of a timeframe for the resumption of negotiations on liability in accordance with Article 16 of the Protocol on Environmental Protection, or sooner if the Parties so decide in light of progress made in approving Measure 1 (2005) – see Decision 2 (2022)				
5.	Assess the progress of the CEP on its ongoing work to review best practices and to improve existing tools and develop further tools for environmental protection, including environmental impact assessment procedures	WG 1 to consider advice of the CEP and discuss the policy considerations of the review of Environmental Impact Assessment (EIA)	Exchange EIA best practices	WG 1 to consider advice of the CEP and discuss the policy considerations of the review of Environmental Impact Assessment (EIA)				
6.	Advance in the implementation of Resolution 4 (2022), including issues related to the development and/or strengthening of research activities and the dissemination of their results	Parties to provide updates on risk assessment approaches taken to identify potential climate change implications for current and future Antarctic, logistics and environmental values		Update from COMNAP on its work with national programmes to use consistent methods to quantify and publish savings made by energy efficiencies and which contribute to				

Priority	ATCM XLIV (2022)	Intersessional	ATCM XLV (2023)	Intersessional	ATCM XLVI (2024)	Intersessional	ATCM XLVII (2025)
	Space agencies – discussion on space-based technologies for observing the Antarctic region in the context of climate change Agree how to deal with any outstanding recommendations from the ATME on Climate Change Implications (2010)		both (a) reducing carbon footprint and (b) reducing fuel consumption				
7. Modernisation of Antarctic Stations in context of climate change	Further discussion on modernisation of Antarctic stations		Parties to continue sharing information and experiences on the environmental, safety and cultural aspects of their construction activities				
8. Review and discuss issues related to increased aviation activity in Antarctica, and assess the need for additional action	Discuss information from the Antarctic Aviation Workshop presented by COMNAP Parties to inform on their aviation-related activities/plans		Parties, Observers and Experts to inform on their aviation-related activities/plans				
9. Contribute to strengthening the consistent implementation of the Polar Code	Further exchange views on national experiences in implementing the Polar Code in Antarctica		Parties to share documents on the national experiences in implementing the Polar Code. A dedicated session will be organized to				

	Priority	ATCM XLIV (2022)	Intersessional	ATCM XLV (2023)	Intersessional	ATCM XLVI (2024)	Intersessional	ATCM XLVII (2025)
				enhance and support harmonized implementation of the Polar Code				
10.	Promote enhancement of hydrographic surveying in Antarctica	Parties to react to IHO's proposal Parties, IHO and IAATO to report on progress in hydrography		Parties to discuss ways and means to implement existing resolutions on Hydrography (refer to ATCM XLIII - IP 4 (2021)) Parties, IAATO and IHO to report on progress in hydrography				
11.	Develop a strategic approach to the management of Antarctic tourism to ensure it is conducted in a safe and environmentally responsible way	Consider outcomes of ICG on permanent facilities for tourism and other non-governmental activities in Antarctica	Second period - ICG on permanent facilities for tourism and other non-governmental activities in Antarctica	Consider further outcomes of ICG on permanent facilities for tourism and other non-governmental activities				
		Further consideration of environmental issues relating to tourism based on any new advice from the CEP		Consider implications of increased tourism activity for search and rescue burdens, including on national Antarctic programs	Consider options to assist and encourage implementation and entry into force of Measure 4 (2004) and Measure 15 (2009)	Review progress on implementation and entry into force of Measure 4 (2004) and Measure 15 (2009)		

Priority	ATCM XLIV (2022)	Intersessional	ATCM XLV (2023)	Intersessional	ATCM XLVI (2024)	Intersessional	ATCM XLVII (2025)
	Consideration of possibly increased search and rescue burdens on national Antarctic programmes due to increased tourism activity in Antarctic	Parties to consider developing proposals for a discussion on how the ATCM can best identify monitoring strategies, including indicators that might suggest tourism trends which could increase risks to effective management or present a risk to the Antarctic environment	Discussion on how the ATCM can best identify monitoring strategies, including indicators that might suggest tourism trends which could increase risks to effective management or present a risk to the Antarctic environment	Interested Parties to consider options for ATCM post visit report forms for land-based tourism activities and air-supported tourism activities. Informal intersessional discussions on possible applicability and use of tourist fees	Assess any growth in tourism or non-governmental activities conducted by non-IAATO operators		
	Further discussions relating to issues arising from the growth of tourism, including any implications of the potential growth in non-IAATO registered operators		Parties and other participants to provide updates on progress with tourism-related environmental monitoring activities they are sponsoring or conducting, as well as compliance monitoring of tourism activities		Request advice from the CEP on the design of a strategic tourism environmental monitoring program, to support a discussion of implementation options		Assess whether the suite of Site Guidelines and other tools adequately cover the locations in which tourism activities occur
	To analyse CEP progress on recommendations 3 and 7 of the CEP Tourism Study			Parties to bring forward advice from their competent authorities on what types or	Consider whether guidance for Antarctic operators on the collection and provision of		

Annex: ATCM Multi-Year Strategic Work Plan

	Priority	ATCM XLIV (2022)	Intersessional	ATCM XLV (2023)	Intersessional	ATCM XLVI (2024)	Intersessional	ATCM XLVII (2025)
					forms and standards of evidence of suspected non-compliance would be useful in exercising their compliance obligations	evidence of suspected non-compliance should be developed		
12.	Enhancing compliance with ATCM regulations relating to non-governmental activities including tourism activities	Working Group 1 to provide advice on how those operating in Antarctica can most effectively gather and share evidence of suspected non-compliance	Secretariat to request Parties to provide advice concerning proper documentation of suspected non-compliance	Working Group 1 to provide advice on how those operating in Antarctica can most effectively gather and share evidence of suspected non-compliance				
13.	Address equality, diversity and inclusion issues, by promoting full participation of underrepresented groups in Antarctic science and operations activities across all Antarctic issues, including science, operations, policy and law	Parties to share information on their plans on these issues		Parties, Observers and Experts to share information on their plans on these issues		Parties, Observers and Experts to share information on their plans on these issues		Parties, Observers and Experts to share information on their plans on these issues
14.	Strengthen coordination on the management of hazardous natural events in Antarctic facilities	Consider any information from SCAR and COMNAP on different aspects associated to the volcanic/seismic events and Antarctic facilities Review and discuss how Parties can adequately deal with these events in Antarctic facilities	Encourage Parties to participate in the COMNAP Technical Collaboration Group through the National Antarctic Programs	Review and discuss how Parties can adequately deal with these events in Antarctic facilities COMNAP to inform on the work of this group at ATCM XLV				

ATCM XLIV Final Report

Priority	ATCM XLIV (2022)	Intersessional	ATCM XLV (2023)	Intersessional	ATCM XLVI (2024)	Intersessional	ATCM XLVII (2025)
			SCAR to inform on seismic activities in Antarctica				

Note: The ATCM Working Groups mentioned above are not permanent but are established by consensus at the end of each Antarctic Treaty Consultative Meeting.

Decision 4 (2022)

Letters on Antarctic Climate Change and the Environment: A Decadal Synopsis and Recommendations for Action report

The Representatives,

Recognising the important role of the Antarctic region in global climate processes;

Welcoming the Decadal Synopsis Report on Antarctic Climate Change and the Environment ("Decadal Synopsis") by the Scientific Committee on Antarctic Research ("SCAR"); and

Concerned by the effects and projected changes to Antarctic environments resulting from climate change outlined in the Decadal Synopsis;

Decide to request the Chair of the Antarctic Treaty Consultative Meeting ("ATCM") to send the letter annexed to this Decision forwarding the Decadal Synopsis to:

1.   the Executive Secretary of the United Nations Framework Convention on Climate Change ("UNFCCC") for conveyance to the President of the 27th Conference of the Parties to the UNFCCC;

2.   the Secretary of the Intergovernmental Panel on Climate Change Secretariat ("IPCC");

3.   the Secretary-General of the World Meteorological Organization ("WMO");

4.   the Executive Secretary of the Intergovernmental Science-Policy Platform and Biodiversity and Ecosystem Services ("IPBES"); and

5.   the Secretary-General of the International Maritime Organization ("IMO").

Dear Executive Secretary of UNFCCC Patricia Espinosa / Secretary of the IPCC Secretariat Abdalah Mokssit / Secretary-General of WMO Petteri Taalas / Executive Secretary of IPBES Dr Anne Larigauderie / Secretary-General of IMO Kitack Lim

At the 44th Antarctic Treaty Consultative Meeting (ATCM XLIV) held in Berlin, Germany, from 24 May to 2 June 2022, the Antarctic Treaty Consultative Parties recognised the important role of the Antarctic region in global climate processes, welcomed the Decadal Synopsis Report on Antarctic Climate Change and the Environment (ACCE report) by the Scientific Committee on Antarctic Research (SCAR) and showed concern about the effects and projected changes to Antarctic environments resulting from climate change outlined in the Decadal Synopsis.

In light of the above, I am pleased to send you the ACCE report. I also kindly request the Executive Secretary of the UNFCCC, Patricia Espinosa, to convey this report to the President of the 27th Conference of the Parties to the UNFCCC, Sameh Shoukry.

Yours sincerely,

Tania von Uslar-Gleichen
Chair of ATCM XLIV

Decision 5 (2022)

Information Exchange Requirements

The Representatives,

Noting Articles III (1)(a) and VII (5) of the Antarctic Treaty;

Conscious of the obligations to exchange information as contained in the Protocol on Environmental Protection to the Antarctic Treaty ("the Protocol") and its Annexes;

Conscious of Decisions of the Antarctic Treaty Consultative Meeting ("ATCM") in relation to the information to be exchanged by Parties;

Desiring to ensure that the exchange of information by Parties is conducted in the most efficient and timely manner;

Desiring also that the information to be exchanged by Parties be readily identified to maximise its utility;

Recalling Decision 4 (2012), which decided that the Parties would use the Electronic Information Exchange System ("EIES") to exchange information in accordance with the Antarctic Treaty and the Protocol and its Annexes and which specified that Parties would continue to work with the Secretariat of the Antarctic Treaty ("the Secretariat") to refine and improve the EIES;

Noting that Decision 4 (2012) requires Parties to update relevant sections of the EIES regularly throughout the year, in order that such information be made available and accessible to Parties as soon as practicable;

Decide:

1.   that the Annex to this Decision represents a consolidated list of the information agreed to be exchanged by Parties;

2.   to request the Secretariat to modify the EIES to reflect the information contained in the Annex to this Decision; and

3.   that the Annex to Decision 7 (2021) is no longer current.

Information exchange requirements

1. Pre-season Information
The following information should be submitted as early as possible, preferably by 1 October, and in any event no later than the start of the activities being reported.

1.1 Operational information
1.1.1 National Expeditions

A. Stations
Names of stations (giving region, latitude and longitude), seasonality, operating period (for seasonal), status, maximum population, and medical support available. Names of refuges (giving region, latitude and longitude), medical facilities, and accommodation capacity. Other major field activities, *eg*, scientific traverse (giving locations).

B. Non-Military Ships
Name of non-military ships, ice strength, country of registry, number of voyages, planned departure dates, areas of operation, ports of departure and arrival to and from Antarctica, and purpose of voyage. Maximum crew, maximum passengers.

C. Non-Military Aircraft
Type of non-military aircraft, planned number of flights, period of flights or planned departure dates for inter-continental flights, purpose. Maximum crew, maximum passengers.

D. Research Rockets
Coordinates of the place of launching, time and date/period, direction of launching, planned maximum altitude, impact area, type and specifications of rockets, purpose and title of research project.

E. Military
- Number of military personnel (officers and enlisted) in expeditions.
- Number and types of armaments.
- Information on military equipment, if any, not included in Section 3.2.D below, including its site name, coordinates (latitude and longitude), type of equipment, and purpose of equipment.
- Ship: Name of military ship, ice strength, number of voyages, planned departure dates, areas of operation, ports of departure and arrival to and from Antarctica, and purpose of voyage. Maximum crew, maximum passengers.
- Aircraft: Type of military aircraft, planned number of flights, period of flights or planned departure dates for inter-continental flights, and purpose. Maximum crew, maximum passengers.

1.1.2 Non-governmental Expeditions[i]
A. Vessel-based Operations
Name of operator, name of vessel, maximum crew, maximum passengers, country of registry of vessel, number of voyages, expedition leader, planned departure dates, ports of departure and arrival to and from Antarctica, areas of operation including the names of proposed visited sites and the planned dates at which these visits will take place, type of activity, whether these visits include landing, (optionally) duration of landing and the number of visitors that participate in each of the specific activities.

B. Land-based Operations

Name of expedition, name of the operator, method of transportation to, from and within Antarctica, type of adventure/activity, location/s of activities and/or routes, dates of expedition, number of personnel involved, contact address, web-site address.

C. Aircraft Activities
Name of operator, type of aircraft, number of flights, period of flights, departure date per flight, departure and arrival location per flight, route per flight, purpose per flight, and number of passengers.

D. Denial of Authorizations
Name of vessel and/or expedition, name of operator, date, reason for denial.

1.2 Visits to Protected Areas
Name and number of protected area, number of people permitted to visit, date/period and purpose.

2. Annual Report
The following information should be submitted as early as possible after the end of the austral summer season, but in all cases before 1 October, with a reporting period of 1 April to 30 March.

2.1. Scientific Information

2.1.1. Forward Plans[ii]
Details of strategic or multi-year science plans or contact point for printed version. List of planned participations in major, international, collaborative science programmes/projects.

2.1.2. Science Activities in Previous Year
List of research projects undertaken in previous year under science discipline (giving location(s), principal investigator, project name or number, discipline and main activity/remarks).

2.2. Operational information

2.2.1. National expeditions
Update of information given under 1.1.1.

2.2.2. Non-governmental expeditions
Update of information given under 1.1.2 plus, for section 1.1.2.A and B: total amount of passengers transported in each journey, total number of crew members on board in each journey and combined activity for section A, B and C. Information on unusual incidents for sections A, B and C, including type of unusual incident occurred (affected people, environment and/or materials/assets), date, place, from whom assistance was received and contact point for more information on the incident (operator or a member of the National Programme or whoever the competent authority considered).

2.3. Permit Information

2.3.1. Visits to Protected Areas
Update of information provided under 1.2.

2.3.2. Taking and harmful interference with flora and fauna
Permit number, permit period, species, location, amount, sex, age and purpose[iii].

2.3.3. Introduction of non-native species

Permit number, permit period, species, location, amount, purpose[iv], removal or disposal.

2.4. Environmental Information

2.4.1. Compliance with the Protocol[v]
Description of measure, date of effect.

2.4.2. Contingency Plans
Title of Contingency Plan(s) for oil spills and other environmental emergencies, copies
(PDFs) or contact point for printed versions.

2.4.3. List of IEEs and CEEs[vi]
List of IEEs/CEEs undertaken during year giving proposed activity, (optionally)
period/length, location, level of assessment and decision taken.

2.4.4. Monitoring activities report[vii]
Name of activity, location, procedures put in place, significant information obtained, action
taken in consequence thereof.

2.4.5. Waste Management Plans
Title, name of site/vessel, copy (PDF) or contact point for printed version.
Report on implementation of waste management plans during the year.

2.4.6. Measures taken to implement the provisions of Annex V[viii]
Description of measures.

2.4.7. Procedures relating to EIAs
Description of appropriate National Procedures.

2.4.8. Prevention of marine pollution[ix]
Description of measures.

3. Permanent Information
The following information can be updated at any time.

3.1. Science Facilities

3.1.1 Automatic Recording Stations/Observatories
Site name, coordinates (latitude and longitude), elevation (m), parameters recorded,
observation frequency, reference number *(eg,* WMO no.).

3.2 Operational Information
A. Stations
Name of stations (giving region, latitude and longitude), status, seasonality, date
established, accommodation and medical facilities.
Names of refuges (giving region, latitude and longitude), medical facilities, and
accommodation capacity.

B. Non-Military Ships
Name of non-military ships, country of registry, ice strength, maximum crew,
maximum passengers.

C. Non-Military Aircraft
Type of non-military aircraft, maximum crew, maximum passengers.

D. Military
- Number of military personnel (officers and enlisted)
- Number and types of armaments.
- Information on military equipment, if any, not already reported in the EIES, including its site name, coordinate (latitude and longitude), type of equipment, and purpose.
- Ship: Name of military ship, ice strength, maximum crew, maximum passengers.
- Aircraft: Type of military aircraft, maximum crew, maximum passengers.

3.3 Environmental Information

3.3.1 Waste Management Plans
Title of Plan, site/vessel, copy (PDF) or contact point for printed version.

3.3.2 Contingency Plans
Title of Contingency Plan(s) for Oil Spills and other environmental emergencies, copies (PDFs) or contact point for printed versions.

3.3.3 Inventory of Past Activities
Name of station/base/field camp/traverse/crashed aircraft/etc., coordinates (latitude and longitude), period during which activity undertaken, description/purpose of activities undertaken, description of equipment or facilities remaining.

3.3.4 Compliance with the Protocol[x]
Description of measure, date of effect.

3.3.5 Procedures relating to EIAs
Same as 2.4.7.

3.3.6 Prevention of marine pollution
Same as 2.4.8.

3.3.7 Measures taken to implement the provisions of
Annex V. Same as 2.4.6.

3.4 Other Information

3.4.1 Relevant National Legislation
Description of law, regulation, administrative action or other measure, date of effect/enacted, giving copy (PDF) or contact point for printed version.

[i] provision of information on Non-governmental expeditions will be allowed for it to be provided as soon as possible after completion of national processes, with the relevant timing description being: 'as soon as possible following completion of national processes, preferably by the pre-season target date of 1 October, and no later than the start of the activity'.

[ii] optional provision of information on Forward plans will be allowed at any time, for example when domestic plans are completed or updated.

[iii] purpose with reference to Article 3 of Annex II to the Protocol.

[iv] purpose with reference to Article 4 of Annex II to the Protocol.

[v] new measures adopted during past year in accordance with Article 13 of the Protocol on Environmental Protection to the Antarctic Treaty including the adoption of laws and regulations, administrative actions and enforcement measures.

vi information on IEEs and CEEs is encouraged to be provided 'as soon as domestic processes are concluded, while maintaining the existing deadline for Parties to submit the information'.

vii Monitoring activities connected with activities subject to initial and comprehensive environmental evaluations (referred to in Protocol Annex I, Art. 6.1 c).

viii Information on measures taken to implement Annex V including site inspections and any steps taken to address instances of activities in contravention of the provisions of ASPA or ASMA management plans.

ix Measures to ensure that any warship, naval auxiliary or other ship owned or operated by a State and used, for the time being, only on government non-commercial service acts in a manner consistent, so far as is reasonable and practicable, with the Annex.

x Measures adopted in accordance with Article 13 of the Protocol on Environmental Protection to the Antarctic Treaty including the adoption of laws and regulations, administrative actions and enforcement measures.

3. Resolutions

Resolution 1 (2022)

Revised Guidelines for the assessment and management of Heritage in Antarctica

The Representatives,

Recalling that Article 8 of Annex V to the Protocol on Environmental Protection to the Antarctic Treaty ("the Protocol") provides for sites or monuments of recognised historic value to be listed as Historic Sites and Monuments ("HSM"), which "shall not be damaged, removed or destroyed";

Recalling also Measure 23 (2021), which adopted the reformatted List of HSM;

Recalling further Resolution 3 (2009), which recommended that the Guidelines for the designation and protection of HSM be used by Parties as guidance on questions related to the designation, protection and preservation of historic sites, monuments, artefacts and other historic remains in Antarctica;

Recalling furthermore Resolution 2 (2018), which recommended that the non-mandatory Guidelines for the assessment and management of Heritage in Antarctica be used by Parties as additional guidance on questions related to the assessment and management of sites/objects with heritage values in Antarctica;

Noting the growing expertise in the management of Antarctic heritage values;

Desiring to support Parties, where appropriate, to develop Conservation Management Plans to appropriately balance environmental protection and heritage conservation considerations in the management of HSM;

Welcoming the work of the Committee for Environmental Protection ("CEP") to develop guidance for conservation management planning for HSM, for inclusion in the Guidelines for the assessment and management of Heritage in Antarctica;

Recommend that their Governments:

1.   replace the Guidelines annexed to Resolution 2 (2018) with the Guidelines for the assessment and management of Heritage in Antarctica annexed to this Resolution;

2.   use the revised Guidelines as additional guidance on questions related to the assessment and management of sites/objects with heritage values in Antarctica; and

3.   request the Secretariat of the Antarctic Treaty to post the text of Resolution 2 (2018) on its website in a way that makes clear that it is no longer current.

Guidelines for the assessment and management of Heritage in Antarctica

1. Introduction

The aim of this document is to provide Parties with some guidance and support in the process of assessing and determining whether a site/object should be managed as heritage, including whether it merits Historic Site and Monument (HSM) listing, both in the context of Annex V and Annex III to the Protocol on Environmental Protection to the Antarctic Treaty (Environment Protocol). Furthermore, it aims to provide guidance as how the heritage site/object can best be managed once a conclusion has been reached. The guidance is non-mandatory, but provides points to consider when a Party or Parties begin to consider HSM listing or other methods of protection for a particular object or site.

The guidance seeks to assist the Committee for Environmental Protection (CEP) and Parties in reaching the following overarching vision:

"To recognise, manage, conserve and promote Antarctic heritage for the benefit of current and future generations."

These guidelines take into account that it is essential that the needs of protecting the Antarctic environment, as set out in the Environment Protocol, are appropriately balanced with the desire to protect important heritage sites and objects.

Article 8 of Annex V to the Environment Protocol provides that any sites or monuments of recognised historic value can be proposed for listing as a Historic Site and Monument (HSM), which shall not be damaged, removed or destroyed.

Resolution 3 (2009) contains *Guidelines for the designation and protection of Historic Sites and Monuments*, and provides guidance to Parties on questions related to the designation, protection and preservation of historic sites, monuments, artefacts and other historic remains in Antarctica. These guidelines provide further guidance as to the implementation of Resolution 3 (2009).

The CEP must consider all HSM proposals, which ultimately must be agreed by the Antarctic Treaty Consultative Parties at an Antarctic Treaty Consultative Meeting (ATCM). No further measures are required or specified in the Environment Protocol or through measures adopted by the Antarctic Treaty Parties. The current document does however provide guidance as to potential and relevant management efforts for a heritage site or object, whether listed as HSM or maintained as a general site or object of historic interest.

This document should be regarded as guidance only, to aid in ensuring that all relevant aspects have been considered appropriately and sufficiently in the process leading up to the decision whether to propose an object or site as an HSM or not. Sites, including any objects they contain, considered for HSM listing will have different qualities, past, current or future pressures and management challenges associated with them, and the specific circumstances will need to be taken into account in any listing process.

In addition to the guidance provided to the proponent(s), it is the long-term aim that this document will contribute a degree of consistency within and comparability between assessment processes (while recognising that each potential HSM will have its own requirements and dynamics), and ensure that the process is sufficiently documented for future reference.

The following materials are relevant reference and framework documents for these guidelines:

- Annex V to the Environment Protocol (specifically Article 8);
- Annex III to the Environment Protocol;
- Resolution 3 (2009) on Guidelines for the designation and protection of Historic Sites and Monuments;

- Resolution 5 (2001) on handling of pre-1958 historic remains; and Resolution 5 (2011) providing a revised Guide to the presentation of Working Papers containing proposals for Antarctic Specially Protected Areas, Antarctic Specially Managed Areas or Historic Sites and Monuments;

- Current list of Historic Sites and Monuments: https://ats.aq/devphBackEnd/api/export/hsm?lang=e

- Annex I to the Environment Protocol

An overview of other relevant background material and documents is included in Chapter 11.

2. Aim of guidelines

These guidelines constitute an element in the CEP's effort to reach the overarching vision of recognizing, managing, conserving and promoting Antarctic heritage for the benefit of current and future generations.

The aim of the material contained in these guidelines is to assist both those making an initial assessment of a potential heritage site/object, both in the context of Annex III and Annex V, and the CEP in evaluating submissions/proposals for new HSMs. The twin objectives of the guidance are:

- Objective 1: Provide guidance to decide whether a site/object should be managed as heritage, including whether it merits/requires/needs HSM listing.

- Objective 2: Provide guidance as to management options for HSMs and other heritage sites/objects.

Figure 1 provides an overview of the process described in this document, consisting of the following steps:

1. Consider whether an object/site has heritage value as specified in Resolution 3 (2009)[1];

2. Determine whether to list as HSM, preserve *ex situ* or plan for retaining for different reasons/removing;

3. All sites/objects listed as HSMs, should consider options for management, including additional protection through Treaty system mechanisms;

4. For listed HSMs and site/objects with other heritage values including any preserved *ex situ*, consider appropriate outreach/dissemination activities.

---

[1] Note: This document touches on the principles of considering heritage values, but does not attempt to provide full and comprehensive guidance to this complex and nationally/culturally framed issue.

Figure 1

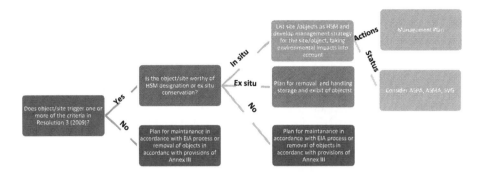

3. Heritage and historic values in the Antarctic context

Humans' presence in Antarctica is, seen in the global context, extremely short. Since the first sighting of the continent in 1820, the extent to which humans have left their mark here is relatively limited. In such a context, the limited historical evidence of a connection between man and land becomes extremely visible and special.

Parties gave full recognition to the historic sites, structures and objects as part of humankind's cultural heritage already at the first Antarctic Treaty Consultative Meeting in 1961.

The Environment Protocol makes the Historic Sites and Monuments (HSM) list[2] the key mechanism for the protection of historic values in Antarctica. The Environment Protocol provisions state that sites and monuments on the HSM list are to be protected from damage, removal or destruction.

Resolution 3 (2009) provides Parties with more detailed guidance on designation, protection and preservation of HSMs. Section 4.2 provides a further description and consideration of these guidelines. Resolution 3 (2009) remains key for determining whether a site meets the criteria for being listed an HSM.

In addition, Resolution 5 (2001) provides Parties with a mechanism for interim protection of pre-1958 historic artefacts/sites until they have had due time to consider their inclusion into HSM list.

The terms "site" and "monument" are fundamental terms in the framework provided by the Environment Protocol. These terms depend largely on national contexts and national legal frameworks, but the following basic definitions and descriptions, drawn on definitions supplied by the ICOMOS International Polar Heritage Committee (IPHC), are relevant to inform our understanding:

- **Site**: the setting in which a monument(s) occur(s) or where artefact(s) are located and which is directly related to the monument(s) or the artefact(s).

- **Object and artefacts**: Every item that is taken to Antarctica is an 'object' (a neutral term), but it may be formally ascribed with significance as an 'artefact' which gives it a heritage value.

---

[2] The HSM list was first introduced and agreed to at the fifth Antarctic Treaty Consultative Meeting (ATCM) in 1968

- **Monument**: all standing structures over the ground that have cultural heritage values.

- **Memorials or commemorative objects**: Memorials are established with the aim of ascribing significance to people, events or cultural traditions and include endeavours associated with achievement, loss and sacrifice. Memorials range from plaques and artworks to philanthropic trusts, which fund ongoing research. They may also be associated with a research institute, community facility or religious structure. An existing artefact or structure can be ascribed memorial status.

4. Determining and assessing heritage and historical values

4.1. Determining whether an object or site has heritage value as specified in Resolution 3 (2009)

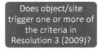

Ahead of assessing any object/site for HSM listing it is assumed that the proposing Party will have made a preliminary assessment to determine whether an object or site has potential heritage value, and should thus be further considered in line with guidance provided in this document, or whether it is simply material with no heritage value remaining from past activities that therefore requires removal from Antarctica in accordance with Annex III to the Environment Protocol.

In many cases this will be obvious, with a clear difference between objects/sites that should be considered worthy of management as heritage versus what can essentially be considered waste. It is to be assumed that the vast majority of objects present in Antarctica should fall under the latter, and thus be removed when their utility in Antarctica has expired.

In a small number of cases the object or site may have heritage value, connoting a product, place, or such that evokes a nostalgic sense of tradition or history, informing us about the past in general terms, and providing tangible evidence of the continuity between past, present, and future.

In making such a preliminary assessment, the process would greatly benefit by drawing on appropriate expertise and stakeholder engagement. See Chapter 11 for information about potential relevant expert resources.

If it is determined that the object/site merits further consideration then Parties should look to Article 8 of Annex V to the Environment Protocol, which very broadly identifies "recognised historic value" as the criterion for listing an HSM. However, Parties have agreed that an object or site having a "recognised historic value" should meet at least one of the criteria[3] listed in Annex to Resolution 3 (2009). The criteria listed in Resolution 3 (2009) are further described and explored below in order to provide guidance in the assessment process. For heritage dating before 1958, Resolution 5 (2001) should be noted and considered.

If the assessment process determines that an object/site does not require consideration for further protection, then these objects should be considered and handled in light of the clean-up provisions of Annex III to the Environment Protocol and supporting documents such as the Antarctic Clean-up Manual (adopted through Resolution 2 (2013)).

---

[3] Cf. Annex to Resolution 3 (2009): Guidelines for the designation and protection of Historic Sites and Monuments

4.2. Guidance to the evaluation criteria contained in Resolution 3 (2009)

The ATCM has, through Resolution 3 (2009), adopted a set of criteria, which provide an indication as to whether an object or site has a "recognised historic value." These are described and explored here in order to aid Parties in their assessment process.

1.   A particular event of importance in the history of science or exploration of Antarctica

Determining the importance of an event in history is both difficult and to a certain degree controversial due to the subjective nature of the issue. As a starting point, one should note that events could be considered those points in history when an act, decision or natural phenomenon altered or informed the direction of a community's evolution, in this case the human occupation of Antarctica being the community evolution. Events are typically not spread over a long time – they are rather sharp and discrete moments. To guide assessment against this criterion it is relevant to consider the following:

- Can the event be defined as a single, discrete event that can also be seen as the inaugural moment of events and activities that follow – and that can be seen as describing the history of that particular theme?

- Does this event have relevance for many people or nations?

- Can the event be connected to a specific site or place?

Historic Site and Monument No. 80 (Amundsen's Tent) is an example from the current list of HSMs that trigger this "event" criterion.

2.   A particular association with a person who played an important role in the history of science or exploration in Antarctica

Individuals of historical significance can typically be either those whose life's work helped define and guide the course of Antarctic history or those whose lives stand as examples for the community. To guide assessment against this criterion it is relevant to consider the following:

- Did the person make, invent or devise an idea or product that was and has continued to be used in the Antarctic context (and possibly outside) that had an impact on the evolution of Antarctica?

- Can the person be said to be representative of an Antarctic activity?

In doing the assessment, the following should also be considered:

- The length of the person or group's influence on/in the Antarctic context.

- The number of people or nation having a connection to the activities of the individual or group.

- Connections to extant site, that is, are there major extant site connections that still exist where the person lived and worked, or is the person buried at an Antarctic site?

Historic Site and Monument No. 3 (Mawson's Rock Cairn) is an example from the current list of HSMs that trigger this "person" criterion.

3.   A particular association with a notable feat of endurance or achievement

This criterion is similar in nature to criterion 1 and the same factors should be considered, although firmly in the context of a notable feat of endurance:

- Feat: an achievement that requires great courage, skill, or strength

- Endurance: the ability to endure an unpleasant or difficult process or situation without giving way

Historic Site and Monument No. 53 (Endurance Memorial Site) is an example from the current list of HSMs that trigger this "feat" criterion.

4.   *Representative of, or forms part of, some wide-ranging activity that has been important in the development and knowledge of Antarctica*

This criterion is similar in nature to criterion 2 and the same factors should be considered, although firmly in the context of increasing knowledge about Antarctica or the wider world. This could for example be a site/object linked to or representative of a particular scientific discovery.

Historic Site and Monument No. 42 (Scotia Bay huts) is an example from the current list of HSMs that trigger this "activity" criterion.

5.   *Particular technical, historical, cultural or architectural value in its materials, design or method of construction*

This criterion aims to consider whether the place or object demonstrates innovative or important methods of construction or design, whether it contains unusual construction materials, is an early example of the use of a particular construction technique or has the potential to contribute information about technological or engineering history. Questions that can help clarify and inform assessments in this regard include:

- Is the place significant because of its design, form, scale, materials, style, ornamentation, period, craftsmanship or other architectural element?

- Does the place demonstrate innovative or important methods of construction or design, does it contain unusual construction materials, is it an early example of the use of a particular construction technique, or does it have the potential to contribute information about technological or engineering history?

- Does the place have integrity, retaining significant features from its time of construction, or later periods when important modifications or additions were carried out?

- Is the site or area a good example of its class, for example, in terms of design, type, features, use, technology or time period?

Historic Site and Monument No. 83 (Base "W", Detaille Island, Lallemand Fjord, Loubet Coast) is an example from the current list of HSMs that trigger this "construction" criterion.

6.   *Potential, through study, to reveal information or has the potential to educate people about significant human activities in Antarctica*

Artefacts and sites can offer an insight into technological processes, economic development and social structure, etc, and thereby provide a broader understanding of both the times that were as well as the present:

- Does the area or place (where the artefact/s is/are located) have the potential to provide scientific information about the history of Antarctica?

- Is the object/site of high real or potential interest to scholars and/or archaeologists?

- Does the object/site hold the potential for new scholarship in a field of study?

- Does the object/site have the potential to make a significant and lasting contribution to a field of study?

- Could the place contribute, through public education, to people's awareness, understanding and appreciation of Antarctica, including exploration and scientific achievement?

Historic Site and Monument No. 4 (Pole of Inaccessibility Station building) is an example from the current list of HSMs that trigger this "study" criterion.

7.   *Symbolic or commemorative value for people of many nations*

With all the other criteria discussed above in mind it is useful to consider the extent to which the values identified are most relevant to the broader Antarctic community. As mentioned above the importance of national heritage should be evaluated in the context of broader significance, considering its importance in the wider history of humankind's activities in Antarctica and/or relevance to several nation states.

Historic Site and Monument No. 82 (Antarctic Treaty Monument) is an example from the current list of HSMs that trigger this "symbolic for many" criterion.

4.3.   Determining whether values merit Historic Site and Monument Listing

Having assessed the various heritage values attached to the site/object against the criteria set out in Resolution 3 (2009) the proponents will have a clear view on whether the site/object should be conserved.

If it is not clear whether it should be conserved then parties responsible for the site/object will need to consider whether it should i) be maintained in Antarctica for a different purpose with the environmental impacts of doing so appropriately assessed; or ii) removed from the continent under the terms of Annex III.

Where it is determined that the site/object should be conserved the next step is to consider whether to seek HSM listing for protection *in situ* in Antarctica or whether is more suited to being preserved *ex situ*.

5. Consider in situ or ex situ conservation

5.1. *In situ* vs. *ex situ* preservation

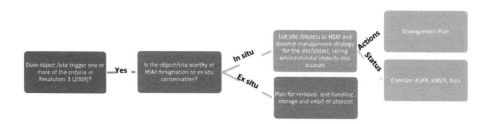

When it has been determined that an object or site has heritage and/or historic value it is time to consider appropriate approaches and needs for protection. First in line in this regard is to consider whether the value is best maintained by leaving it in place in Antarctica or by moving it or by other means maintain the value outside of Antarctica.

The potential environmental impacts must be considered appropriately both when assessing whether to maintain the object *in situ* and when to maintain *ex situ*, this to ensure that the environmental principles set out in Article 3 (2) of the Environment Protocol are respected. It may often be appropriate to do so through an environmental impact assessment (EIA) process as set out in Article 8 (and Annex I) of the Environment Protocol. See "Section 12 – Resources" for examples of EIAs related to HSMs.

Most often it is natural to maintain any fixed objects (such as infrastructure) associated with the site *in situ*, although in some instances it may be more appropriate and relevant to remove and restructure such objects *ex situ* (for example by relocating to a museum).

Any movable objects, on the other hand, can be maintained both *in situ* and *ex situ*. There can be both advantages and disadvantages to both approaches.

- *Relevance to the setting*: The object can best/only be understood and appreciated in full in its original setting (e.g. coldness, isolation, and wilderness).

- *Local interest and enthusiasm for protection*: Heritage belonging to or 'adopted' by a local population (i.e. a nearby Station) will normally be adequately cared for.

- *Long-term maintenance expenditure and resource usage*: Although there could be short term saving of resources by not moving the object, adequate maintenance over time will normally be costly (logistics and conservation resources).

- *A smaller audience*: The visitation potential for sites and objects in remote locations will never match more central locations.

- *Local interest (and therefore care) may be less than interest shown from outside*: No or limited number of people in the area will make heritage maintenance dependent on continued high interest from temporary populations.

Considerations that may guide a decision as to whether *ex situ* conservation or *in situ* protection of fixed and movable objects would be most appropriate include:

- *Ex situ* conservation may be relevant and appropriate if the objects are at risk from natural degradation processes.

- *Ex situ* conservation may be relevant and appropriate if it is obvious that it will be too costly or difficult to maintain the objects *in situ* over time.

- An assessment of how important it is that the object can be seen and appreciated by a large number of people could be useful in considering *ex situ* vs. *in situ*.

- *Ex situ* conservation may be relevant and appropriate if the objects are located in a particularly sensitive environment where protection of this environment may be a higher priority. Preserving *in situ* may be relevant and appropriate if there is a high risk of damage were objects to be removed.

- The ability (logistically and financially) to maintain objects *in situ* will have bearings on the decision.

- If an object cannot be portrayed appropriately in a contextual setting and the object loses its value by being removed from its surroundings, it may be more appropriate to consider protection *in situ* rather than removal for *ex situ* conservation.

- If it has been shown through an appropriate assessment that the existing suite of Antarctic HSMs already adequately covers the value of the object in question, it may be useful to consider *ex situ*. However, if the object/site is considered representative (e.g. examples of an important class of significant items) or rare (unusual aspect of Antarctic history or heritage), where no similar object/site is listed, it may be more appropriate to consider *in situ* maintenance.

In cases where highly important heritage objects are in danger, copies may be made while the original is inaccessible. A foreign *ex situ* setting may be partly alleviated by using various effects to give an impression of the original setting.

Removal of objects for *ex situ* conservation should only occur after having consulted and agreed with all Parties that have or may have a connection to or interest in the object at hand, as well as on basis of assessment and advice from heritage expertise. This is particularly important as legal and other related issues may arise in terms of the origin or ownership of an object or artefact.

5.2.   Documentation

If it is determined that *ex situ* conservation may be most appropriate, a thorough documentation of the site is advisable for it to be available in archive form. Rigorous documentation provides a means by which scholars and the public comprehend a site that has since changed radically or disappeared.

New technologies have opened up new opportunities in the process of documenting historic heritage. Filming, 3D scanning, photography, interviews and storage of archival records are all accepted recording methods.

With modern technology it is possible to create virtual realities, used *inter alia* to avoid impacts or to provide "access" to remote and inaccessible sites.

6. *Historic Site or Monument Listing*

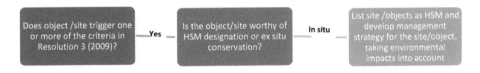

Once a site/object has been determined to trigger one or more of the criteria of Resolution 3 (2009) a decision must be made as to whether the object should be managed as a heritage value associated with national operations or whether it merits listing as an HSM. The strength of the value (against the HSM criteria in Resolution 3 (2009)) will likely have provided substantial basis for making this decision. Some details regarding how the assessment and potential listing process is achieved are provided below.

Article 8 (2) of Annex V to the Environment Protocol stipulates that any Party may propose a site or monument of recognised historic value for listing as an HSM, to be approved by the ATCM.

The following steps are useful to follow to determine and propose an object or site as an HSM:

- **Step 1**: Assess site/object – cf. Section 3 and 4.

- **Step 2**: Decide whether HSM listing is appropriate.

- **Step 3**: Consult with Parties with an interest in the site/object in question in accordance with Resolution 4 (1996) and reiterated in Resolution 3 (2009), which stipulates that during the preparations for the Listing of an HSM, adequate liaison is accorded by the proposing Party with the originator of the HSM and other Parties, as appropriate.

- **Step 4**: In cooperation with interested Parties, develop management framework.

- **Step 5**: Prepare and submit proposal to the CEP. The following information should be included in the proposal in a format that can be easily moved into the formal HSM list[4]:

Introduction
- *HSM name*
- *Original proposing Party:* List proponent(s)
- *Party undertaking management:* Name the country/countries which are committed to following-up (with management approach specified for the object/site)
- *Type:* Building (hut, station, other building remains etc.), site, other remains (expedition cairn, tent, lighthouse, etc.) or monument/commemorative (plaque, bust)

Description and documentation of the site
- *Site Location*: Provide both place name and coordinates (where known) relevant for site/object. Describe materials, construction, function, use. Physical Features & Local/cultural landscape. Provide pictures showing the site, monument and the location in the surroundings.

Historical / Cultural features
- *Description of the historical context*: Overview of the site in question. It would be useful if the information also clearly indicates which primary evaluation criteria contained in Resolution 3 (2009) the object/site in question triggers.

Management
- *Describe management and/or monitoring actions planned for the object/site in question – cf. Section 6 and 7, as well as pt. 5 in Annex to Resolution 3 (2009)*, as well as measures, which will be taken to limit any environmental impacts that the management of the HSM may cause.

- **Step 6**: In cooperation with interested Parties, implement management framework (cf. Section 7).

---

[4] The items here listed are in large part based on requirements contained in Resolution 3 (2009).

7. Determining management actions for an HSM

7.1 Methods of management

Once it has been determined that an object or site should be maintained *in situ* as an HSM, an assessment of its particular challenges and sensitivities is advisable, along with consideration of the options available for its management. In considering management approaches, it is also necessary to take into account the requirements of Annex I related to EIA as well as monitoring and mitigation measures. These elements are relevant as basis for the development of any management and/or conservation plan for the object or site.

"Minimal intervention" is an overarching aim in global heritage conservation. The decision that has to be made with regard to the site or object in question is whether a non-intervention approach or active management (some intervention) is to be the guiding light, balancing the need to protect the HSM with the environmental protection principles of the Environment Protocol.

In certain instances, it may be appropriate to allow a site, even though recognised as an important site, to be managed according to the principle of controlled deterioration, which is allowing natural decay to proceed with only limited protection. However, health, safety and environmental considerations usually make this impractical and some minimal maintenance is usually required in order to ensure a site is not dangerous for either humans or wildlife.

Active management involves people managing change to a significant place in its setting, in ways that sustain, reveal or reinforce its cultural and natural heritage values. Conservation is not limited to physical intervention, for it includes such activities as the interpretation and sustainable use of places. It may simply involve maintaining the status quo, intervening only as necessary to counter the effects of growth and decay, but equally may be achieved through major interventions; it can be active as well as reactive. Change to a significant place is inevitable, if only as a result of the passage of time, but can be neutral or beneficial in its effect on heritage values. It is only harmful if (and to the extent that) significance is eroded.

Issues to consider when determining what level and type of management action is required and desired include the following:

- Identification of the current use of the object and site and consideration of any need for an appropriate change of use;

- The condition of the object and any need for repair: Repair is work beyond the scope of normal maintenance, to remedy defects caused by decay, damage or use, and is normally carried out to sustain the significance of the building or place. Repairs should normally be done with minimal or no changes to the original fabric of the structure and in like materials, and if possible using the same methods as first created. Such work would greatly benefit by drawing on appropriate expertise.

- Actions needed to conserve or restore the object: Restoration indicates bringing an object back to a former position or condition. Focusing on conservation, the absolute maximum amount of the original material, in as unaltered a condition as possible, is preserved. Any repairs or additions must not remove, alter or permanently bond/cross-link to any original material. Such work would greatly benefit by drawing on appropriate expertise.

- Potential impacts on the environment that may arise from the deterioration of the object.

- Servicing needs.

- The costs of the various recommended measures.

- The likely resources available for the asset, both immediately and in the future.

- Education and outreach. Note, further guidance and examples provided in Section 9.

7.2. Supplementary management approaches

When considering how best to manage/maintain a site/object of historic heritage value there are a number of formal approaches that could be considered, some of which have formal status within the Treaty system and which afford various degrees of protection.

7.2.1. Conservation management plans

A Conservation Management Plan (CMP) can provide a useful guiding document for the conservation and management of a heritage site or object. Through such a plan it will be possible to identify what policies are required to ensure the heritage values of the site/object are retained in its future use and development. A CMP will also provide an important framework for ensuring that the management of the heritage site or object has the least possible impacts on the environment. Each CMP will vary and will need to be tailored to each site/object, based on the type and size of its place, heritage attributes and needs. A CMP provides guidance in managing change in the heritage site or object without compromising the heritage significance of its place.

At its most basic, conservation management planning is a valuable tool to enable a greater understanding of heritage. Questions concerning significance, interpretation, threats and risks, opportunities for improvements and potential for use are all considered during the process and the answers should create a better understanding and a clear plan for its future.

A considerable amount of information has been published which can inform good decision-making for heritage management, and there are many exemplars of excellent heritage stewardship from Antarctica and around the world (see references).

The guidance contained in Appendix A, informed by international standards and best practice, offers suggestions on what might be included in a CMP. This guidance is not intended to be a template nor to provide a strict set of instructions. Each HSM will be different and may require its own approach. It should be noted that a CMP may not be appropriate for every HSM; it's important that the approach is fit for purpose.

7.2.2. Site Guidelines for Visitors (SGV)

The Antarctic Treaty Parties have since 2005 developed and utilised Site Guidelines for Visitors as a management tool. The aim of the guidelines is to provide specific instructions on the conduct of activities at the most frequently visited Antarctic sites. This includes practical guidance for tour operators and guides on how they should conduct visits in those sites, taking into account their environmental values and sensitivities. SGV are developed based on the current levels and types of visits at each specific site, and such SGV would require review if there were any significant changes to the levels or types of visits to a site. Heritage and historic values at highly visited areas may benefit from the development of specific SGVs, whether formally adopted as HSMs or not, and in this manner guide visitors' activities in this area to reduce potential for negative impact, damage and destruction.

Relevant examples of such SGV include:

- SGV No. 8: Paulet Island[5]
- SGV No. 14: Snow Hill[6]
- SGV No. 17: Whalers Bay[7]

7.2.3. Antarctic Specially Protected Areas (ASPA)

Article 3 (1) of Annex V to the Environment Protocol specifies that any area may be designated as an ASPA to protect *inter alia* outstanding historic values. According to Article 8 of Annex V sites or monuments that are designated as ASPAs shall also be listed as HSMs. Managing the site as an ASPA would give added value through the development and adoption of a formal management plan for the area, as well as requiring permits for entry into the area. Such a management approach may be particularly useful in situations where it is important to regulate, limit or control visitor pressure.

Guidance material is already available for the designation process for ASPAs:

- ASPA No. 155: Cape Evans, Ross Island[8]
- ASPA No. 158: Hut Point, Ross Island[9]
- ASPA No. 162: Mawson's Huts, Cape Denison, Commonwealth Bay, George V Land, East Antarctica[10]

7.2.4. Antarctic Specially Managed Areas (ASMA)

Article 3 (1) in Annex V to the Environment Protocol specifies that any area may be designated as an ASMA to protect *inter alia* outstanding historic values. According to Article 8 of Annex V sites or monuments which are designated as ASMAs shall also be listed as HSMs. Managing the site as an ASMA would give added value through the development and adoption of a formal management plan for the area. Such a management approach may be particularly useful in situations where there are a number of ongoing, potentially competing activities and interests, where coordination is required to ensure appropriate control of activities in order not to put the historic values of the area at risk.

Guidance material is already available for the designation process for ASMAs:

- ASMA No. 4: Deception Island[11]
- ASMA No. 5: Amundsen-Scott South Pole Station, South Pole[12]

8. Environmental Considerations

It is important to take environmental issues into account throughout the process for assessing a potential heritage site/object; indeed environmental considerations should be at the forefront of thinking on how to handle a site/object.

As noted, assessment of environmental impacts of actions and decisions taken are needed throughout the assessment process, and it is likely that the relevant member will find it necessary to complete an EIA at some point in the process. Not only is an EIA likely to be a

---

[5] https://guidelines.ats.aq/GuideLinePDF/ea07581b-ee37-49bf-94c3-68dd20fef6a9/8_Paulet_2018_e.pdf
[6] https://guidelines.ats.aq/GuideLinePDF/974720a7-faaf-417c-a40a-40584bf98c51/14_Snow_2019_e.pdf
[7] https://guidelines.ats.aq/GuideLinePDF/30c44ada-60be-404c-9665-331b79c81ecf/17_Whalers_2018_e.pdf
[8] http://www.ats.aq/documents/recatt/att572_e.pdf
[9] http://www.ats.aq/documents/recatt/att574_e.pdf
[10] http://www.ats.aq/documents/recatt/att549_e.pdf
[11] http://www.ats.aq/documents/recatt/Att512_e.pdf
[12] http://www.ats.aq/documents/recatt/Att357_e.pdf

formal requirement for many actions described in these guidelines but it can also be a useful tool.

Clearly the impact on wildlife (and the wider ecosystem) will need to be seriously considered under all scenarios. Clean up, which will be the primary outcome for most sites of human activity, and indeed *ex situ* preservation (which will require objects to be removed from a site) will both require careful environmental assessment and planning.

Meanwhile different conservation options will also require varying degrees of environmental assessment, with the option of natural decay for example needing particularly careful appraisal.

The decision on when and to what level an EIA is required will need to be determined on a case-by-case basis but this decision should be done in the context of the continual review of the environmental impacts.

When initiating and conducting an EIA process, reference should as appropriate be made to and guidance taken from Annex I of the Environment Protocol and the Guidelines for Environmental Impact Assessment in Antarctica (as adopted by Resolution 1 (2016)).

If and when an EIA has been completed as part of an assessment process leading to an HSM proposal, it would be helpful to the CEP if proponents were to reference the conclusions of the EIA in the Working Paper presenting the proposal for consideration by the CEP.

9. Education and outreach

Whatever the form of protection determined necessary for individual sites/objects it is essential that appropriate methods of outreach are considered. Given that only around 40,000 tourists currently visit Antarctica every year, it is clear that Antarctic heritage is not and will not be accessible to the wider public. While protecting heritage is important for its own sake, its value can diminish somewhat if it cannot be seen. This is partly why *ex situ* conservation in some instances should be given serious consideration, allowing people to view Antarctic heritage in a museum or some other form of public display. Likewise, this is also why *in situ* objects should form part of wider outreach and education process, considering that most people will not be able to experience the heritage on site. Many methods can be used to help alleviate the fact that not everyone can visit or see everything in person.

Some of the tools described in Chapter 5.2 make this process easier than it was in the past, with the details of HSMs now potentially available online to anyone who wishes to see them in the form of photos, video tours or digital maps, alongside more traditional approaches such as literature. It should also be possible to draw together records of the sites together with archival material and testimonials.

Proponents should consider building education and outreach into their management plans, making it an integral part of managing a heritage site/object. Parties should also consider outreach within their own countries, especially with children, to ensure the Antarctic heritage is shared and appreciated as widely as possible. Central to heritage management are ongoing outreach and education endeavours that inform and inspire the public about the values the specific Antarctic heritage carries with it. This enhancement is important when engaging the public with Antarctic heritage.

10. Terms/Acronyms

ATCM: Antarctic Treaty Consultative Meeting

CEP: Committee for Environmental Protection

HSM: Historic Site and Monument

Memorials or commemorative objects: Memorials are established with the aim of ascribing significance to people, events or cultural traditions and include endeavours associated with achievement, loss and sacrifice. Memorials range from plaques and artworks to philanthropic trusts, which fund ongoing research. They may also be associated with a research institute, community facility or religious structure. An existing artefact or structure can be ascribed memorial status.

Monument: All standing structures over the ground that have cultural heritage values.

Object and artefacts: Every item that is taken to Antarctica is an 'object' (a neutral term), but it may be formally ascribed with significance as an 'artefact' which gives it a heritage value.

Site: The setting in which a monument(s) occur(s) and which is directly related to the monuments.

11. References

11.1. ATCM decisions

- Resolution 4 (1996): https://www.ats.aq/devAS/Meetings/Measure?Length=4&id=237
- Resolution 3 (2009): https://www.ats.aq/devAS/Meetings/Measure?Length=4&id=444
- Measure 3 (2003): https://www.ats.aq/devAS/Meetings/Measure?Length=4&id=296
- Resolution 1 (2016): https://www.ats.aq/devAS/Meetings/Measure?Length=4&id=637
- Resolution 2 (2013) Antarctic Clean-up Manual: https://www.ats.aq/documents/recatt/att540_e.pdf

11.2. ATCM/CEP Documents

- ATCM XXXIII - WP 47 (Argentina): Proposal for the discussion of aspects related to the management of Historic Sites and Monuments
- ATCM XXXIV - WP 27 (Argentina): Report of the Informal Discussions on Historic Sites and Monuments
- ATCM XXXV - WP 46 (Argentina): Final Report of the Informal Discussions on Historic Sites and Monuments
- ATCM XXXIX - WP 12 (UK): Managing Antarctic Heritage: British Historic Bases in the Antarctic Peninsula
- ATCM XXXIX - WP 30 (Norway): Consideration of protection approaches for historic heritage in Antarctica
- ATCM XXXIII - IP 22 (Argentina): Additional information for the discussion of aspects related to the management of Historic Sites and Monuments

12. Resources

12.1. Organizations

- International Council on Monuments and Sites (ICOMOS): www.icomos.org/en
  - ICOMOS Australia. Burra Charter, 2013. http://australia.icomos.org/publications/burra-charter-practice-notes/
  - ICOMOS. The Nara Document on Authenticity, 1994. https://www.icomos.org/charters/nara-e.pdf
  - ICOMOS. Xi'an Declaration, 2005. https://www.icomos.org/xian2005/xian-declaration.pdf
  - ICOMOS. Charter for the Protection and Management of Archaeological Heritage, 1990. http://wp.icahm.icomos.org/wp-content/uploads/2017/01/1990-

Lausanne-Charter-for-Protection-and-Management-of-Archaeological-Heritage.pdf

- o ICOMOS' International Polar Heritage Committee (IPHC)

- ICOMOS: IPHC Statutes. http://iphc.icomos.org/index.php/statutes/

12.2. International agreements

- The UNESCO Convention on the Protection of the Underwater Cultural Heritage, 2001. http://www.unesco.org/new/en/culture/themes/underwater-cultural-heritage/2001-convention/

- The UNESCO Convention concerning the Protection of the World Cultural and Natural Heritage, 1972

12.3. General heritage literature

- Logan, W., M.C. Craith, and U. Kockel, eds. 2015. A Companion to Heritage Studies. Chichester. Wiley-Blackwell.

12.4. Case studies

- New Zealand. 2015. Ross Sea Heritage Restoration Project, Historic Huts at Cape Adare

- Russia. 2016. Restoration of the Buromsky Island Cemetery (HSM 9) within the programme of the Russian Antarctic Expedition activities.

12.5 Environmental Impact Assessments

- New Zealand. 2009. IEE. Removal of artefacts from historic sites in Antarctica for the purpose of restoration and protection.

- New Zealand. 2012. Initial Environmental Assessment Ross Sea Heritage Restoration

12.6 Conservation Management Planning

The content of external websites and other resources does not necessarily reflect the views of the Consultative Parties. Links to external websites are provided as a convenience and do not indicate an endorsement of any information contained on the linked sites.

Selected Bibliography

- Petzet, Michael. (2004) Principles of Preservation: An Introduction to the International Charters for Conservation and Restoration 40 years after the Venice Charter. https://www.icomos.org/venicecharter2004/petzet.pdf

- Semple Kerr, James. (2013) The Conservation Plan. 7th Edition. Australia ICOMOS https://australia.icomos.org/publications/the-conservation-plan/

Organisations

- The World Heritage Centre https://whc.unesco.org/

- International Council on Monuments and Sites https://www.icomos.org/

- http://openarchive.icomos.org/2146/

- https://www.iccrom.org/sites/default/files/2018-02/1998_feilden_management_guidelines_eng_70071_light_0.pdf

- UNESCO World Heritage Centre can provide detailed guidance and case studies of heritage management.

Existing Conservation Programmes for Antarctic HSMs

- UK Antarctic Heritage Trust
  http://www.ukaht.org

- NZ Antarctic Heritage Trust
  https://nzaht.org/

- Mawson's Huts
  http://www.antarctica.gov.au/environment/cultural-heritage/mawsons-huts-cape-denison

Appendix A: The approach to developing a Conservation Management Plan

The following guidance offers suggestions of the sort of information that may be useful to include in a CMP. While each of the sections below might not be relevant for every HSM, it can be a useful exercise to work through them. A good CMP can be divided into five sections, which can be as detailed or as brief as is appropriate. Photographs, illustrations, drawings, historical documents and maps are all extremely useful as supporting information.

1. **Description of the heritage**
    - Describe each of the different elements of the heritage on the site including artefacts, buildings, structures, vehicles, and archaeology, as relevant.
    - Describe the context of the heritage, explaining where it is and what is around it, including any important environment, wildlife or landscape elements.
    - Describe its condition, including completeness and repair status (individual details on this can be stored in an appendix).
    - Describe its history, including how it became to be there, and what has happened to it over time. Here is a good place to use historical sources to illustrate its story.
    - Describe how it relates more widely, including how it compares with other sites or events.
    - Describe how the heritage is currently looked after, how the site is managed and by whom.
    - Consider the use of digital referencing for the site and associated individual objects. This could aid future monitoring, as well as identification of artefacts for particular management actions.

2. **Significance of the heritage**
    - Describe what is important about this heritage, and to whom. It might be a whole site, or there may be elements within the site that have special significance. The description could include:
        - Whether the heritage is part of any wider designation (such as an ASPA or ASMA).
        - Historical associations - people, events, activities, stories.
        - Aesthetic value, if the heritage is an integral part of the visual landscape.
        - Scientific value – landscape, geology, wildlife, scientific data collection.
        - Rarity – is it, or are elements of it, unique or rare?
    - Describe clearly those elements that are crucial and cannot be lost or compromised.
    - Describe also elements of the heritage that might not be original. In the case of restorations, some elements will be historic, while others might be the result of modern interventions.
    - It would be useful to include summaries of archaeological reports, results of research, or other expert analysis that may contribute to the understanding of the heritage's significance.

3. **Risks and Opportunities**
    - Describe the ways in which the heritage might be vulnerable and any threats to its future survival. These could include:
        - Environmental risks: including from climate change and environmental conditions, as well as wildlife.
        - Ongoing science operations: if the site is still used or part of an operational site, operations may impact the heritage. There may be tensions between conservation and operation.
        - Resource requirements: are there sufficient financial resources and expertise to look after the heritage?

- o Access: consider whether the heritage site can easily be visited for inspection. Does the site receive large numbers of visitors, and what are the associated risks (wear and tear damage, theft, vandalism)?
- Describe any risks to the environment from deterioration of materials, or dispersal of fabric from the heritage.
- Describe particular hazards or hazardous materials. If the site deteriorates does it become more dangerous? Is access difficult or potentially dangerous?
- Describe also the opportunities for improving protection of the heritage, and creating better access to it. These could include:
  - o Considering whether conservation actions would improve the longevity of the site or elements of it.
  - o Considering whether visits could be better managed, including by improving safety or accessibility to the site, or improving the site's sustainability.
  - o Considering alternative ways to tell the site's story, such as by using digital technology to engage people virtually.

4. Managing the heritage - policies

- It is important to set out the policies that will guide actions and activities to manage the heritage. These policies may be as brief or comprehensive as needed, and will likely be guided by the level of intervention required to manage the heritage (which could range from minimal intervention to a full-scale conservation programme). As a minimum, it is important to set out the overarching aims for the future of the heritage (for example, to maintain and preserve the historic site, to provide a visitor experience, or to protect the whole site and its character). Clear aims and guiding policies will inform all future activity related to the heritage. Relevant policies may include:
  - o Conservation and repair – description of how the condition will be maintained, including any principles or guidelines that should be followed during repair or maintenance work.
  - o Access and visiting – how visits to the site should be managed, including any requirements for booking, supervision, and reporting.
  - o Health and safety – description of any policies for hazards, fire, disasters, or incident reporting.
  - o Managing the environment – policies for any environmental or wildlife considerations.
  - o Research – description of policies related to further surveys or study of the heritage (including archaeological, digital, geophysical, or ecological) and any constraints around the techniques to be used (use of RPAS, laser scanning, excavation).
  - o Climate change and environment – description of the vulnerability of the site to a changing climate and description of policies for mitigation or adaptation to the impacts of a changing climate.
  - o Documentation of interventions – description of how repairs and other measures taken to preserve, stabilise, or maintain the site and artefacts should be documented to keep a history of changes.
  - o Information – description of how information and data about the site will be managed (including where the information will be stored, and whether it will be made publicly available).

5. Appendices

- Supporting detailed information related to the conservation management of the heritage should be included in appendices. Any available data or information can be useful in understanding and managing the site. Helpful information could include data from archives, surveys, and research projects, action plans and reports, or images.

Resolution 2 (2022)

Site Guidelines for Visitors

The Representatives,

Recalling Resolutions 5 (2005), 2 (2006), 1 (2007), 2 (2008), 4 (2009), 1 (2010), 4 (2011), 4 (2012), 3 (2013), 4 (2014), 2 (2016), 1 (2018), 2 (2019) and 3 (2021) which adopted and updated lists of sites subject to Site Guidelines for Visitors ("Site Guidelines");

Believing that Site Guidelines enhance the provisions set out in the Guidance for those organising and conducting tourism and non-governmental activities in the Antarctic annexed to Recommendation XVIII-1 (1994);

Confirming that the term "visitors" does not include scientists conducting research within such sites, or individuals engaged in official governmental activities;

Noting that Site Guidelines have been developed based on the current levels and types of visits at each specific site, and aware that Site Guidelines would require review if there were any significant changes to the levels or types of visits to a site;

Believing that the Site Guidelines for each site must be reviewed and revised promptly in response to changes in the levels and types of visits, or in response to any demonstrable or likely environmental impacts;

Desiring to keep the list of sites subject to Site Guidelines and the Site Guidelines up to date;

Recommend to their Governments that:

1.   Wordie House, Winter Island be updated in the list of sites subject to Site Guidelines annexed to this Resolution and that the Site Guidelines for that site, as adopted by the Antarctic Treaty Consultative Meeting ("ATCM"), be added to the Site Guidelines;

2.   Torgersen Island, Arthur Harbor be removed from the list of Site Guidelines;

3.   the Secretariat of the Antarctic Treaty ("the Secretariat") update its website accordingly;

4.   all potential visitors are urged to ensure that they are fully conversant with and adhere to the relevant Site Guidelines; and

5.   the Secretariat post the text of Resolution 3 (2021) on its website in such a way that makes clear that it is no longer current.

List of sites subject to Site Guidelines

Site Guidelines	First Adopted	Latest Version
1. Penguin Island (Lat. 62° 06' S, Long. 57° 54' W)	2005	2005
2. Barrientos Island - Aitcho Islands (Lat. 62° 24' S, Long. 59° 47' W)	2005	2013
3. Cuverville Island (Lat. 64° 41' S, Long. 62° 38' W)	2005	2013
4. Jougla Point (Lat. 64° 50' S, Long. 63° 30' W)	2005	2013
5. Goudier Island, Port Lockroy (Lat. 64° 49' S, Long. 63° 29' W);	2006	2006
6. Hannah Point (Lat. 62° 39' S, Long. 60° 37' W)	2006	2013
7. Neko Harbour (Lat. 64° 50' S, Long. 62° 33' W)	2006	2013
8. Paulet Island (Lat. 63° 35' S, Long. 55° 47' W)	2006	2018
9. Petermann Island (Lat. 65° 10' S, Long. 64° 10' W)	2006	2013
10. Pleneau Island (Lat. 65° 06' S, Long. 64° 04' W)	2006	2013
11. Turret Point (Lat. 62° 05' S, Long. 57° 55' W)	2006	2006
12. Yankee Harbour (Lat. 62° 32' S, Long. 59° 47' W)	2006	2019
13. Brown Bluff, Tabarin Peninsula (Lat. 63° 32' S, Long. 56° 55' W)	2007	2018
14. Snow Hill Hut (Lat. 64° 21'50'' S, Long. 56° 59'31'' W)	2007	2019
15. Shingle Cove, Coronation Island (Lat. 60° 39' S, Long. 45° 34' W)	2008	2008
16. Devil Island, Vega Island (Lat. 63° 48' S, Long. 57° 17' W)	2008	2018
17. Whalers Bay, Deception Island, South Shetland Islands (Lat. 62° 59' S, Long. 60° 34' W)	2008	2018
18. Half Moon Island, South Shetland Islands (Lat. 62° 35'24'' S, Long. 59° 55'13'' W)	2008	2019
19. Baily Head, Deception Island, South Shetland Islands (Lat. 62° 58' S, Long. 60° 30' W)	2009	2013
20. Telefon Bay, Deception Island, South Shetland Islands (Lat. 62° 55'27'' S, Long. 60° 39'47'' W)	2009	2018
21. Cape Royds, Ross Island (Lat. 77° 33' 11" S, Long. 166° 10' 7" E)	2009	2021
22. Wordie House, Winter Island, Argentine Islands (Lat. 65° 15' S, Long. 64° 16' W)	2009	2022
23. Stonington Island, Marguerite Bay, Antarctic Peninsula (Lat. 68° 11' S, Long. 67° 00' W)	2009	2009
24. Horseshoe Island, Antarctic Peninsula (Lat. 67° 49' S, Long. 67° 18' W)	2009	2014
25. Detaille Island, Antarctic Peninsula (Lat. 66° 52' S, Long. 66° 48' W)	2009	2009

Site Guidelines	First Adopted	Latest Version
26. Removed		
27. Danco Island, Errera Channel, Antarctic Peninsula (Lat. 64° 44' S, Long. 62° 36' W)	2010	2013
28. Seabee Hook, Cape Hallett, Northern Victoria Land, Ross Sea, Visitor Site A and Visitor Site B (Lat. 72° 19' S, Long. 170° 13' E)	2010	2021
29. Damoy Point, Wiencke Island, Antarctic Peninsula (Lat. 64° 49' S, Long. 63° 31' W)	2010	2013
30. Taylor Valley Visitor Zone, Southern Victoria Land (Lat. 77° 37.59' S, Long. 163° 03.42' E)	2011	2011
31. North-east beach of Ardley Island (Lat. 62° 13' S; Long. 58° 55' W)	2011	2011
32. Mawson's Huts and Cape Denison, East Antarctica (Lat. 67° 00'31'' S; Long. 142° 40'43'' E)	2011	2014
33. D'Hainaut Island, Mikkelsen Harbour, Trinity Island (Lat. 63° 54' S, Long. 60° 47' W)	2012	2012
34. Port Charcot, Booth Island (Lat. 65° 04'S, Long. 64 °02'W)	2012	2012
35. Pendulum Cove, Deception Island, South Shetland Islands (Lat. 62°56'S, Long. 60°36' W)	2012	2018
36. Orne Harbour, Southern arm of Orne Harbour, Gerlache Strait (Lat. 64° 38'S, Long. 62° 33'W)	2013	2013
37. Orne Islands, Gerlache Strait (Lat. 64° 40'S, Long. 62° 40'W)	2013	2013
38. Point Wild, Elephant Island (Lat. 61° 06'S, Long. 54°52'W)	2016	2016
39. Yalour Islands, Wilhelm Archipelago (Lat. 65° 14'S, 64°10'W)	2016	2016
40. Astrolabe Island (Lat. 63° 17'S, Long. 58° 40'W)	2018	2018
41. Georges Point, Rongé Island (Lat. 64° 40'S, Long. 62° 40'W)	2018	2018
42. Portal Point (Lat. 64° 30'S, Long. 61° 46'W)	2018	2018
43. Cape Evans (Lat. 77° 38' 12"S, 166° 25' 15"E)	2021	2021
44. Hut Point (Lat. 77° 50' 44.7"S 166° 38' 30.3"E)	2021	2021
45. Cape Adare (Lat. 71° 18' 27.5"S, 170° 11' 29"E)	2021	2021

Resolution 3 (2022)

Air Safety in Antarctica

The Representatives,

Recalling Resolution 6 (2021) on air safety in Antarctica;

Welcoming the advice provided by the Council of Managers of National Antarctic Programs ("COMNAP") in regard to the review by the Antarctic Treaty Consultative Meeting ("ATCM") of Resolution 6 (2021);

Concerned by the increasing diversification of aviation activities and the potential for increasing numbers of non-governmental aircraft movements;

Understanding the need to ensure that measures for improved air safety apply to all flights in Antarctica;

Noting the importance of ensuring effective communications between all actors involved in Antarctic air activities, including air operators, National Competent Authorities and COMNAP, and consistency of information across the various data repositories within the Antarctic Treaty System;

Recognising the importance of safe air operations in the Antarctic and that the principal body of knowledge and experience of Antarctic air operations, and its current challenges, lies with the operators of National Antarctic Programmes;

Acknowledging that any technical criteria must not impair the right of aerial observation granted in Article VII of the Antarctic Treaty;

Desiring to contribute to air safety in Antarctica through updated recommendations;

Recommend to their Governments:

1.   for the purpose of ensuring that measures for improved air safety apply to all flights and all aviation-related infrastructure in the Antarctic Treaty area, measures to improve air safety set out in paragraphs 2-10 taking into account the International Civil Aviation Organization ("ICAO") criteria and the specific features of Antarctica as well as existing practices and services;

2.   that, for the purpose of the safety of air operations in the Antarctic Treaty area, Parties should exchange, preferably by 1 September and no later than 15 November each year, information about their planned air operations in accordance with the standardised format of the Electronic Information Exchange System ("EIES");

3.   that, for the purpose of improving air safety in Antarctica, all operators, governmental and non-governmental, operating aircraft or managing air-related infrastructure, camps or aviation facilities or services in the Antarctic Treaty area should be provided, at the request of their Competent Authority or National Antarctic Programme, with a continuously updated compendium produced by COMNAP, known as the COMNAP Antarctic Flight Information Manual ("AFIM"), describing ground facilities, aircraft (including helicopters) and aircraft

operating procedures and associated communications facilities in the Antarctic Treaty area (out of the use of which questions of liability will not arise) and, therefore, that they should:

(a)   facilitate the ongoing revision of AFIM by collective action through COMNAP;

(b)   adopt a format in which information provided is kept in a manner that facilitates updating of information;

(c)   request their Antarctic operators to provide timely, current and accurate information for the purpose of maintaining the AFIM; and

(d)   ensure consistency of information across the various data repositories within the Antarctic Treaty System;

4.   that, for the purpose of ensuring mutual awareness of current air operations and exchanging information about them, Parties should designate:

(a)   Primary Air Information Stations ("PAIS"), which coordinate their own air information and information from their Secondary Air Information Stations (if any) for the purpose of notifying current air operations to other PAIS. These PAIS should have adequate communication facilities able to transmit information by appropriate and agreed means; and

(b)   Secondary Air Information Stations ("SAIS") which comprise stations/bases (including field bases and ships), which provide air information to their parent coordinating PAIS;

5.   that, for the purpose of ensuring effective communications between PAIS, Parties and other operators should ensure that their PAIS have adequate facilities for communicating with other PAIS;

6.   that, for the purpose of avoiding air incidents in areas beyond the range of very high frequency ("VHF") radio coverage of PAIS and SAIS:

(a)   aircraft outside the areas covered by PAIS and SAIS should use a specific radio frequency to apply the Traffic Information Broadcast by Aircraft ("TIBA") procedure, laid down in Annex 11 to the Convention on International Civil Aviation;

(b)   transponders in all aircraft must be switched on at all times during flight in the Antarctic Treaty area; and

(c)   in addition, operators should strongly consider the installation and use of Automatic Dependent Surveillance – Broadcast ("ADS-B") In and/or Traffic Collision Avoidance System ("TCAS") technology in all aircraft operating in the Antarctic Treaty area;

7.   that, so as to ensure compliance with Article VII, paragraph 5 of the Antarctic Treaty and also Recommendation X-8, Part IV, Parties should keep one another informed about non-governmental flights and should request COMNAP to provide access to AFIM to any operator of a non-governmental flight or infrastructure within the Antarctic Treaty area;

8.   that, so as to provide for the improved collection from, and for the exchange within Antarctica of meteorological data and information of significance to the safety of, Antarctic air operations, Parties should:

(a)   encourage the World Meteorological Organization ("WMO") in its work towards this end;

(b)   take steps to improve meteorological services available in Antarctica, specifically to meet aviation requirements; and

(c)   take account of the International Antarctic Weather Forecasting Handbook;

9.   that, for the purpose of consideration of emergency response that might be required, Parties should consider that any increase in air activity brings with it increased risks that must be managed or mitigated, and in cases of search and rescue ("SAR") or emergency response, it is the National Antarctic Programmes that are often called upon to respond. This should be considered when Parties are made aware of non-governmental applications for air activities that are not in support of science;

10.   that, for the purpose of improving air safety in Antarctica, Parties should request that all Antarctic air operators, government and non-governmental alike, ensure that they are aware of safety requirements, have identified alternative landing sites and communicated their intentions in advance directly to the operators of the alternative landing sites, reflecting that many airfields in the Antarctic Treaty area have limited and seasonal capacity and there should be no presumption of capabilities, operations or ability to assist;

11.   that, to improve chances of survival in the event of an air accident, the operators of all personned aircraft should ensure that, at least, recommended minimal survival equipment is maintained and carried onboard their aircraft. Such recommended minimal survival equipment is to be based on a risk-based approach that considers type of aircraft, number of persons onboard and proposed specifics of the operations, such as whether the operations are intra-Antarctica or inter-Antarctic. The list of recommended minimal survival equipment shall be maintained through COMNAP and reviewed regularly by all operators; and

12.   that Resolution 6 (2021) is no longer current.

Resolution 4 (2022)

Antarctic Climate Change and the Environment: A Decadal Synopsis and Recommendations for Action report

The Representatives,

Recalling the Washington Ministerial Declaration on the fiftieth anniversary of the signing of the Antarctic Treaty, in which Ministers from all Antarctic Treaty Consultative Parties noted their concern about the implications of global environmental change, in particular climate change, for the Antarctic environment and dependent and associated ecosystems and confirmed their intention to work together to better understand changes to the Earth's climate and to actively seek ways to address the effects of climate and environmental change on the Antarctic environment and dependent and associated ecosystems;

Recalling also the importance of the Committee for Environmental Protection's ("CEP") Climate Change Response Work Programme and its vision of preparing for, and building resilience to, the environmental impacts of a changing climate;

Welcoming that the Decadal Synopsis Report on Antarctic Climate Change and the Environment ("Decadal Synopsis") by the Scientific Committee on Antarctic Research ("SCAR") draws on the best available science representing current understanding of and projections for climate change and its impacts in the Antarctic;

Welcoming also SCAR's advice that urgent action is required to prevent irreversible changes to Antarctica and consequential implications for the planet;

Concerned by the effects and projected changes to Antarctic environments resulting from climate change outlined in the Decadal Synopsis;

Recalling Resolution 8 (2021) on climate change response and remaining committed to seeking ways to address the effects of climate and environmental change on the Antarctic environment and dependent and associated ecosystems;

Determined to address the policy and research recommendations of the report;

Recommend that their Governments:

1.   ensure that their respective departments and agencies charged with climate change negotiations receive copies of the Decadal Synopsis and have an opportunity to be fully briefed and fully consider its findings and recommendations for action;

2.   ensure that national Antarctic science and research bodies and funding agencies receive copies of the Decadal Synopsis and have an opportunity to be fully briefed and fully consider its findings and recommendations for action;

3.   encourage dissemination of the findings of the Decadal Synopsis and of ongoing Antarctic climate change research to the general public and the media; and

4.   continue to welcome updates by SCAR on Antarctic climate change and its implications.

Resolution 5 (2022)

Permanent facilities for tourism and other non-governmental activities in Antarctica

The Representatives,

Recalling the designation of Antarctica as a natural reserve, devoted to peace and science in Article 2 and the Environmental Principles contained in Article 3 of the Protocol on Environmental Protection to the Antarctic Treaty;

Recalling Resolutions 5 (2007) and 7 (2009);

Conscious of the Antarctic Treaty Consultative Meeting's ("ATCM") consensus that tourism in Antarctica should be undertaken in a safe manner that will not contribute to the long-term degradation of the Antarctic environment and its dependent and associated ecosystems, or the intrinsic natural wilderness and historical values of Antarctica;

Recognising the International Association of Antarctic Tour Operators ("IAATO") Bylaws that tourism will have no more than a minor or transitory impact on the Antarctic environment;

Desiring to take a pragmatic and precautionary approach in order to prevent wilderness degradation in Antarctica;

Desiring to prevent additional strain on search and rescue ("SAR") support and National Antarctic Programmes to respond to safety emergencies;

Emphasising that, given recent plans for such facilities, National Competent Authorities may urgently need advice;

Recommend that their Governments make every effort to prevent, and not authorise, permit or approve, the construction and/or exploitation of any structure or facility exclusively for tourism and other non-governmental activities to be operated in Antarctica over multiple seasons, where its construction, operations or removal is expected to have more than a minor or transitory impact on the Antarctic environment and its dependent and associated ecosystems, or the intrinsic natural wilderness and historical values of Antarctica. Examples include, but are not restricted to, buildings, wharves and jetties, and graded runways on exposed ground.

Resolution 6 (2022)

Revised standard Post Visit Report Form

The Representatives,

Conscious of the provisions of the Antarctic Treaty Consultative Meeting ("ATCM") in relation to the information to be exchanged by Parties and of the obligations to exchange information as contained in the Protocol on Environmental Protection to the Antarctic Treaty ("the Protocol") and its Annexes;

Recalling Resolution 3 (1997), which sets out a standard form for advance notification and post visit reporting on tourism and non-governmental activities;

Noting also Resolution 10 (2021) which recommended the use of a revised standard Post Visit Report Form to exchange information on activities carried out by tourist and non- governmental vessels in Antarctica;

Recalling Decision 7 (2012), which decided that the Parties will use the Electronic Information Exchange System ("EIES") to exchange information in accordance with the Antarctic Treaty and the Protocol and its Annexes and which specified that Parties would continue to work with the Secretariat of the Antarctic Treaty ("the Secretariat") to refine and improve the EIES;

Noting also that Decision 4 (2012) requires Parties to update relevant sections of the EIES regularly throughout the year, in order that such information be made available and accessible to Parties as soon as practicable;

Noting the convenience of obtaining consistent information that would facilitate analysis of the scope, frequency and intensity of tourism and non-governmental activities;

Desiring to ensure that the exchange of information by Parties be conducted in the most efficient and timely manner;

Desiring also that the information to be exchanged by Parties be readily identified;

Recommend that their Governments:

1. amend the standard Post Visit Report Form annexed to Resolution 10 (2021) to incorporate the changes indicated in the Annex to this Resolution; and

2. request the Secretariat to make the amended standard Post Visit Report Form available on its website.

Revised standard Post Visit Report Form

For the purpose of this Resolution, an unusual incident is *"An undesired or unforeseen event deviating from the activity described in the environmental impact assessment, or the failure of planned mitigation measures, resulting in environmental impacts exceeding those predicted in the environmental impact assessment; and/or negative effects on people; and/or damage to materials or assets; and it may also have led to the cancellation or interruption of the assessed activity and/or required the need for external assistance from outside the Operator's company or organization."*

As agreed by ATCM XLIV, items 2, 3 and 4 of section D "Report on Expedition by Expedition Leader" in Part 1 of the PVR form annexed to Resolution 10 (2021) now reads:

Item 2. Were there any unusual incidents affecting people, environment and/or materials/assets?

Item 3. If there were any unusual events, whether assistance was required or not. And, in case it was, if assistance was required from National programme, tour operator, private expedition, fishing vessel, RCC or other.

Item 4. A summary description of the incident being reported and the consequences, and the data (name/mail/national programme) to which the incident detail report is to be sent.

Heads of Delegation picture

1. Antonio Quesada (Spain), 2. Juan Camilo Forero Hauzeur (Colombia), 3. William Muntean (United States), 4. Mbulelo Dopolo (South Africa), 5. Jana Newman (New Zealand), 6 Emil Ruffer (Czechia), 7. Konrad Marciniak (Poland), 8. Stephanie Langerock (Belgium), 9. Michael Pistecky (Netherlands), 10. Augusto Arzubiaga (Peru), 11. Orazio Guanciale (Italy), 12. Caroline Krajka (France), 13. Mike Sparrow (WMO), 14. Adam McCarthy (Australia), 15. Claire Christian (ASOC), 16. Jose Xavier (Portugal), 17. Phillip Tracey (WG2 Co-chair - Operations, Science and Tourism), 18. Dmitri Cherkashin (Russian Federation), 19. Filipe Nasser (Brazil), 20. Mohd Nasaruddin Abd Rahman (Malaysia), 21. Elizabeth Moreano (Ecuador), 22. Francisco Berguño (Chile), 23. Jane Rumble (United Kingdom), 24. Fausto Lopez Crozet (Argentina), 25. Mette Strengehagen (Norway), 26. Miriam Wolter (Germany), 27. **Tania Von Uslar-Gleichen (ATCM Chair)**, 28. Andriy Fedchuk (Ukraine), 29. Manfred Reinke (Host Country Secretariat), 30. Albert Lluberas Bonaba (Antarctic Treaty Secretariat), 31. Dimana Dramova (Bulgaria), 32. Vijay Kumar (India), 33. Zha Hyoung Rhee (Republic of Korea), 34. Jenny Haukka (Finland), 35. Céline Le Bohec (Monaco), 36. Theodore Kill (WG1 Chair - Policy, Legal and Institutional Issues).

Made in the USA
Middletown, DE
25 November 2022

15924016R00161